ONTHEGAME.IE
PROSTITUTION IN IRELAND TODAY

STEPHEN ROGERS

Gill & Macmillan

Gill & Macmillan Ltd
Hume Avenue, Park West, Dublin 12
with associated companies throughout the world
www.gillmacmillan.ie

© Stephen Rogers 2009
978 07171 4491 4

Typography design by Make Communication
Print origination by Carole Lynch
Printed in the UK by CPI Mackays, Chatham

This book is typeset in Linotype Minion and Neue Helvetica.

The paper used in this book comes from the wood pulp
of managed forests. For every tree felled, at least one
tree is planted, thereby renewing natural resources.

A CIP catalogue record for this book is available
from the British Library.

5 4 3 2 1

CONTENTS

01 | **INTRODUCTION**
FROM SEX IN THE CITIES
TO SEX IN THE SUBURBS

Paul Humphreys sat counting the €30,000 in crisp banknotes in his kitchen, meticulously tallying it against the work-sheets that lay before him.

Life was good for the 63-year-old Corkman, a former cruise-ship chef: the two-shift system at his brothels was paying off. The prostitutes liked the clean premises, and the fact that they were paid in full according to the terms they had agreed with Humphreys. He had a happy business spread over at least three brothels in Dublin city centre. The success of the operation meant he was taking in as much as €780,000 for himself annually, quite a bit more than he could have expected from his previous employment.

Little did Humphreys expect the Gardaí to burst through the door in the midst of his bookkeeping. The raid was part of 'Operation Quest', set up to investigate organised prostitution in Dublin.

What detectives uncovered was one of the city's most successful prostitution rackets. Prospective clients of the ten prostitutes working the two shifts at the apartments would ring one of the ten mobile numbers liberally advertised on a range of web sites. They would reach a 'call centre' where the receptionists would direct them to one of the brothels at Cecilia Street, West Essex Street or Gallery Quay (Grand Canal Square). As appointments were made they would be recorded at the call centre and the brothel, and the dual record was used to tally the takings when the money was collected daily.

As detectives expanded their search to the other premises they discovered a further €11,000. They examined the worksheets and were able to ascertain that the brothels were staffed by anything up to five women at a time, working shifts. The women, mainly from eastern Europe, charged €150 for half an hour and €250 for a full hour, of which they were allowed to keep half.

On the night before the Garda raid forty-seven clients visited the brothels between 7 p.m. and 5 a.m., and a total of €8,730 was taken in during that period. Humphreys' address in Dublin was given to the court as Harty Court, Lower Ormond Quay, but in reality he lived most of the time in a hideaway in Cyprus, returning only to collect his takings. Bank accounts in Cyprus were frozen as part of the investigation into the brothel-owner's affairs. The Gardaí discovered that Humphreys would tell prospective landlords that he was a property developer from Cyprus who needed an Irish base.

The weight of evidence against Humphreys was strong, and in Dublin District Court he had little choice but to plead guilty to knowingly allowing premises to be used for the purpose of prostitution between 31 August 2005 and 26 March 2006.

His defence counsel made a valiant attempt to make Humphreys appear to be a man simply running a business. He said that Humphreys had no involvement with human trafficking and did not employ under-age women or those with a 'specific vulnerability'. He said his client came from a good family and there was nothing in his past that would lead him towards this kind of activity.

However, these attempts did not impress Judge Frank O'Donnell, who told the court that he disagreed with the maximum fine allowable for the sentence compared with the amount of money Humphreys would have made. 'It is wrong that he should be walking away with money in his pocket,' he stated. However, he backdated the beginning of the two-year sentence to the arrest and suspended the rest pending the payment of €40,000. Even though the judge was unhappy to let Humphreys walk away a rich man, insufficient evidence meant he could not confiscate the pimp's assets.

The state sought the confiscation of €670,000, as the estimated profits from five brothels run by Humphreys. It was put to the court that Humphreys was estimated to have earned as much as €780,000 from the business. The prosecution said that the Gardaí had taken testimony from the women working in the brothels and had examined the accounts. These showed that Humphreys had made a profit of €663,751.

The defence opposed the confiscation, submitting that the court did not have the jurisdiction to interfere with bank accounts and with property abroad. A lot of money belonging to Humphreys and his wife had been sunk in the property in Cyprus as well as in accounts belonging to Mrs Humphreys. The defence said she had not been served with any documents by the state in relation to the forfeiture application. It argued that the court did not know if the property was obtained with legitimate funds.

In his deliberations the judge said he did not know what Humphreys' wife worked at in Cyprus. 'She could be a high-flying banker, a lawyer or a barrister making a fortune in Cyprus.' He refused the application to confiscate the money, because he said there was not enough evidence to allow it. 'It galls me that this man was drawing disability from the state and the Irish taxpayer while he was making money for himself by working these unfortunate women,' Judge O'Donnell said. He stated that there was no valuation for the property the couple owned in Cyprus and there was no way to determine whether it had been purchased with legitimate or illegitimate funds.

Paul Humphreys was just another man making the most of what many people are sick of hearing called the 'world's oldest profession'. The reality, however, is that the cliché is far from inaccurate. Paying for sex has been a part of society for thousands of years, as women have been bought and sold, or have hired themselves out, to satisfy the wants of men—either voluntarily or against their will.

However, the way that sex is sold today, the type of sex on offer and the way profits are being generated are all very new. Only twenty years ago the main way for women to sell their bodies was to take the old-fashioned route of walking the streets. Each city had its own 'red-light district', where women would gather. It was the traditional side of the industry known the world over.

Now, however, if one were to go onto the streets of Dublin or Belfast or any Irish city on any night of the week, the number of prostitutes gathered there would be a small fraction of what it was previously. The only reason why one would see more of them is that there are fewer punters cruising the myriad back-roads looking for them.

So where have these men gone?

It is not that the demand for anonymous sex has diminished in any way. It would be naïve to think it had. Irish society, on the contrary, has become more and more sexually charged, and the demand for sexual services has never been greater. Popular culture is now permeated with graphic sexual references. On our television screens, the way goods are sold to us in advertisements and the role of actors—both men and women—have been sexualised to a degree that would simply not have been expected, or accepted, less than a quarter of a century ago.

Viewing figures show that risqué television is what draws the crowds, whether it be through salacious story lines in a soap opera or the likelihood of a romance on a reality show. In essence, television has been 'dumbed down' to reach our most primeval urges.

There are areas of popular culture where this is more deeply apparent, areas that were previously taboo. Without leaving the sitting-room or the television set, the examples are there. Satellite television packages offer whole swathes of channels dedicated to scantily clad women. After the 'watershed' hour of 9 p.m. they tease with simulated sex on the basic channels, while those willing to pay several euros per minute can even talk to the women as they sit on the screen before them, entreating them to simulate an act that particularly turns the watcher on. They can then look forward to the feeling of guilt when the phone bill drops through the letterbox. If the satellite subscriber is willing to pay that little bit extra, far more graphic scenes of sex are available on the typing of a credit card number.

Sky and the rest would not put these channels into their packages if they did not think they would get the viewers. They are simply following the best marketing trick in the trade: sex sells.

The evidence is even more apparent as one goes outside the front door. Stand in any city centre in Ireland and you are almost guaranteed to be within ten minutes' walk of a sex shop. Here there is no fancy marketing, no need for undertones. It is uncompromising sex, in a bewildering array of forms, with videos, magazines, sex aids and contact sheets vying for counter space.

These and the lap-dancing clubs that are also multiplying have a very thin veneer of acceptability. Men flock to the lap-dancing clubs for stag nights, they ogle the women, pay an exorbitant price for an up-close and personal dance, and then go home to their wives or partners with a relatively clear conscience.

All these areas have brought sex out into the open. It is no longer men's dirty little secret. In some respects the way prostitution has gone is almost the opposite. Whereas before there was a very public face to the scene—it was on the street corners—it is now much harder to stumble upon. Men have to go looking for it. And they do.

There is a distinct, almost traditional view of prostitution in Ireland that it is not as prevalent here as in other countries, such as Britain. Pick up a British 'lad's mag'—not necessarily the top-shelf pornography but men's equivalent of *Cosmopolitan*—and there will be a number of advertisements for 'escort agencies'. Even in some of the women's magazines there are advertisements for women willing to work in such agencies.

The acceptance of prostitution in 21st-century society was blatantly revealed on a British prime-time television programme— ironically aimed squarely at women; and it was an Irish woman who caused the furore. In 2005 the former singer Coleen Nolan revealed on 'Loose Women' that she had promised to let her son go to the red-light district in Amsterdam if he passed his exams, and added that her then fiancé could have a one-night stand during the proposed trip as well. She said she had offered to finance the trip, but only if her partner accompanied the boy.

> He [her son] said, 'Well, then, Ray [her fiancé] might sleep with a prostitute too.' I said, 'Oh, that's all right, it's only a prostitute.' I wouldn't throw away the father of my children and all that for the sake of lads being lads—as long as he comes back and tells me about it. I'm not joking, I'd love it. There's something a little bit kinky about me.

There was an immediate uproar, with agony aunts describing her as an irresponsible parent. However, she was unrepentant, saying that her son had been sexually active since he was fifteen, and that she and he had always had a 'fantastic open relationship', talking about everything, including safe sex. 'As soon as you mention prostitute and the words "paying for it," everyone is, like, "gasp",' she said. This sums up an attitude that has pervaded society.

In another episode that was not quite so blatant, Lucy Baxter, a mother whose 21-year-old adopted son has Down's syndrome, contemplated helping him visit a prostitute so he could lose his virginity. She pointed out that her son, and other people with Down's syndrome, were no different from others. She has three other adopted sons with the same condition.

> I'd like all my boys to find love and enjoy sex. I would have no problem if he went to a brothel in Amsterdam. I always look at what other people are doing, and why shouldn't they do the same things? I strongly believe, and have always said, that society has a learning disability when it comes to Down's

syndrome. Why should these people be kept separate and pigeon-holed when they have the same emotions, desires and feelings as so-called normal people? He has the same expectations as everybody else.

Back in Ireland, while the traditional view of prostitution pertains to a certain extent, the way we look at the sale of sex has evolved in recent years. Trish Murphy, a psychotherapist, told 'Prime Time' in 2006:

Fifteen or twenty years ago prostitution in Ireland was seedy. It was something you would be ashamed of if you were caught being involved in it. Now it has completely changed. It is happening in salubrious surroundings. People would not necessarily brag about it but would not hold their hand in shame either.

In its publication *Globalisation, Sex Trafficking and Prostitution: The Experiences of Migrant Women in Ireland,* the Immigrant Council of Ireland quoted Judith Lewis Herman, professor of clinical psychiatry at Harvard University Medical School, as saying that she was perplexed at what she called 'mass social dissociation' or the social denial about prostitution in society.

She asks how we live knowing and not knowing about it—'a worldwide enterprise that condemns millions of women and children to social death and often to literal death, for the sexual pleasure and profit of men,' and that thrives everywhere, answered the question. The denial can be partly explained by the tacit acceptance of the objectification of women and the mainstreaming of what has become known as 'raunch' culture. The public performance of the erotica infuses our culture with an iconography of style known as the 'pornochic'.

Like many other capital cities, Dublin has been at the hub of the way prostitution has evolved, and other cities around the country have followed suit.

In the nineteenth and early twentieth century Dublin even had the largest red-light district in Europe, the Monto district. Reputedly housing up to 1,600 women at one time, Montgomery Street (now Foley Street) had as the key to its success the nearby British army barracks, whose many soldiers, far from home, were more than willing to avail of its services. Ironically, while many celebrated Britain's withdrawal from the 26 Counties, the prostitutes saw their livelihood all but wiped out as their main clientele returned home. The final nail was hammered into the coffin of the district by the Legion of Mary in the 1920s, who also nailed a picture of the Sacred Heart on the door of every brothel.

At that point it became 'every woman for herself,' and they took to the streets—where they have remained, to varying degrees, ever since. This has particularly been so since drugs began to take hold in the cities. The need for money to support a chronic heroin addiction has seen hundreds of women selling themselves to pay their dealer and sate their habit. (See chapter 3.)

However, since the 1970s the indoor trade has once again taken off and in the last ten years has exploded. A 'mobile brothel' touring the country even offered 'sex in the suburbs'.

There was no shortage of people willing to exploit Ireland's flimsy prostitution laws for their financial gain. Several enterprising individuals rented out as much cheap property as was fiscally possible close to the city centre, and advertised for women willing to pay a percentage and to 'service' as many men as could get through the door. All the owners had to do was sit back and count the profits.

——

Brothels really came to the fore in the 1990s, when Mike Hogan began publishing thinly veiled advertisements for women in *In Dublin*, previously a hard-hitting and controversial news magazine. When Hogan took over, its attentions were turned even more blatantly to sexual advertising, and soon a large proportion of its income was derived from the sex trade. Hogan had bought the magazine for £6,500 in 1992 and would later say that the advertisements were already there, running alongside ads for telephone sex lines. A married man with three children, he defended himself on the grounds that 'I don't hold myself out as being the moral guardian of the nation.'

The brothel-owners would pay up to £400 for one-eighth of a page, usually weakly disguising themselves as massage parlours. With twenty-six issues annually, Hogan could expect to earn £400,000 a year from the advertisements alone. When it seemed that the ads were drawing too much attention from the Censorship Board, he ordered his staff to moderate the images and the language used. Nevertheless he was unable to escape the attentions of the Gardaí. The ads for 'massage parlours' came especially to their attention following the murder of Belinda Pereira, a young prostitute killed in 1997. During the investigation into her murder it was revealed that she had advertised in *In Dublin*. The Gardaí brought Hogan to court on charges covering the period from 19 June 1997 to 12 August 1999. The premises involved in the ten charges were named as 'Flamingos', 'Tropical Paradise', 'New Imperial', 'Angels', 'Emmanuelle's', 'Personal Services', 'Tiger Lilies', 'Secrets of Seduction', 'Leather and Lace', and finally 'Xclusive', which sought staff.

Detective-Inspector John McMahon told the court that 64 per cent of the men interviewed in the brothels raided revealed that they had got directions to the premises from *In Dublin*. Hogan was fined £50,000 when he pleaded guilty to ten sample charges of publishing advertisements for prostitution. Since then the entrepreneur has moved into selling ring tones for mobile phones.

When this easy advertising source was taken off the market the brothel-owners had to become a little more enterprising. The advent of the internet provided the ideal opportunity (as can be seen in chapter 2). It also brought the sale of sex outside the capital. Now every county has a booming sex industry, and sex is sold within yards of every street. In the suburbs the sale of sex is rife.

A shop in a reasonably affluent residential area of Cork had built up a good passing trade for many years, selling a range of convenience products to customers who did not have the time, the energy or the inclination to go to the slightly more distant super-market. The owner sold a limited range of each product and so was able to keep a close eye on stocks of the various items. Gradually he began to realise that he was selling out of cans of whipped cream a lot more rapidly than previously. He increased the order with his supplier, and began to take a curious interest in why this mundane product was suddenly selling so quickly. He noticed that a pretty blonde woman would often come in and buy the cans in twos and threes. He had a good rapport with his usual customers, but there was something about this woman, a certain air, that made him refrain from questioning her motives.

After months of this unusually fast-seller rushing off the shelves he noticed that sales suddenly plummeted, and the increased stock of cream was building up on the shelves. It was only weeks later that he heard from a garda acquaintance that a brothel had been investigated and closed down within a few streets of his business.

———

A compelling study carried out in London in 2008 revealed the extent of prostitution in 21st-century cities, as well as the depths to which people, mainly women, are forced to sink in the sex trade. The Poppy Project recruited and trained male researchers to phone brothels between the autumn of 2007 and the spring of 2008. They asked precise questions about the women and the services available, as well as the nature of the establishment itself.

The research was thorough, all results were cross-referenced, and details obtained from the brothels were verified by follow-up phone calls. Although approximately 1,500 brothels were identified, a little under a thousand premises were surveyed, partly because some advertised numbers were defunct, while calls to other numbers continually went through to voice mail or were left unanswered.

As a result of the detailed analysis the researchers were able to draw a number of startling conclusions. They found that there was an 'absolute minimum' of 1,933 women working only through advertisements in the print media. They said the 921 brothels that provided information were only the 'tip of the iceberg' of sex premises in London. While the declared age of the women was between eighteen and fifty-five, and the average age twenty-one, the researchers speculated that under-age women were available, given that a number of brothels offered 'very very young girls' or 'baby-faced girls', without divulging ages. The women were of seventy-seven different national origins, with 55 per cent stating that they were from Europe and 30 per cent from Asia.

Full sex was available for as little as £15, ranging up to £125, with the average £61.93. Prices for penetrative sex (vaginal or anal) without a condom began at £10 extra, bringing the total average up to £71.25. Of the 921 brothels surveyed, 19 admitted to providing penetrative sex without a condom, though the great majority told the researchers to negotiate directly with the women, meaning that it was undoubtedly available in many more.

The men hired to carry out the interviews could barely contain their shock at what they discovered. One said:

> I found it very strange how much they were willing to discuss over the phone, how blunt they were, and how little persuasion they needed to tell their exact whereabouts. One was particularly worrying, as she'd drive and meet the punter in abandoned buildings or the countryside. I thought she was really endangering herself.

Helen Atkins, joint author of the book *Big Brothel*, said:

> It has been said that we are never more than six feet away from a rat in London. Apparently, something similar applies to

brothels, places where thousands of women are regularly exploited by men who buy sex. This research shows the disturbing prevalence of the sex industry in every corner of London—fuelled by the demand for prostitution services. Multi-media misrepresentations of commercial sex as a glamorous, easy and fun career choice for girls and women further contribute to the ubiquity of London's brothel industry. However, for most women involved in prostitution, the reality is a cycle of violence and coercion, perpetuated by poverty and inequality.

Many of the brothels discovered by the Poppy Project advertised themselves as legitimate businesses, licensed as saunas or under the guise of massage parlours.

In the following chapters this book attempts to show that what was found by the authors of *Big Brothel* in London is just as prevalent in Ireland but is simply not in the public eye, because there is a concerted effort to ignore what is virtually in everyone's back yard. It will look at the people who are making the money, the people who are suffering, the surprisingly large number of men who are regularly paying for sex, and the social and health consequences this 'industry' is creating.

Since you got up yesterday morning at least a thousand Irish men have paid for sex. They have received sexual gratification from a man or woman in a hotel room, in a dingy back-street 'massage parlour' or in a comfortable city-centre pad.

Men no longer need to drive the streets of Dublin, Cork, Limerick or Belfast hoping to find a woman willing to satisfy sexual longings. If they go on the internet they can find a woman or man who will be at their door within half an hour. If they don't want the woman they claim to love to find out (love has nothing to do with this) they need simply pop out for a 'meeting'. 'Just put my dinner in the oven; I'll be back in an hour . . .'

A quick web search for an 'escort' (or prostitute with a bigger bank balance) will bring up listings for more than a thousand men and women in cities and towns in every corner of Ireland. Pictures of the prostitute in little or no clothing are accompanied by the vast range of services they offer and, without fail, a mobile contact number.

Fast surfers will be able to find within minutes a man or woman of whatever nationality, age, size and sexual preference their whim has pushed them towards. After a sometimes enjoyable, probably guilty and certainly expensive dalliance they will often log back on to the web site to give a review of their latest costly conquest. She didn't look like the picture, she made me wait for ages at the door, she let me 'do her' without a condom . . .

When the bank balance allows, the internet will spew forth a few hundred more options. The 'world's oldest profession' is taking on a distinctly 21st-century gloss. Yes, you can still find women huddled on street corners offering back-seat or dark-alley sex, but they are vying with international beauties who can offer not just a bed but also what all the men crave: no chance of being caught. That guarantee is the holy grail that makes the punter look past the fact that the woman might not be lying under them willingly, that she hates herself for every second, and every one of the men, that he may be putting his life and that of his partner and his children at risk. Sex has never been this easy, this available, this seemingly inconsequential. It has also never been this dangerous, both for the punter and the prostitute.

This book explains what has become thousands of men's most guilty secret. It asks how Catholic Ireland has let its social halo slip so far, and why the law seems to penalise no-one, preferring to keep the problem under wraps from the right-thinking in the community.

One organisation that features prominently in these pages is Ruhama (Hebrew for 'renewed life'), which deserves great praise for the tireless work it does with women in prostitution. Ruhama was founded in 1989 as a joint initiative of the Good Shepherd Sisters and Our Lady of Charity Sisters, both of which had a long history of involvement with marginalised women, including those involved in prostitution. The organisation's initial service was based on the women's need for the opportunity to discuss their issues, and the problems they face, with someone who would not judge them but would be able to offer advice and support. To do that it set up an outreach service where workers would go out into the red-light districts each night. This service, which still exists today, offers women a hot drink, a friendly ear and a neutral and safe environment in which to talk to the staff and volunteers.

From that beginning the organisation has developed into a more professional non-governmental organisation with a staff of fourteen, more than thirty volunteers, and a range of services. It now also offers a casework service, counselling, and a referral and support system to assist women involved in prostitution in obtaining access to such services as housing, addiction recovery schemes, and immigration and legal services. It also offers court accompaniment for offenders or victims of crime. 'We have supported women who were raped or trafficked throughout the criminal process,' it points out. The organisation has also supported women who are victims of sex trafficking by offering safe accommodation as well as aiding with their repatriation.

There are many people and organisations for which Ruhama is a thorn in their side. Its belief that prostitution is violence against women and is a violation of women's human rights, as well as its determination that the great majority of prostitutes, both indoors and outdoors, are forced into it—whether through blatant trafficking or by less attributable circumstances—is, not surprisingly, not welcomed by a lot of pimps and the owners of 'escort' web sites. They say that Ruhama is using its religious ideals to push a view of the scene that simply does not exist. Readers will have to make up their own minds on this as they read on.

Ruhama is also far from popular with the authorities, as almost weekly it draws attention to the flaws in legislation and the policing of the sex trade as well as the pitiful support for women trafficked into Ireland. Where possible it has sought—with mixed success—a number of amendments to legislation on the sex trade that has been introduced over the last twenty years. It would say that legislation has either been long overdue or has been inadequate to meet the issues that affect women forced into prostitution.

Ruhama is all too aware of how the sale of sex has changed during its twenty-year existence. The following quotation encapsulates Ruhama's view of prostitution, which it is not ashamed to promote but which is questioned by a number of people with a vested interest in the sale of sex.

> When Ruhama was set up, most women involved in prostitution were in street prostitution, often to cover additional expenses for particular events—Christmas, first Communions etc. Generally from socially and financially deprived backgrounds, with low levels of education and little marketable skill, they had few employment opportunities. Many had been brought up in care, had weak family and social networks and few support mechanisms. Rarely younger than their early twenties, their substance abuse was generally limited to alcohol.
> Over the last ten years this profile has changed significantly:
> — some 95 per cent of women in street prostitution are drug users; their drug of choice heroin or cocaine.
> — the incidence of homelessness has increased sharply
> — relationships between the women and their partners is more exploitative, with many young women being pimped directly by their partners
> — while the age range remains broad, the numbers of very young women involved in prostitution is increasing rapidly, with most living extremely chaotic lives without the support of their families or community networks. Their vulnerability, isolation and powerlessness to take control of their lives are very apparent, and this is reflected in the level of support they need from Ruhama staff and volunteers.

Ruhama has also had to change its modus operandi to reflect the explosion in the indoor prostitution industry made possible by the internet.

It made its first contact with a woman who was a victim of sex trafficking in 2000, and it is convinced that over the past decade Ireland has become both a significant transit route and a significant destination for trafficking.

Similarly, the Immigrant Council of Ireland's report *Globalisation, Sex Trafficking and Prostitution: The Experiences of Migrant Women in Ireland* provides a good basis from which to work. For the moment, one small part of that report summarises well the sex trade in Ireland.

- There is a minimum of 1,000 women in indoor prostitution in Ireland at any one time
- While some women operate independently (the proportion of which is not known), other women are linked to prostitution agencies, which exercise different levels of penalty, control and violence that is difficult to determine due to the clandestine nature of prostitution
- There are 51 different nationalities of women available to men in indoor prostitution
- Of women advertised on the internet, 41 per cent were described as 'touring escorts'. These women move around Ireland and some travel internationally
- Between 3 and 13 per cent of the women in indoor prostitution are Irish, which means that up to 97 per cent are migrant women
- Nearly 40 per cent of migrant women in prostitution attending the Women's Health Project (HSE) have children and, for a minority of women, their children reside with them
- The largest group advertising on the internet self-identify as being from one of the EU 15 countries. Caution needs to be taken in interpreting the findings in relation to nationality. It is possible that some women who claim to be from the EU 15, particularly from Spain and Italy, are of South American origin or from Eastern European countries. The second-largest group are from South America/Caribbean

- The women's ages range from 18 (with some evidence that girls as young as 16 years are involved) to 58 years. The average age is estimated at 25.

02 | IT'S SEX, DEAR, BUT NOT AS WE KNOW IT

Charlie is a thirty-year-old 'Irish lady born and bred' who says she is more attuned to the finer things in life but also has a down-to-earth essence about her. She offers seven different services to male clients for half an hour; the cost will be €150. Oral sex without a condom is an extra €50, but if the client haggles he might get away without paying that. A full hour of her charms will set the client back €250, with a further €180 for every hour after that. For €2,200 the energetic client can spend twenty-four hours with her.

This tall blonde (5 feet 6 inches), who lives in Phibsborough, claims that with her 'long blonde hair and stunning good looks, your first impression of her will certainly be WOW.' She also claims a body that just wants to be stroked and kissed all over, and prospective clients can bet their pay-cheque they will never forget any experience of Charlie, as she just loves to French kiss, and an erotic time is guaranteed.

Charlie services Dublin Airport and has showers available for her clients to use, or perhaps to share with her, at her accommodation. Parking is available at Phibsborough Shopping Centre. She offers appointments from 9 a.m. to 2 a.m. Past clients say she looks like the glamour model Jordan and that, while she is a 'little bit heavier than the photos,' her 34DD breasts 'certainly make up for it.'

I have never met this woman, only talked to her on the phone for less than ten seconds. So how do I know all this? Because every detail a punter would want to know is on the internet. There are photographs of Charlie, some showing her in underwear, others topless. She is just one of more than four hundred women (and, to a far lesser extent, men) who are on or have been on *escort-ireland.com*, which quite credibly claims to be Ireland's leading escort site, as it does seem to have the lion's share of the women.

The title 'escort' is a veneer. Escorts, under the traditional meaning of the word, offer protection or companionship. But can companionship by the half hour with sexual services as the focus be described as anything other than prostitution?

Another of the web sites, *irishindependentescorts.com*, draws a distinction between the two terms. 'Essentially an escort charges for their time where as a prostitute charges for a service,' it claims. But there can be no arguing that the premise is the same. Therefore *escort-ireland.com* shows what can only be described as predictability and a spurious naïveté when it states:

> All the escorts listed on Escort Ireland charge for their time and companionship only. Anything else that may occur is a matter of coincidence and choice between consenting adults so far as Escort Ireland and the escorts listed on Escort Ireland are concerned. We do not condone prostitution.

The 'time and companionship' mantra is on practically every page of the web site, even though hundreds of the women listed clearly describe the sexual services on offer.

The web sites on which the women promote themselves are not illegal, as the majority of agencies are licensed, and the owners' addresses are outside the state. If they were licensed here they would be subject to the full rigours of the law; outside Ireland they are untouchable. They are extremely well run, strictly monitored by their owners, and updated regularly, if not daily or even hourly. They have to be exact.

There is competition. *irishindependentescorts.com* has a growing number of women on its books and so can expect to attract nearly as many hits daily as its big rival, *escort-ireland.com.*

Neither site is advertising women who are under their own control. There is a clear distinction between those sites that advertise a particular brothel only and those that claim they are only advertising sites on which escorts and brothels can advertise themselves. 'All escorts or agencies just use us to advertise and they work for themselves,' claims David, joint owner of *irishindependent escorts.com.* 'The escorts listed on this site do not work for us, we just make their information freely available to the public.' It does more than that. At one point the site launched a reception service for the women and agencies, with a former 'escort', Mandy, to act as receptionist. David tells punters:

> Over the years we have had many requests from both clients and escorts to offer a reception service so clients need only remember one telephone number and escorts can still accept bookings while unable to answer their own phone.
>
> So no need to carry multiple phone numbers or duck and dive to the nearest internet cafe to retrieve tens of numbers, many of which will be unavailable. Just call Mandy on one of the new IIE telephone numbers below for Ireland or Northern Ireland and let an experienced escort and receptionist organise your appointment.

The site's owners are fully aware, and even boast, that even though they are advertising the women in this jurisdiction they are based outside the country, where they know they are immune from prosecution.

> This site is not hosted in the Republic of Ireland and both owners live in a country where it is perfectly legal.

This supposed detachment also enables this site, and others like it, to give every detail, no matter how sordid, of what the women will offer. For this service the site's owners are paid €100 per month for independent escorts and €300 per month for agencies. It has spread its speciality beyond the women who are available for sex in person: it also has several links to sites that host women who are willing to have sex either by themselves or with a partner on live webcams. These women, all apparently foreign, lie for hours on end at the other end of the camera, waiting for punters who will ask them for a 'private show', for which they will charge them exorbitant prices by the minute.

escort-ireland.com certainly has no need of such distractions on its web site. According to its own description, it is the creation of a former Dublin 'escort', Patricia Albright, who saw a niche in the market in 1998 following the collapse of *In Dublin*, which had been the stronghold of the sex advertising market. Women pay up to €250 per month to advertise on *escort-ireland.com*, and agencies can expect to pay up to €750 to tout their women. The site, which describes itself as the product of a 'reputable and fully registered UK company,' is registered to a company called E Designers Ltd. 'Patricia' looks after everything else, according to the site. It is obviously doing well. On one day the site boasted:

> Today we have 487 Irish Female Escorts, 11 Irish Male Escorts, 18 Irish Transsexual Escorts, 5 Irish Transvestite Escorts, 8 Irish Escort Duos and 3 Irish Escort Couples listed.

The numbers fluctuate daily, according to how many of the foreign women are in the country at the time, and can reach as high as 550. If each of these women is paying £250 per month, that would reap almost €140,000 per month.

The group's operations also include *escort-england.com*, *escort-scotland.com* and *escort-wales.com*; but those operations on the other side of the Irish Sea seem not to have reached the dizzy heights of the Irish enterprise. In mid-2009 *escort-england.com* listed forty-five escorts working, *escort-scotland.com* thirty. *escort-wales.com* seemed hardly to have taken off: 'Today we have 1 Welsh Female Escorts, 1 Welsh Male Escorts, 1 Welsh Transsexual Escorts, listed.'

To bolster what it sees as its legitimacy, *escort-ireland.com* states:

> We are a female owned and operated business that cares about the escorts that advertise with us, the clients that use our website and the overall well-being of our industry. We work very hard to provide a top quality service to our advertising customers and website users. We are often asked how it is that we are so successful, how it is that no other Irish escort website has ever caught up with us. We feel our integrity and dedication to consistently working hard to provide the very best service we can is the key to our success.

The web site is exceptionally professional. After logging on, punters use drop-down menus to choose the woman they want to visit according to (among other things) nationality, ethnicity, hair colour, age, height, bra size, services offered, and sexual orientation. The men on offer are too few to require such a graded system. There are reviews of the women from previous customers, as well as a glossary of terms explaining what such terms such as 'tea-bagging', 'Russian' and 'rimming' mean.

It even has a media section, runs competitions, and expresses concern about the problems of human trafficking, pointing out that

> we have been taking constructive action by educating our industry about this issue and working with organisations that work against human trafficking. We have also made several donations to charities that work with trafficking victims.

Nonetheless, it does not provide details of the ways in which it vets its advertisers to ensure that they are not exploiting trafficked women. (See chapter 9.)

Obviously, the site's services are centred mainly around the Dublin area. It lists 249 escorts in Dublin alone, with the majority, all but approximately twenty, portraying themselves as 'independent', i.e. not working for a brothel. A handful of couples, 'escort duos' (two women working together), male escorts, transvestites and transsexual escorts are added to the mix. Most who are not based in Dublin will return reasonably regularly, knowing they are guaranteed high levels of business, even in recessionary times.

In addition, *escort-ireland.com* offers contact details for escort agencies, with an average of five women working in each. Some offer far more, as many as fifteen to twenty, though at any one time the site may list only thirty-five agency escorts. The number of actual agencies listed fluctuates, depending on whether the brothels are raided. In 2008 a Cork agency listed on the site was raided, and within days it was no longer on the site.

As well as offering information about sexual health, details of lap-dancing clubs and 'glamour' photographers that the women can use, the site takes a shot at traditional prostitution, claiming, with breathtaking hypocrisy:

> These days, if you see a lady working on the streets in Ireland, you are probably looking at a drug addict. Using the services of such ladies is not only against the law, it is also supporting drug-addiction, exploiting vulnerable persons and blighting Irish communities. So, please, don't do it!

The nationwide escort sites have links to the web sites of individual escort agencies, and it is here that it becomes apparent that the industry is still growing rapidly. Many of the agency sites in each part of the country have an 'employment' section, which allows women to apply to join them. Some are more discerning than others. At one point one of the web sites states:

> If you are a pretty young lady, highly desirable, sized 8–12 and aged 18–30, and are interested in exploring the possibility of becoming a Dublin escort, please fill out the form below.

For others, size and age are not quite so important if other attributes are apparent.

One of the most popular sides of the site is the Escort-Ireland 'message board section', comments from which are reproduced throughout this book. It offers contributors the opportunity to engage in general chat about the sex trade, with cutting, complimentary or self-indulgent comments about the women, or about other punters. Another message board allows the escorts to warn other women about certain punters, and allows the punters themselves to make complaints about certain women. It even lists warnings about robberies and attacks that the women and the punters have experienced.

One example of such a message is the following by 'Brenda Beauty Babe', who warned her fellow-prostitutes about men in Cork and their apparently dodgy money.

Girls in Cork, be careful ! There are many guys with fake money around!
Always check all the money from every single client! If u don't know how to check it, u can also buy UV pen or UV lamp. Stay safe!

Another, from Cassie.ca, is much more sinister. Despite her poor English, the danger she faced is all too clear.

Hello to everybody,
i JUST REGISTER HERE TO WARNING ALL LADIES WHATS WRONG TO ME AND MY FRIEND its Cassie. I would like to warn you all as i don't want you to experience the same like me and my friend yesterday. It was really horrible and we are still shocked. One client who sounded young ordered him self to visit me for 30 mins yesterday. When he got to the place i told him and all was ok i geve him the directions to my apartment. All was ok, i had his number, he sounded ok but when he came up to the doors i even check him throw eyelet. BUT when i opened the door suddenly another guy

showed up and both got in. Firstly i thought the other one is comming to my friend, but i was wrong. They went straight to the lilving room and to both bedrooms. When they checked all rooms (against our banning) then one of them took out gun and pointed it at us asking if we are an agency which we of course aren't. We were both shocked and i started screaming and quickly run out. I didn't stop screaming, they got out after me and run away as i didnt stop screaming. It was so terrible . . . We don't know what they wanted. What is it all about. We have never heard this happend before in Dublin. We live near O'Connell street and thought we are save. I have no idea what would have happend if i had a diffrent reaction. They were shouting at me to shut up but i wasnt able to notice anything else then the gun. I am sending you a description how they looked like, where it happend, when it happend and their numbers. Whats going on here??? We always thought Dublin was save but more and more i hear some bed stories. How we are suppose to protect our selves? How to avoid this? Also we are thinking why it was us? Did this happend before to anybody else? Were they just trying to scare us or did they wanted to rob us or hurt us? I have million thoughts in my head. So please be careful. They were 2 very young irish guys. They were wearing grey training suit, one had dark hair and second red. Both were red in their faces and weren't too tall. It happened last night . . .

One of the most popular message boards is the escort advertising section, which allows the women to give details of when they will be returning to Ireland and any special offers they might be using to entice more men. In early April 2009 'Leah', who describes herself, with nude pictures, as a 'genuine 32-year-old British lady who has been told I am a bit of a head turner,' wrote the following message:

30 MINS 100 EURO, EARLY EASTER SPECIAL ;-) xXx. Hi Guys since I leave on good friday I am doing a special offer as

of now for the rest of my dubin tour . . . 30 mins 100 euro's 45 mins 150 euro's 60 mins 220 euro's. Call now & mention this discount when you call but please dont ask for more of a discount. TOYS & UNIFORMS AVAILABLE See you soon. Love & kisses, Leah xxx.

The internet is not the only essential technology for the 21st-century 'escort'. The mobile phone is equally important. Land lines are traceable. In the thousands of advertisements for Irish prostitutes on the internet, the most important piece of information she can get out is her mobile phone number. Then it is simply a matter of waiting until the men start calling. Generally they will—up to twenty a day. The fact that numbers can be changed, that pay-as-you-go numbers can be obtained without an address, guarantees the women a degree of anonymity. Just as important is the demand that the client also not use a suppressed number. If the number does not come up on their display, the women will simply not answer. The most successful and technologically savvy brothels and prostitutes will even have equipment that will read and store the mobile numbers of existing and prospective clients. For the former it is a security policy, which can be used to ensure that they have something with which to trace the punter, to make sure that if anything goes awry they have some form of identification for the person. It also means that if the punter causes trouble, makes the women uncomfortable or is suspected of being a detective, they can file the number on the system and not answer it again.

For existing clients, the number display feature will identify the customer for the woman, and she can then be comfortable enough to be unguarded about the full details of what she is prepared to offer.

The freedom and the reach that mobile phones give prostitutes were evident in 2003 when the Gardaí raided an 'express sex centre' in a Limerick apartment. One local newspaper reported that clients from all parts of the country were linked to a wide-spread prostitution network by phoning the call centre, which was in an apartment in the city. To cope with the huge volume of bookings, the call centre was equipped with up to twenty mobile phones, which were answered by a group of 'co-ordinators'.

The Gardaí said the list of mobile phone numbers was passed around in pubs all over the country. 'Such was the volume of calls,' one garda said, 'they would have needed a switchboard. But of course a switchboard was out of the question, as the operation could be easily traced. With mobile phones the call centre could be moved anywhere at short notice.'

While those in charge of this business were Irish, most of the women were not. After hiring women, the organisers sent them to various parts of the country and provided them with accommodation. In this way they managed to set up a nationwide prostitution network. Prostitutes in nearly every county, city and large town were on call to the operators of the service. The *Evening Echo* reported:

> Once a call was received at the Limerick centre, the punter would be asked what part of the country he was ringing from and told the price of various services on offer. With this information the on-call prostitute operating in that area would be given the punter's mobile.

As well as dealing with Sex Express calls, the centre processed all money transactions. The system enabled those in charge of the centre to keep a tab on every transaction and to know what each prostitute owed after collecting from clients.

A man and a woman, both Irish, were arrested in the raid on the apartment. They were questioned at Henry Street under sex offences legislation but were released without charge.

The dependence the women have on mobile phones was also evidenced by the case of Deena Edridge, a 28-year-old English woman who in 2007 had the dubious honour of being the third person, and the first woman, to be jailed for organising prostitution. Herself a former prostitute, Edridge, with an address at Wentworth Place, Naas, managed a brothel at Bachelor's Walk in

Dublin city centre, which was monitored by gardaí from August to October 2005. When they finally raided the apartment on 10 October, as part of Operation Quest, they knew it was being run as a brothel, seven days a week, in a day shift from noon to 7 p.m. and an evening shift from 7 p.m. to 5 a.m., with five to seven women working at any time out of a total of sixteen. At the time of the raid there were four prostitutes on the premises and one customer as well as Edridge and an accomplice.

When Edridge was brought before the courts Detective-Sergeant Séamus Holohan told the judge that thirty-five mobile phones had been found during a search of another premises at Beresford House in the International Financial Services Centre at Custom House Quay, which operated as a 'call centre' for Bachelor's Walk. Thirty-two of these were switched on and were being answered by two women employed as receptionists, directing customers to the brothel. The men rang the mobile phone number in the advertisement, and the receptionists told them where to go. All the mobiles were 'prepay' or 'ready-to-go' numbers, on various networks, which could not be traced.

The detective described the prostitution industry as 'extremely reliant on mobile phones,' and said that within two days fourteen numbers used by the seized phones were back in operation.

One of the factors that was Edridge's undoing was her effective bookkeeping, a legacy of the course she had taken in business administration in her previous life. In fact the court was told that her management skills could have stood her in good stead in the commercial world. Edridge managed the finances as well as hiring women, greeting customers, lining up the women to allow customers make their choice, and managing the off-site call centre. The Gardaí found that 'meticulous records' had been kept in the brothel, listing the number of women working on a particular day, the number of customers, the duration of their stay, and how much money had been paid. From these records the detectives were able to estimate that the takings over the four shifts before the Garda search had been €22,000, while the annual takings were thought to be about €4 million.

Customers were charged €130 per half hour and €220 per hour for sex and other activities. There was also a 'call-out service', whereby customers could order women to a hotel room or to their own home. The women gave half their takings to the brothel, along with additional deductions of €15 for working the day shift and €25 for working the night shift. The business was advertised through web sites and magazines under the cover of seventeen different escort agencies.

Edridge had rented the apartment, under a false name, but had never lived there, using it solely as a brothel. She was not even the main operator but was paid a salary of €50,000. Her male accomplice, Martin Morgan, a well-known pimp, was the main culprit. While he was not brought to account at that time, we will see later how he finally got his comeuppance at the hands of the courts.

Edridge pleaded guilty to organising prostitution and controlling the activities of more than one prostitute. Her defence counsel said that she was originally from Britain and had come to Ireland five years previously. Edridge, she said, had suffered greatly as a child as a result of her parents' divorce, and when both parents subsequently remarried it was claimed that Edridge's father 'threw money' at her, allowing her to 'live a high life style' until she was eighteen. At that point, for reasons that were not made clear, he stopped financing her activities, leaving her with no way to pay off a number of credit card debts that she had accumulated. Panicking, she attempted to take out a loan. However, she fell into debt again, and at that point she felt she had no option but to answer an advertisement in a newspaper for work as a prostitute.

The defence said that Edridge had been robbed and had had a number of frightening experiences while working in the sex trade. She had been employed to answer the phones for the business, but she took full responsibility for the offences with which she was charged.

Judge Katherine Delahunt told Edridge: 'You are in many ways a victim and fell into an illegal trade because of abandonment by your father.' However, she stated that Edridge was a 'major player who had a significant and trusted role in running the business,' and imposed two twelve-month sentences, to run concurrently.

———

As much as mobile-phone technology is a winner for the prostitutes, it can be a curse for the punter. On occasion, men who have used their own mobile-phone number have been left floundering for words when the women have phoned them back when they are with a colleague or even a partner. More than one man on the message boards vented his spleen at the fact that a prostitute had called or texted him back while he was not in a position to talk, and his partner had taken the call or read the text. There have also been instances when the women have used the mobile-phone numbers registered to the men to make contact with them afterwards so as to blackmail them.

The storage of information created a furore at the beginning of 2009 when it emerged that a number of 'escort' web sites had pooled information on 'good and bad' clients. One woman, calling herself Abby, set up a data-base on which to record 'all my personal bad and good client numbers for my own use.' However, over time the spreadsheet began to include details other than phone numbers and locations, including the men's sexual preferences and their physical appearance.

> This was done so that I could quickly use the search function within the spreadsheet and search the number of an incoming call to see if that number had been recorded by me. This would allow me to make a quick decision on whether I should see the caller or not, and avoided me storing numbers on my own phone.

She admitted that she also took numbers listed on escort forums as 'bad clients'.

Abby began sharing her information with other escorts. To protect clients' confidentiality, she said she reduced the numbers to six digits.

We truly believed that it was a quicker and more efficient way of working when we could not get hold of each other for client references for whatever reason. Often a client would want booking at short notice, and even though he was happy to give the name of an escort he had seen previously, often, the escort wasn't available to give a reference.

The spreadsheet was available by invitation only, and was protected by password. However, within four months of her beginning to share the information, twenty-seven prostitutes had access to it and were contributing to it.

The problem was that Abby, as she admitted herself, was not IT-savvy. The list was put up as a spreadsheet on Google.

I had no control over what was being added and made no demands on anyone. I didn't run it so to speak, it ran itself. It was simply 'there' for trusted girls to access by password. It very quickly became a tool that we all relied upon on a daily basis for our safety only and nothing else.

By the time problems began to arise, there were ten thousand numbers on the list.

Abby claimed she had set up and shared the list with the best of intentions.

Because there is 5000 bad numbers that means 5000 bad incidents (at least). Many go unreported. it's very easy with sim cards being so ready available for a bad client to change their number, a good number, even a partial one gives the girl a sense of reassurance during these bad times, without compromising her clients confidentiality.

However, what Abby described as a 'bad egg' took the information, and it was forwarded to others. With such a wide base of people now knowing about the list it was only a matter of time before its existence got out; and the reaction of the punters was predictable. One asked:

> I have been wanting to go to a girl for a while now but as soon as I pluck up the courage to go this list comes out. What guarantees do we have that it's safe to go without our private lives being compromised?

Another said:

> Client confidentiality has definitely been broken here. This is how the whole operation runs, is by people being discreet. Keeping lists of clients numbers—on a spreadsheet that can be accessed over the internet!—is far from being discreet. How on earth did none of these women not see this??

With so few digits missing, the numbers would not have been hard to work out, making the people easily contactable.

The biggest fears expressed by the men was that somehow their numbers would be used to blackmail them, by telling family members, or would be exposed by journalists. It didn't help when a tabloid newspaper published an article that told even more people about the existence of the list. It was no consolation to the others when one punter pointed out that with the tabloids it would only be famous people who would be subject to the typical loud exposé. Another pointed out the limited worth of any such list.

> Lads, just change your SIM. I've had a punting phone for years. You go out and buy a new SIM every few weeks, or better yet after every punt. Just make sure you call the provider (O2, Meteor, or Vodafone) and cancel the SIM after you switch. You don't want old SIMs floating around. You can buy SIMs in store in O2 for a €10 and they give you a €10 credit! You can get them for free here: O2 Ireland Free SIM cards for you and your friends. Without phone numbers thier lists mean jack shit.

As we will see later, mobile-phone technology allowed the Gardaí to track the activities of one of the country's most notorious paedophiles—himself a former garda—who tried to pay prostitutes to bring him children to have sex with. However, another form of technology nearly brought another set of prostitutes into the clutches of the Gardaí in 2004.

The women had quite a successful operation running in Clonmel when a member of the public stumbled on their advertisement. He had been hoping to get a stripagram for a stag party and had searched the internet for a suitable service. However, when he opened one listing for 'Tipp Babes' he realised they were offering something more than a staged striptease. He notified a local radio station, Tipp FM, which got one of its reporters to ring the number. The reporter was offered an hour-long service with a 'quite naturally big-busted' 27-year-old Caribbean woman with a 'lovely, tanned complexion.' The station made a number of calls to the brothel, and then broadcast recordings on one of its programmes. Within hours the Gardaí raided the premises, an apartment near the Oakville Shopping Centre in Clonmel; but the women had already fled, and had even managed to disconnect the mobile number they had been using. The only people who could be tracked down were the apartment's embarrassed owners, who were dumbstruck when told of their tenants' activities. Their solicitors quickly issued a statement insisting they had no idea of what was going on in their property.

———

The technology with which prostitutes attract men is not the only thing that has moved on as Ireland's sex trade has grown and expanded. The services the women offer have become mind-boggling, some of them demanding a premium on top of the already inflated price tag. Whereas previously women might have offered straight sex or oral sex, perhaps charged a bit extra to put on a nurse's uniform, that is not nearly enough these days. The terminology they use would baffle the most worldly-wise individuals if they were not acquainted with the sex trade. Those who are, however, would know that 'GFE' refers to 'girl-friend experience', 'O-levels' and 'A-levels' refer to oral and anal sex, and 'hardsports' refers to behaviour that need not be explained here except to say that it is extreme and uncompromising and can only be degrading for the woman.

The fact is that while some owners of these internet sites, as well as those who contribute to their message boards, would claim that the women even enjoy what they do, the services they offer in the 21st century can only eat away at their own self-worth, as 'Gemma' admitted.

> You might think we enjoy when they ask us to beat them. I suppose I do like that sometimes especially if the day has been as bad as some of the ones I have had lately. But when they are asking me to pretend to love them, when they want me to do around the world (Slang for kissing the entire body), when they want to French kiss me I find it hard not to gag. That's just the old-fashioned ones. Then you get the ones who have seen something in a porn film and want to try it out. Let's just say people who know what I do think I must be raking it in charging them €150 basic. Frankly, I think they are getting it cheap. There are some sick bastards out there.

Pain appears to be the aphrodisiac that attracts the highest extra charges. Whips, chains and domination have been part of the sexual landscape for several years. However, the level of degradation that has crept into the sex trade is horrifying. In later chapters, attacks on prostitutes are discussed; but it is worth pointing out that some of the violent behaviour men expect the women to put up with as part of the 'service' is verging on the actionable. One punter on one of the message boards summed up the mentality of those men who cannot see past a woman being an object for their satisfaction.

> Met [. . .] was really happy when she opened the door. As soon as I got in there I paid up and then showed her who the boss

was. Once you pay the money she is on your time. I think she liked it when I threw her around the bed. She didn't complain no matter how rough I gave it to her.

To ensure that the women are made to feel like objects, the internet sites on which the women advertise allow the men to write reviews, not only of their performance but also of their appearance, the place where they live or work, and whether they are good value for money. Like a sordid holiday review site, men are asked to say whether they would recommend the woman to another punter, or whether they themselves will return. In the comments the men offer they may claim that the woman is older or fatter than in the photographs on the web site.

This girl is 8–10 kg overweight in my opinion.
Got the feeling that if you got drugs with ya, you might get discount.
She was totally unshapely and the location was dingy and uncomfortable.
The surgeon that gave her the boob job must have been blind.
She had a mass of spots or a rash or something all over her back. To say this girl is rough is been polite.
Ws thinkin that she is pregnant but she just seems to like mc D too much.

On the women's performance, the men are equally unflattering.

I should have saved my money and went into ann summers and bought a blow up doll. Yet another girl that goes through the motions. Her use of the english language is very limited but she is very experienced in the use of the phrases 'that is extra' and 'no you can't touch there.'

Even with her limited English it would be interesting to hear how this woman would return the favour. Certainly one prostitute told me:

I have had a few bad reviews from punters saying I don't look the picture on my profile. Those photos were professionally taken to make me look my best and maybe I don't always look at my best when I have been working hard trying to entertain a load of men in the space of a few hours. But even so the comments are a bit rich coming from these lads who probably have beer guts, comb-overs and smell like a bin lorry.

03 | WHO'S THAT GIRL?

In 2009 a 32-year-old Brazilian woman was refused entry to Britain when she arrived at Newcastle Airport with luggage containing only T-shirts, a dressing-gown, and lingerie—hardly suitable clothing for typical British weather.

Border Agency officials were immediately suspicious of the woman, who had arrived on a flight from Geneva. She seemed to be woefully under-resourced for staying the length of time she appeared to want to remain in the country. They suspected that she was involved in the sex trade. They became more suspicious when she could not say what she would be doing in Britain, other than 'seeing Newcastle city centre.' Investigations revealed that three months earlier she had been refused entry at Belfast City Airport. She sought to conceal this by replacing the passport containing the refusal stamps with a new Brazilian passport. A Border Agency spokesman said:

> We routinely make checks to ensure that people wanting to visit the UK have not previously tried to circumvent our immigration laws. Visitors to the UK must play by the rules. Those who do not are refused entry and sent home.

The spokesman said that the same woman had been refused entry at Belfast on 15 January after a baggage search revealed a collection of sexual 'paraphernalia' and details of escort agencies and sex sites.

This woman was only one of the thousands who flock to Britain and Ireland to sell sex to men at a high price. There are various women's groups that state that all women entering prostitution have been trafficked or forced into the industry, but that is simply not true. There is certainly a significant number of women offer ing sex to Irish men who have been brought here against their will; but of the approximately one thousand women regularly engaging in prostitution it would be inaccurate to say they are all here under duress. So why do these women enter prostitution?

In some ways, distinctions can be drawn at this point between street workers and indoor 'escorts'. As will be seen in chapter 4, women on the streets, particularly in Dublin, tend to be there because something is compelling them. Either they have a sub-stance addiction—mainly to heroin—that a social welfare benefit cannot satisfy or they are so dependent that they simply cannot function well enough or for long enough to find legitimate work. In fact many spend their daytime hours shooting up the drugs or drinking the alcohol paid for by the previous night's work. It is these women who are willing to take the biggest risks.

'Julie' was working in the area around the Peppercanister Church in Mount Street Crescent, Dublin, one cold January evening, and despite the temperature she was skimpily clad. A man walked past her. 'Are you looking for business, love?' she asked him. Not wanting to cause offence, he simply replied, 'Sure in this recession I couldn't afford such a thing.'

Before he knew what was happening she had laced an arm through his. 'For €50 you could have a bareback [no condom] blowjob [fellatio] and do whatever you want to me,' she told him. She admitted afterwards that he looked down at the veins on her arms, shook her off, and swore at her to get away from him.

With a few exceptions, this desperation is typical of the women on the streets. They are there because they see themselves as having no other choice. They do not have either the looks, the money or the self-control to be able to work in one of the more lucrative apartments, where they could charge much more. Instead they must go out on the streets, night after night, normally well after midnight, and stay there until dawn, hoping to pick up some drunk or drugged men coming out of one of the clubs whose common sense has been dulled but libido enhanced.

Those working in the apartments would say they are much less inclined to have as visible a drug problem; those who have hide it well. They would also claim they are much less likely to have the same desperation for money to sate an addiction and so are less likely to provide services that put them in a risky situation that they cannot control. Without such dependence they are also less likely to have ravaged features, and their healthy complexion means they can charge more money.

There are a number of reasons why women enter indoor prostitution, apart from trafficking. They would argue that they are simply putting what they see as their best asset, their looks, to good use.

There is no doubt that the pictures of the women on the web sites show them to best advantage and in positions that they hope will portray an appearance of quality to justify the €250 price tag for their company. One of the biggest complaints among punters is that often the woman who meets them at the hotel or apartment door does not match up to those pictures.

A large number of the women have an apparently high level of intelligence: web sites list them as speaking several languages, able to communicate well in any given circumstance if the client desires them for more than just sex. In many instances it is their business acumen that sets them apart from their street-walking rivals. They are well dressed, base themselves in expensive parts of cities, in apartments or hotel rooms that are clean and attractive to the punters. They offer their clients off-street parking, a glass of wine, and shower facilities (which are often incorporated in the service). From the ability to travel to where their clients are to ensuring that their premises are even accessible by wheelchair, it seems they try to have every angle covered.

Speak to these women and they will say they have found a job that, while possibly not pleasant at times, is fiscally stimulating and allows them to be their own boss, working in their own time. However, according to Ruhama all the appearances of self-choice these women portray are a smokescreen. Gerardine Rowley of Ruhama says:

> Traditionally indoor prostitution has been regarded as more glamorous and acceptable than street work, not least because alcohol and other substance abuse are not tolerated, their mandatory health checks and shift work can add an air of normality. Ruhama's experience however, suggests, that women involved in indoor prostitution experience more psychological problems and are in some ways more damaged by the process than those who work on the streets. The reasons women get involved in prostitution vary not just on the street but also off-street. It is often background issues like debt, lack of real alternative opportunities of making money, lack of education, mental health issues, abusive background, addiction issues and low self-esteem. They could also be involved in current abusive relationships that coerce them into prostitution.

The trafficking of foreign nationals is dealt with in detail in later chapters. However, Gerardine Rowley insists that the traditional view of someone being tricked into coming to Ireland and being exploited is not the best definition of 'trafficking'. She maintains that most women in the sex trade are trafficked when a true definition of the word is applied.

> Trafficking is not necessarily across borders. *Smuggling* is across borders. Therefore Irish women can be trafficked too and there needs to be a greater understanding of that. We need to start looking at the Irish women who have been duped into prostitution, coerced and deceived. Trafficking is movement of people by means of force even within borders for the purposes of labour or sexual exploitation. It does not talk about cross

borders and that is why we are unhappy that it is linked to the Immigration Bill.

We would believe [that] the majority of women in Ireland fall under the victims of trafficking to some degree. There are the extreme cases where a woman is kidnapped and forced into sex and receives no money. However, there is also a level of trafficking involving a woman's position of vulnerability, as talked about in the UN Protocol that defines trafficking and in the Convention of Europe. They talk about a woman being vulnerable through a lack of education, a lack of opportunities or an abusive background, who have been coerced and brought to Ireland and sold a wonderful story. The conditions which they agreed to in prostitution have developed into more exploitative situations and the long term harm is worse than they expected. They may still be victims of trafficking even though they are not at the extreme end.

One only has to look at the profile of those operating supposedly independently, she says, to see that many are under huge pressure.

We have met women from Eastern Europe who knew they were coming here to become involved in the sex industry, but the industry by its nature was controlling and they did not get the money they expected and found themselves under [the] surveillance of those running the sex industry. When you look at their background you may find characteristics which mean they have remained in the situation voluntarily much longer than they otherwise would have.

Working in this area for a long time and speaking to these women, some of whom are coming out the other side, we find they say they get trapped in the sex industry and to survive and to hold on to any sense of dignity and self-esteem they have to tell themselves they are doing what they are doing out of their own choice.

Listening to women, the point at which they enter prostitution is not after sitting down and really making an informed decision. Usually it is at a point of crisis at that time and even though there may be other options they cannot see them. Then they get trapped in the cycle that because they are selling their bodies, their self-esteem goes down and they need money to build it up is again through prostitution because they [have] no other opportunities. Also women who were drug users say they became addicted to money.

Women have spoken about losing their identity. Being a prostitute becomes who they are. They take on the persona that the punter wants and forget who they really are.

When one looks closely, it is clear that there are significant differences between the way the women on the streets and the women indoors perceive what they are doing.

There is quite a different profile between those indoors and those outdoors. Women in street prostitution, and many nights we will hear them talk in our van, will say they cannot believe they have let themselves go so much that they are having to sell their bodies to get drugs. Some will say 'I hate what I am doing, I wish I could get out of it.'

Women in street prostitution use numbing substances—previously it was alcohol such as a half bottle of vodka—now it is hard drugs. The numbing substance does not necessarily come first. We know women who were in prostitution and had to take the drugs to numb what they were doing.

However, with indoor prostitution, it is normalised much more, particularly at an international level. It seems to groom women much more into the mindset that this is legitimate work. The women in the apartments and hotels, where they are much more regulated, will not be tolerated by their pimps if they are on hard drugs because they wont be able to perform like they should and also because they are harder to control and are less predictable on drugs.

Therefore the women indoors, to survive, take on a normalisation in their minds. They convince themselves that they are in control and it is their body to do with as they wish. We have found that the women who try to leave the off-street scene and come to us are more psychologically damaged because they were constantly training their minds to separate from what they were doing. That also makes them more susceptible to the grooming process. But when they come out they realise the harm that has been caused to them.

One of the most comprehensive studies of women who had worked or were still working as prostitutes in Ireland was carried out by TSA Consultancy Ltd on behalf of Ruhama. The survey involved fourteen women aged between twenty-one and sixty. Of these, six had become involved in prostitution before they were eighteen, the remainder while in their twenties or thirties. The least amount of time spent in the sex trade was seven years, the highest twenty-six years. Six women had been involved in street prostitution only, one solely in off-street; the rest had been in a mixture of environments.

The ways they ended up in the streets was fairly similar. Three had grown up away from their families, in care or in foster homes, and most of the rest had left home in their early teens. None had education past the age of sixteen, and some had left school at thirteen. Confirming Ruhama's view that few women enter prostitution without pressure, only three had started off on their own. One was brought into the sex trade through her extended family and the rest by 'friends and peers.' Surprisingly, only two of those women believed they had been pimped, the rest considering that they had been introduced to it by the third party.

The ways they ended up on the streets or in brothels were similar in a number of instances, in that they felt they had no alternative. Four admitted spending the whole night working in order to support a drug habit. One said:

All I knew is that I kept getting into debt with the heroin. My boyfriend never did anything, never made any effort, wouldn't even beg. He just left it up to me. I'd done everything else, robbed my family, pawned jewellery, the lot. It was the only place to go.

For another it was drink that forced her to sell her body.

To me there were no choices. Being an alcoholic and not having education you're not going to get employment because you're at work but you're thinking where you are going to get the next drink or going in with drink on you. The money was easy to make and I didn't know anyone else who might help.

For others it was simply being unskilled or in low-paid employment that they felt could not support them.

When I left care, I had to get work where there was accommodation. So I did nursing home and hospital work but you were paid a pittance. I was not happy so I left the workforce. Then I got married.

And it was her husband who got her into prostitution.

Another woman told the researchers she had worked in hairdressing but couldn't afford to live on the wages once she left home. For another it was as simple as not being able to afford child care and having no family to look after her child. She began working as a prostitute to pay for the care.

Those who were not forced into prostitution and were without an addiction would often develop one to numb the pain of what they were doing. One admitted that once she began working the streets she was never sober, another that she had to take what she described as 'nerve tablets' to keep her calm while she was working.

There was more stark evidence of how much the women had to put up with. One woman said that young men in particular showed violent tendencies. 'The younger generation were bad, more bad, forcing, tearing your clothes, wanting to try every way.' For others the experience was even worse.

Guns put up to me, knives, hammered on my head, taken up the mountains and raped. I could go on and on. I got a black eye one Christmas and let on I was drunk and fell at the fireplace.

Another woman seemed to have come across a similar type of punter. 'I've had broken jaws, a couple of hidings. I was raped once up the Dublin mountains.'

The risk of violence was so high that they had to develop protection strategies. The women told how they would always make sure they directed the punter to somewhere that was not too dark, would always keep their window open so that any screams would be heard, and always said they wanted to get out immediately if the punter locked the doors. Another woman had advice about dress. 'Don't wear earrings or scarves,' she advised.

However, all the protection strategies could never guarantee their safety. They were as likely to be attacked by a man in a suit as by any other.

Most of the time they had such charm that you'd think they were genuine, just going for the sex. Then the simplest thing and their personalities would change. Some girls had regulars for years and they'd suddenly change.

But, as is common in countries where women are prosecuted for prostitution, most of the fourteen women interviewed admitted they would never report their attackers.

The women also told how hard it was to escape the sex trade. The few who had tried told how once they made the leap they found it next to impossible to find alternative work. First of all they had to explain the gap in their employment history. Others would find that their past would come back to haunt them when the prospective employer wanted to see if they had previous convictions. It was not that they didn't have a lot to offer. One woman pointed out how her painful experience with drugs would have made her an ideal person to work with young people affected by drugs.

I'd understand, have empathy. Also I'd know if they were using or at risk of using. Because of all the work I have done on myself I would know how to spot the behaviour, see the patterns, know if a child was insecure and might turn to drugs.

For others they simply wanted the chance of finding out what they could do. As one of the women put it,

Just a little while ago, I was in another world. I never got the chance to do anything decent. I don't know what talent I have. I just know I am not a bad person.

In fact the paucity of drug treatment schemes and the long delays for placement left a number of the women in prostitution for longer than they might have been otherwise. 'Drug services, waiting lists. Madness that you have to be clean before you can get help,' said one.

There was also the lure of the fast buck. Several of the women reported that the money was one of the hardest things they had to give up. As one put it, 'I have left before but the money brings you back. I did stop for a while but the money pulled me back in.' Another said: 'After I had done it that one time and I was back in regular work it would go through my head when I was having lunch. I'm earning £2 an hour and I could be earning such good money out there.'

———

The Next Step Initiative, organised by Ruhama, was one of the few studies anywhere in the world that examined how prostitution affected women's relationships with their partners. A number of these partners knew what their wife or girl-friend was doing, and from what the women said it had a hugely detrimental effect.

[Boy-friend] accepted me working when I met him . . . he knew I had been working on and off since I was 15. He doesn't mention it but sometimes if I am sore, you can get very sore, and I don't want to have sex with him he might ask me if I enjoy having sex with my clients just to hurt me. Other times he would tell me I am never going to have a life, that I am nothing without him.

One of the other women gave an even more harrowing account of why she simply could not have a sexual relationship with a man outside prostitution.

I don't go out with men now because of the work I did. I'm seven years separated from my ex and I haven't gone out with anyone. I always have the fear of them finding out what I did and turning violent and taking advantage of me and getting me back into prostitution so they can take the money.

One of the main 'escort' web sites periodically uploads 'interviews' with the escorts who advertise on its pages. These tend to feature the same questions and, very often, very similar answers. Certainly when one compares the answers with those obtained from one interview by the author with a prostitute, the differences are stark. One of the interviews on the web site went as follows:

How long have you been escorting?
Since January 2000
What was the reason you became an escort?
That's an easy one I just love the sex
Do you enjoy working as an escort?
I love it
What was the worst experience you have had working as an escort?
Never had one
Have you ever been scared working as an escort?
No

What about your best experience as an escort?

A booking with two American footballers in a Newcastle hotel

Have you ever worked for an agency?

No

Have you ever been forced to work as an escort against your will either here in Ireland or in another country?

No

Is there a certain type of client that you prefer?

Not really I enjoy all the different types

Have you ever fancied a client?

No but when I retire there are a couple I would pay to see me lol [laughing out loud]

Have any clients now or in the past ever harassed or stalked you?

No

How long do you think that you will be escorting until?

Until I don't enjoy it anymore

What do you want to do once you retire from escorting?

Lie on a beach somewhere

Where will you live when you retire?

Somewhere nice and warm.

Do you think working as an escort is wrong?

Daft question if I thought it was wrong I wouldn't do it

If you had a choice to work at something else, what would it be and why?

I do have a choice but I love what I am doing

Would you like it if another member of your family worked as an escort? e.g. sister, brother, daughter, mother?

No I can't say it would bother me

If you were being harrassed or attacked by a client or a pimp for that matter, would [you] feel ok going to the police?

If someone ever harassed or attacked me I would never have a problem reporting it, as for the pimp thing I would never work for one

Do you think the Police/Garda give enough help to escorts when they are in trouble?

Yes

Do you think the laws should be changed so the Police/Garda can help escorts more when they are in trouble?

Why change the law, they can already help

Lastly, what puts a smile on your face?

A very proficient tongue (male or female)

Now compare those answers with those given in an interview between the author and an indoor prostitute. Emma (not her working name) has been working in Ireland on tours from her native England since she was twenty-four. Now twenty-nine, she began working on the streets in the north of England when she was seventeen but was then taken on by a pimp. Unlike many of the other women, she managed to keep £80 out of every £100 she earned when she was working for that man in a brothel. After three years working for him she left the brothel and began working out of an apartment for herself and then as part of a partnership. She flies into Ireland every three months or so and works out of hotels and apartments in Dublin, Cork, and Belfast.

What got you into prostitution?

When I started working on the streets it was because my mother kicked me out of the house just before my seventeenth birthday. We had had a pretty volatile relationship since I was about thirteen, and in the end it was a fight over babysitting my little brother, which got out of control, that made her kick me out. I was going out with a fella at the time, so I stayed with him for a few weeks, but then we broke up and I went into a shelter. There wasn't much to do there so I started hanging out with the other ones my age, drinking and that.

There was a girl there who was on the game, and she told me it was easy to make money. I left school when I was fifteen and didn't know how to do anything, so I let her take me out one night to watch. Every time a car pulled up she would go over to the guy and I would just walk away. Then one night I downed a half bottle of vodka and just went for it. The first guy wasn't too bad. He was an old fella. He was pretty ugly but at least he was pretty kind, not like some of the other bastards I came across later on. He got that excited when I told him he was my first ever punter, and I think that was why he blew it fairly quick. I was a bit naïve. I let him give me only a tenner. [. . .] nearly killed me when I came back and told her that.

For the next few weeks I went with a load of different men. I was quite popular, which pissed off a few of the girls who were already working. One of the nights one of them smacked me. She was quite old, in her forties, and I was scared to hit her back, so I just steered clear. The men were all right mostly—a few were way too rough, but, unlike some of the other girls, none of them raped me, though one did try to make me have sex with him bareback. I jumped out of the car and he just drove away. [. . .] had told me to act tough and direct with them the second I got into the car, and I think that helped.

I was stopped by the police eight or nine times with punters, but mostly I just got a warning and the punter got either a warning or got done. You should have heard some of the excuses they came out with, even though the police knew exactly what was going on. There were some of them who were nice to us, but the women police always tried to get us done. Most times I was brought to the nick and then let go again with a caution.

I must have been one of the few girls that was working the streets who wasn't using. I think that's why [. . .] took me off the street. He could see I wasn't off my head. He came to me first just like any other punter. He came back three or four times and then one night asked me did I want to come and work for him. Because I had been with him a few times I thought [he] seemed all right, so I said I'd think about it. I knew one of the girls on the street who had worked in a massage parlour and she told me what that was like, and told me what I needed to do. The next time he came I said Okay.

What was the brothel like?
It wasn't too bad. I didn't have to see as many men, 'cause I was charging more. On the street the average punter gave me about £25. These guys had to pay me £70 or £80 so I was doing all right, even though I had to give 20 per cent to [. . .].

There were two other girls working there when I started. We would take it in turns answering the phone, and then when a punter arrived whichever ones weren't with someone would come out and meet him, and he would choose. Just like on the streets, you got some bastards and some who weren't too bad. It felt a bit safer, 'cause you had the other girls or [. . .] just down the corridor.

For the first year we had adverts in top-shelf mags and a few classifieds which made out we were a massage studio. Then [. . .] got an advert on a web site, and the number of customers shot up. It was only a small site but we got photos taken that were put onto it, and that seemed to bring in loads of business.

We would normally see five or six each a day, working from about midday to 10 p.m., but I found I was getting more than my fair share—up to ten a day. I think it was 'cause of that that I eventually went out on my own.

To be fair to [. . .], he was fine about it. I had earned him some good money, so he did well out of me. He didn't even mind when I took a few of my regulars with me.

How did you set up on your own?
I had seen how well [. . .] did out of the internet, so I just focused on that. I got professional photographs taken and put them on an escort web site. Because internet escorting hadn't taken off by then, the web site owners weren't looking for as much to advertise—not nearly as much as I have to pay now.

I had got an apartment with the money I earned in the brothel, and for a while I just did in-calls out of that. The work was just the same as the brothel, except I wasn't on a rota. To be honest, for the first few weeks I was pretty scared, 'cause I was on my own and there was no-one there to help if a punter turned on me. Then one day one got nasty with me 'cause I wouldn't let him go bareback, just like on the street. He told me I wouldn't catch anything off him, but I told him No. Then he started yelling at me and calling me all the names under the sun. I told him my boy-friend was in the next room, and he believed me and left. But that really shook me up. All I could think was what if he came back—he could be waiting outside the front of the apartment block for me or anything.

Eventually I decided I wasn't going to work from my home any more, because I was so shook up. I almost went back to [...].

But then I saw an advert from another escort in my area looking for a duo partner. She wanted someone to work with her so that she could get clients who were looking for two girls at once. I met up with her and we agreed to share the cost of renting an apartment. It worked quite well. Men would pay a lot to have 'parties' with both of us together. The two of us also started doing tours to hotels and apartments around the rest of Britain and Ireland.

Do you enjoy this work? Have you encountered any violence from punters or agency owners?
I think any escort who says she enjoys doing this is either kidding herself or lying. I have been seeing men for quite a few years and I still feel nervous the first time a new punter arrives at the door. It was okay in the brothel, and it hasn't been too bad since I started working with [...], because at least I know someone is only a room or two away as well. Sure there have been a few good-looking men who I would have been interested in in another world; but there and then I just want to get through the appointment, get my money, and get them back out the door.

I have had a few run-ins with punters, as I've already said. The worst night of my life was only last year. I was doing a tour in Scotland, and [...] agreed to do an out-call, so I was left in the hotel on my own. I had an appointment with this young guy. He didn't want anything too strange, and things were going all right when he suddenly got off the bed and started muttering. I asked him what was wrong, and he told me to 'shut the fuck up.' I was tempted to tell him not to speak to me like that, but I was getting scared. Next thing he opened the minibar and drank a couple of the shorts down, and then just sat down. I presumed he was going to come back, but he just kept sitting there staring at me and then at the ground. He kept muttering under his breath.

I asked him again if he was all right, but he just kept staring at me. Then he threw one of the empty bottles through the door of the bathroom and it smashed on the floor. I was really shitting myself then, but he just got up, got dressed and walked out. By the time [. . .] came back I still hadn't calmed down.

Another guy demanded I give him his money back afterwards, saying he did not like my service. I told him where to go, and he went for me. Luckily I was closer to the door than him and I ran out of the room and into the kitchen, where [. . .] was. When he came in and saw the two of us there he let it go.

She actually had a far worse experience than me when she was working on her own. Some guy just started laying into her while the two of them were in the bed. They had just finished and he gave her a beating. She should have told the police, but she had only started working and thought she would end up getting done.

If you don't enjoy this, why do you keep doing it? Will you keep doing it?
What else am I going to do? I got out of school when I was fifteen, so I'm not qualified to do anything, and I can't see myself going and training for anything. A few times I thought about setting up an agency, but I think I would be shit at it. I'm useless with money, and the ones working for me would probably rip me off. [. . .] looks after getting apartments and hotel rooms and all that at the minute.

I'm only twenty-nine, so I could keep doing this for a while yet. I've earned a good bit of money and I'm still getting a good number of clients, so I'm not rushing to stop for a while yet. But I suppose I do want to do the whole getting-married-and-having-kids thing. I've been out with a few fellas and haven't told them I have sex for money—they just think they're onto a winner 'cause I'm good in bed. Even if I found a guy I really loved I couldn't tell him I had been doing this. Doesn't matter at the minute anyway. There's no-one.

If you do settle and have kids, what would you say if you found out that your daughter was working as an escort?
I suppose I could lie and say that it's her life. But really I think I would bloody kill her. My mum knew I worked the streets, but when we made up a few years ago I didn't tell her I was still doing it. I think she's sort of guessed but isn't saying anything. We may be talking, but we're still not that close, so it's not really an issue.

Do you think prostitution should be legalised here in Ireland? Have you had much hassle from the police here or in Britain?
I do think it should be legalised, 'cause it would make it safer to work. For one thing, we could hire a hire legit security firm instead of having to get some fella through an escort web-site ad. At the minute none of the proper ones will touch us, because if word got out they were working with escorts their other clients wouldn't take them on.

Legalising the industry would also allow them to bring in mandatory testing. I'm fairly regular in getting tests done, but I know a load of girls who aren't. I don't want to pick anything up 'cause some punter has been with one of them. All the same I tend to look out for myself. I'm one of the few girls that doesn't offer oral without.

Touch wood, I haven't had any hassle from the police here or in Britain since I started working indoors. A few of the hotels here have given me a few strange looks, but they've still let me check in. Only one asked me to leave, and that was 'cause the guy's girl-friend got wind of where he was going and went mental with him when he went down to reception. Unfortunately, I went down from the room a couple of minutes after he left, 'cause I wanted to go to the shop. There he was standing there with her going mental. Somehow she knew I was the woman her fella had been seeing and started screaming at me. I presume the hotel staff put two and two together, or had been watching my room or something, 'cause they knocked on the door the next morning and asked me to leave.

Do you believe there are women trafficked into the industry here?

I haven't met any or even heard of any in Ireland, though I have heard of a few in England. Again I haven't met them. I wouldn't expect to, really. That's one thing I am thankful for. If I wanted to stop tomorrow I could—though God knows where I would get money then.

Do you regret getting into the industry?

What do you think? When you've been doing this for more than ten years you have a lot of regrets—like if I hadn't left school when I was fifteen, or if I hadn't got myself kicked out of my mum's house, what else I could be doing. Doing this isn't exactly like wanting to be a teacher or a nurse when you grow up.

Anti-prostitution groups say that, no matter what they say, women working even as high-class escorts are invariably forced into the sex industry, either by an individual or circumstance. What do you think of that? Is it a generalisation? Has your self-esteem been badly affected?

I wasn't forced by anyone to do what I do. I started working the street because I had no money, just like someone takes any job to get money. I would not have done this if I had another option, but at the end of the day it was my decision and my decision only. It's all very well these do-gooders making us all out as victims, but it's no different from someone else doing a job they didn't like. My self-esteem is pretty low having sex for money, but at the end of the day I can still look myself in the mirror every morning. I'm doing what I need to do to get by.

What do you think of the men who pay to have sex with you?
It really depends which ones you're talking about. I have some clients that have been with me for years. Fine, I don't fancy them, so I don't enjoy having sex with them. But they pay me well, they are always polite, and I'm not scared when I'm with them. Obviously there are quite a few that, as soon as they walk in, give me a bad vibe. They barely speak, and I'm always wondering what they are thinking. It's always a relief when the door swings closed again with them on the other side.

There are the first-timers, who are quite sweet. Those are probably the easiest, 'cause they are so nervous that half the time they are nearly wanting to get it over quicker than I am. I hate the cocky ones. They walk in as if they own the place, making their demands. Some will even say such-and-such does that better, or tell me I'm charging too much compared to other girls. Since I started advertising on the web sites it has been those bastards that have written the shitty reviews, just 'cause I didn't let them do one thing or another or because they had it better somewhere else.

I suppose a load of the men who come to me are probably married or with a girl. Sometimes I do think what it would be like for them if they found out. Some of the regulars that I know better have started talking about their wives and have even shown me pictures of their kids. I just smiled and said nice things, but really I just felt sorry for them.

There are many classes of women who become embroiled in prostitution, but one of the most common occupations given by the women is 'student'. Hundreds of women advertise themselves in the sex trade as students. It would seem they believe this gives them, firstly, the appearance of being young, secondly, the appearance of being intelligent, thirdly, the appearance of being in need of money, and, finally, the appearance of being independent and merely working in the industry to pay their fees.

Of course there are a number of women working in the sex trade who really are students and who feel there is no other way to finance their life-style while they are still enjoying home comforts. In 2006 the *Scotsman* reported that dozens of Scottish students were travelling to Ireland for 48-hour periods over the weekend to service Irish punters before returning in time for classes on Monday morning.

The trend would appear to be spiralling out of control in England, with some students in the Universities of Oxford and Cambridge turning to prostitution. One student in Cambridge told the university newspaper that she was charging men £50 per hour and slept with forty to fifty in a two-month period in her first year at university. She said she was certainly not the only Cambridge student having sex for money.

> I met other students who did it too. Once you've done it, it is tempting. If you need quick easy money, it's there. Clients did like the fact that I was a Cambridge student and so did the agency. They liked having a classier girl there—it was good for business. In the end I left of my own accord. I just didn't fancy doing it any more. It did affect my studies, but it was good while it lasted.

In Ireland there are fewer reports of students engaging in prostitution, though obviously it is happening to some extent. The following description, which appeared on one of the Irish 'escort' web sites, is typical of what is happening throughout the sex trade.

> Laura is a stunning newcomer to Dublin, this exquisite young lady is extremely friendly and loves to laugh, cuddle, and play. Laura is currently a student studying at a top Dublin

university. Intelligent, creative and multi-talented, Laura is truly a delicious dish for any man's appetite!

On one message board 'student-Alison' described herself as a twenty-year-old Dublin student looking for work. 'I am available for escort, photography and film work,' she wrote. Within a few months she had replies from several men and agencies offering to avail of her services. While Alison was more open about her intentions from the beginning, other students will simply log on to the internet, find agencies, and submit a résumé.

In Ireland, as well as genuine students who turn to prostitution to make money, there are those who come here on a student visa but who then work as prostitutes. One of three Brazilian women found running a brothel in Limerick in early 2009, forty-year-old Maria da Silva, entered the country the previous year on the pretext of coming here to study. During her trial, Limerick District Court was told that she spent only one day on an educational course in Dublin. Together with 32-year-old Joiceline Costas dos Santos and 31-year-old Ana Christina dos Santos she pleaded guilty to keeping a brothel at Clancy Strand, Limerick, and to obstructing the gardaí who went to raid it. They had to force their way in because the women, realising who they were, refused to open the door. When the gardaí finally gained entry they found that the apartment had all the signs of being a brothel, with €500 in cash, six mobile phones, and a laptop computer. The laptop revealed that the brothel had been operating for a number of months. The Gardaí had suspected not only that the women were operating the brothel of their own volition but also that Maria da Silva, the supposed student, was in charge.

Each of the women was sentenced to six months' imprisonment for keeping a brothel, with the sentences suspended on condition that they leave Limerick within seventy-two hours. In an act of leniency the judge directed that the €500 be returned to them to help them leave the country.

In another case of a supposed student engaging in a different type of work a Chinese national, Wang Jingjing, was jailed for four months at Kilkenny District Court after she pleaded guilty to managing and operating a brothel in the town. She was also fined €900. During the hearing it emerged that she had trained as a nurse in China and had come to Ireland on a student visa. Her solicitor said she had taken a nursing course in Dublin but wanted to do another one, which cost €11,000. She could not make enough money from pubs and restaurants and so had set up a Chinese massage business. She published advertisements in local media, but no land-line number was published. That had aroused the suspicion of the Gardaí. Two detectives were offered sexual services when they phoned the mobile number. In court it emerged that Wang had been turning over €900 a day through the business, which operated for approximately five weeks. She even hired another Chinese woman to provide 'massage and other services.'

——

A number of women—and a smaller number of men—are selling sex under the veneer of massage, as emerged in 2009 at the expense of the popular classifieds web site Gumtree. The site featured more than a thousand advertisements for massage-related services in Ireland—a large proportion of which were legitimate professional businesses. However, its owners in Britain were unaware that a significant number of the operations, often listed under 'full-body massage', were a front for sex services. A number of the men and women were willing to confirm on the phone that they offered 'oral or hand relief' as extras, in addition to the massage.

One woman who answered the phone appeared to be acting as a pimp in a full-blown prostitution service. When asked what services were available she offered massage 'with oral or hand relief' from two different women in two different parts of Dublin. She added that if a 45-minute appointment was booked the women would have full sex with the punter for €200. She even admitted that one of the women was prepared to offer oral sex without a condom. Other women who answered the phone said that any 'erotic extras' would have to be negotiated with the women who were doing the massage when the client arrived.

The majority of the women offering the dubious massage services are eastern European or Asian. However, one woman, who described herself as a 'black north American,' said she offered 'covered oral sex' (i.e. with a condom) with massage for €100 or hand relief with massage for €60. On 17 February one of her ads on Gumtree offered 'with happy ending,' but that ad was removed by the following day.

The Gumtree site also featured advertisements from men looking for sexual services in addition to massage. One poster advertised: 'Male 30s looking for masseuse in Naas area for full body massage with hand relief.'

When the media raised the issue with Gumtree it issued a statement in which it said:

> Gumtree.com is a local community notice board that facilitates face-to-face trade, similar to classified ads in local newspapers. The advertisement of sexual services is against Gumtree's posting rules.
>
> Ads in the Massage Services section of Gumtree must include relevant qualifications and state that they are not offering a sexual service.
>
> Gumtree encourages its users to alert us to any suspicious ads that do not comply to these rules via the community reporting system on the site, and our dedicated safety team will take appropriate action as soon as possible. In this instance, we will investigate the adverts that you have brought to our attention and remove them from the site if they are found to be inappropriate.

The proliferation of such advertisements in various media led the Irish Massage Therapists' Association to seek greater regulation of the industry in order to eliminate the stigma that these other services are bringing to their business. Fine Gael said the Government must act to allow legitimate massage therapists to work without the stigma thrust upon them by the dubious services. The party's spokesperson on immigration, Denis Naughten, claimed:

> Criminal elements are exploiting the lack of regulation of the legitimate massage industry to provide legitimate cover for brothels which are trafficking women into this country. As a result of complete inaction by the Minister for Health and the proliferation of sex advertisements appearing as professional classified ads, the Irish Massage Therapy industry has been forced to consider regulating itself. The failure by the Department of Health to implement the 2005 recommendations of its own working group on the regulation of the legitimate massage therapy industry, is providing a legitimate cover for many brothels to operate and exploit vulnerable migrant women. That the gardaí are now monitoring some of these premises means that the situation requires urgent action. In its recommendations the working group called for the 'development of a robust system of voluntary self-regulation' for this industry, yet nothing has happened in the intervening years. This lack of regulation cannot continue. It is undermining the legitimate complementary therapy sector and allowing for the proliferation of such brothels, which in many cases are trafficking women into this country to work in the sex industry. It is clear that the Minister for Health does not believe that this area needs to be prioritised for regulation. This is sending out a clear message to international criminals that Ireland continues to be a soft touch.

There is no doubt that either the women or their pimps are often enterprising in their approach to the prostitution business. They realise that as well as having to be one step ahead of the Gardaí they have to make their product as marketable as possible and therefore are paying above the odds to advertise their wares on the web sites with the greatest traffic, paying for high-quality photographs and renting rooms or apartments in city-centre areas that will allow punters easiest access.

They are also aware of the limitations of their market. This was nowhere more clearly shown than when the economic crisis began to take hold at the end of 2008 and beginning of 2009. As one punter put it,

> the escort trade is bound to be affected by the recession like everything else at the moment. With people having less money to splash around and with an uncertain future. Escorting is something that will suffer as it's a luxury people can't afford anymore on a regular basis.

There was an acceptance among a large number of women that many of their customers, no matter how strong their sex drive, simply could not afford to pay the exorbitant prices being charged. To do their bit, the women began offering discounts. Many reduced their half-hourly rate of €150 by as much as a third, or began offering special hourly rates. One such offer, by 'sexyloola', read:

> hi guys due to the many calls i get about prices and the recession im going to reduce my rates for the weekend only::: 120 30mins,,,,180 an hr i offer all xxx services and i will be available all weekend untill 12pm sunday,,when ill be returning home . . . xxxxxxxxxx give me a call . . . xxxxx

Unlike many of the Irish shops that suffered hugely for not matching euro to pound when Christmas sales started to slump, one Englishwoman realised that she should give her clients a fair exchange and wrote on an escort message board:

> I am currently charging the same as i do in the UK, due to the economic climate at the moment. The value between the £ and € is the exact same, so it would be silly to charge more. I currently charge €100 for 30min or €150 for hour.I also have 160 reviews, so my services can't be that bad . . . lol.

Even *escort-ireland.com* acknowledged the depths of the economic crisis, writing:

> 2008 did of course bring a global financial crisis and Ireland has not been untouched by this. However the sex industry in Ireland is as recession-proof as it gets. A recession will always leave some clients thinking more carefully about how they spend their money, and in response escorts may have to make sure their pricing is competitive, but the number of clients seeking escort services in Ireland and the number of escorts available in Ireland continues to grow!

One person on the site went so far as to launch a crudely named 'Riding out the Recession' section, advertising women offering cut-price services.

One enterprising punter put up a section on one of the sites to publicise women who were offering the cheapest services. Calling himself 'recession eddie', he began listing the women in Cork, Dublin, Limerick and Belfast who had contacted him to tell him about their special offers. One of the web sites seized on the idea and introduced an 'up to 100 section'. This was most welcome to the clients. Said one:

> I really don't understand how some of the girls have the neck, to charge €150 a lot of them are just off the plane and unreviewed. Obviously they still think that thick Paddy will still pay this amount of money. I myself will not pay more than €100 for the last year. You will notice that there is now approx 30 girls in the €100 section, this is a lot compared to last year where the standard price was €150. I have also made deals with some girls recently I was with a girl who advertises here for €150 for €80. Obviously she is not going to advertise this. I don't agree about not making deals. Maybe these lads are in a comfortable financial position but to the ordinary punter a €100 is plenty to hand over. As I have said previously the average European price is €50 for 15 min which does most lads, however that option is not available here.

Not surprisingly, however, some of the women were not impressed with the others reducing their prices, saying that it lessened the value of their service. 'I'm still getting €150 or more for halfhour so why I should shag for less money?' said one woman when asked if she would reduce her prices.

> Shag for €100 . . . and so shag 10guys every day if I wanna hav a €1.000?? No fucking way! Why I should do that if I can shag only 6guys for the same money? If u can't afford it, don't bother to call the good girls which have fixed prices. And don't ask for cheaper service, beg for discount, for lower price, oh, how all the loosers doing it those days, beggars . . . There are plenty of guys which can afford it and they are happy with the price and also with the service. So, there are also plenty of girls with lower prices, those girls are for the guys which can't afford it, so that for you.

More proof, if it were needed, of how enterprising the women and the pimps can be is seen during one week each year, usually in July. The Galway Races attract thousands of people each day of that week to the Ballybrit racecourse. The city comes alive, its coffers swelling with the tourist dollars. In 2008 the carnival atmosphere was bolstered by the festival overlapping with the August holiday weekend.

Enterprising sex workers saw their opportunity. Aside from the prostitutes permanently living in the city, the number of touring 'escorts' working in Galway shot up for the week. In a normal week ten or fewer came to the city as part of a tour; in that week there were sixty-five advertising on one web site alone. The *Irish Independent* quoted Patricia Albright, self-proclaimed founder of *escort-ireland.com*:

> For escorts there is simply no other event like the seven-day racing festival in the Irish social calendar. It wouldn't be the same without escorts. Irish men have come to know they can always get lucky at the Galway Races. It is famous for attracting

a massive volume of horny Irish men to the region. Galway will be flooded with punters from tomorrow, a great many of whom will be hoping to enjoy more than just a flutter on the horses.

Even men who don't normally avail of escort services know they are available in Galway during Race Week, because in years past escort agencies have blitzed the area with flyers. For many men, the Galway Races represents the best opportunity they'll get all year to have a few days away from home—and with all the drinking and gambling going on anyway it's only natural [that] thoughts turn to other vices.

Usually any escort visiting Galway during race week will be inundated with bookings. There aren't so many agencies around now as there used to be, but there are plenty of independent escorts in their place.

Sensing that they would face strong competition, several of the women offered discounts off the usual €150 per hour.

As it s race week treat ur self 2 time wit me 100 half hour 200 hour i provide a good service and want 2 make u feel good so y not call me 4 the time off ur life

said 'tracey', before giving out her mobile number. Rachel decided to get into the racing lingo:

Galway special . . . Back a winner ! why put ur money on a donkey? when this FINE filly will make u cum first past the post !

2nd circuits welcome,and im the PERFECT course 4 STAYERS. NOVICES 100 for half an hour STAYERS 200 per hour. geldings STAY AWAY.

Because she expected to be inundated with visitors, 'Sasha Eve' posted a message on a message board asking if anyone could propose 'a serious person' to offer her security during the race week as well as 'a few days per month every month in Letterkenny. Only serious applicant thanks,' she demanded. A fellow-prostitute, Anita, warned her to be careful, saying, 'You might need security from the security,' while a regular punter advised that it would need to be a non-local, 'because it would be a bit awkward if he ran into a client who happened to be someone he knew.' One helpful contributor pointed her towards a personal security company, even saying he would track down one that his family had used and post the details later.

04 | BABY, IT'S COLD OUTSIDE

'I've been split open, raped, beaten up. But I've been out here for ten years because I'm on gear.' That is the stark admission of Clare, who at 2:30 a.m. on a cold January morning has just come onto the streets of the red-light district around Fitzwilliam Square in Dublin to sell her body. She told the author she expects to stay out until 6:30 a.m. to try to get men coming out of clubs who are willing to pay €50 for 'hand relief', €80 for oral sex and €100 for full sex.

Clare has children at home, who do not know what their mother is doing. As she disappears to get a coffee, her friend Ann admits that her own son thinks she is out for a few drinks with her friends. Ann has been on the streets for seven years. She too has been raped several times, and she too accepts less than €100 to prostitute herself. Both women hope to see anything up to ten clients in a night, though the post-Christmas lack of money has hit their trade too. 'We get all ages: eighteen to nineteen, eighty to ninety,' says Ann. 'Once they get through puberty they're down here. Winning the lotto is the only way I'm going to get out of this.' She says she needs the money to put her son through college, but the way her pupils are dilated and the gaunt expression on her face tell a different story. She has a heroin addiction, like so many other women on the darkest streets of Dublin.

Twenty minutes before I met Ann and Clare a lone garda on patrol pointed out one of the women slipping off down a side street with a punter, and then pointed to the canal, where the shadow of a slight young woman is barely visible away from the street lights. Once reassured that I am not a punter, he is happy to share information about where the women are.

The woman in the shadows is far less confident than the others. While the first two seem hardened about what they do, 'Emma', with only three months' experience on the game, is still exceptionally nervous. 'I'm all the time scared of who I'm going with and if I'm going to come back alive,' the attractive young woman says. 'Most serial killers, the first person they come after is the girls on the street.' She looks little more than twenty but does not tell me her real age.

Emma is also having sex with up to ten men a night—and earning more than €1,000 a day on occasion—to feed her crippling heroin addiction. 'Every girl on the street is involved in drugs. It's the only reason they're down here,' she says. She is determined to stop what obviously disgusts her as soon as possible.

> I'm waiting to get on a methadone programme. Whenever I get on the programme I'll be stopping all this. But there's a three-year waiting list to get on the methadone, so I don't know when that's going to happen. My family don't know I do this. If they found out I'd be better off dead, because I'd be killed anyway, one way or another.

The seedy underworld of this area has been well known for years, and one of those who has been here the longest is 'Paula'. She has worked the streets for twenty-three years, ever since she lost her catering job. She is a formidable-looking woman, with her small, squat stature in thigh-high leather boots giving the impression that she is not someone to be messed with.

Paula is reminiscent of the old image of prostitutes, women who have sex for money to pay the bills but do not let it rule their lives. 'Most of the guys I know are regular clients who will tell me everything that's happening in their lives, about how their wives are spending too much money,' she says, after telling me she charges €100 when she thought I was a client. She does not work past midnight,

> because that's when the junky ones come out to feed the habit. I wouldn't stay out after that. Those women are loose cannons. All of them have pimps, usually their drug dealers, who are always hanging around. Thing is if we stay out when their girls are working, they will start coming at us trying to move on. I ain't messing with them. It ain't worth it.
>
> It's 'catch 22' for those girls. I don't drink, I don't do drugs. If I don't do anything tonight I can go home quite happy. I don't need a fix from the money.

Fitzwilliam Square, she says, has earned a reputation as the more upper-class area among the clients and one where the clients don't give trouble. She says she and a group of other women, all of whom know each other, have a good arrangement.

> We look out for each other, help each other out. We may be competing for punters but we're still friendly enough to keep an eye out. I have only had one bad client. He was violent, but I got out of it okay. It shakes you up.

All the women on the streets are united in their dislike of the women working behind closed doors. They say they would not work in that environment, because so many indoors are under the control of a pimp. 'The amount we would earn indoors, we'd earn twice as much on the street,' says Emma.

The women also condemn the way the escorts and those in brothels offer services without a condom. 'I wouldn't touch his dick without a condom,' said Ann. 'As soon as I did I'd pick something up.'

These assertions, however, simply do not square with the anecdotal evidence. Firstly, it is the women on the streets, mainly the drug addicts, who are typically the ones who will provide full sex without a condom in exchange for extra cash for heroin. As we will see later, women who have escaped the streets will openly admit that. As to being controlled by a third party, once again in a large number of cases it is the women on the streets who are not free of control. When I walked the tour of the red-light district on two separate nights a motorcyclist was a permanent presence in at least two of the streets. Dressed completely in black leathers, riding a black motorbike and wearing a black helmet with tinted glass, he was a foreboding presence. From a distance I could see him stopping every few minutes to speak to the women when no-one was near them. As soon as another car came past or someone on foot he would move off. He constantly circled throughout the early hours of the morning.

When questioned, none of the women would talk about who he was, and there was no visible sign of money changing hands. However, it was clear from the women's body language that this man was not some random person having a harmless chat with them.

A slightly less obvious presence but equally imposing in his physical appearance was the driver of a small Japanese hatchback car. His appearance was notable because he seemed to barely fit into the driver's seat. While the motorbike rider would constantly be on the move, talking to different women, the driver of the car sat in one spot and watched at least two women who appeared to be under his control. At one point late in the night he got out of the car and went over to speak to one of them before strolling back over to the car. He sped off and then returned with take-away food for the women.

Inevitably, another conspicuous presence around the red-light district is the dozens of potential punters, and the gawkers. From seven o'clock they circle the Peppercanister Church before heading over to the other pick-up spots around the canal favoured by the women. The men actively seeking women drive slowly, hoping to catch one of the prostitutes before any other cars come close. They barely keep their eyes on the road as they hunt for a sighting. Other men appear to have developed a route that encompasses all the red-light streets. They will not stop, only watch what the women are doing. Many prostitutes report that the men will follow them to the spot where they have chosen to take a punter, hoping to catch a sight of them in the act. Some will continue to circle the area for most of the evening and night. Paula jokes, 'They probably spend more on petrol than they would simply by stopping at the first one and having sex with her.'

One of the women who is on the streets early and who remains only for a few hours is Nadia. Even in the dark, dank surroundings of the roadside beside the canal this young eastern European woman, with her fashionably cut bright blond hair and statuesque looks, stands out from the other women. Whereas the others are struggling to get customers in the post-Christmas slump, punters driving past nearly swerve to pull in beside Nadia, and she is whisked away to a nearby quiet spot that she said she has been using for a few weeks. Each time she returns she talks readily to me about the man she has just met: she tells me what they wanted, and how much they paid, and gives a brief description of them. Most of the punters she describes are forty-plus, of average looks, and pay between €60 and €100, depending on the service. 'I get more money here than I could earn in a week back home,' she says, though she refuses to tell me what country that is. 'When I come here I had job in hotel as cleaner, but I get fired. I was hooker at home for few months, so I try this now.'

At one point she notices a young man who, with his rucksack slung across his back, looks like a student. She ushers me away, and a few minutes later she and the young punter slip down a side road and under the awning over the entrance of an office building that has closed for the night. It is an ideal spot, completely hidden from the main road. She returns a few minutes later, €70 better off. She says she has just given him oral sex with a condom, 'and let him feel me.' I returned to that entrance early the next day. Seven used condoms lay there, a pleasant sight for the first workers to arrive each morning.

Nadia seems to buck a lot of trends. She insists she has no pimp, no boy-friend who takes half or all her money. She admits that she drinks 'some' but is adamant that she does not do drugs. She seems exceptionally lucid and aware of her situation. I asked her whether, given her apparent intelligence, confidence and looks, she has ever considered turning to the indoor trade, but she says she needs to earn more money first, and she would need to become 'more good with computers.'

For three hours Nadia seemed to be almost cheerful when she talked to me. However, after going off in a car with one man it was almost as if a different woman returned. Suddenly she seemed to change completely. First she seemed angry, demanding to know why I was bothering her. Then she broke down and cried. I have no idea what happened to change her demeanour so markedly. She walked away, and I did not see her again.

———

One of the aspects of street prostitution that the women on the street willingly comment on is the way the gardaí, for the most part, look out for them. In 2002 the late Tony Gregory TD asked the Minister for Justice to secure a report from the Gardaí regarding the action they were taking to deal with the widespread street prostitution in the region of Montpellier Hill in the Oxmantown area of Dublin. The minister, Michael McDowell, replied:

I am informed by the Garda authorities that the Montpelier Hill area receives ongoing daily attention from both mobile and foot patrols. Community gardaí also provide a uniform presence. I am further informed that Operation Encounter and the Garda beat that covers Benburb Street have been extended to cover the Montpelier Hill area. The Garda adopts a proactive approach in dealing with both clients and prostitutes and the situation is monitored on an ongoing basis. I am assured by the Garda authorities that additional resources will be assigned to the area if necessary.

A tour of the red-light district does indeed bring one into contact with gardaí, and one would have to acknowledge the small safety net that this gives the women. Emma said: 'They wouldn't let us go away with a punter in front of their eyes, but at the same time if we went away with a punter and something happened they would be behind us 100 per cent.' Paula said it depended on the unit how much hassle the Gardaí would create, but she also said it was the client who would be given the attention. 'If you were a punter and the gardaí pulled up, most would just say, "Oh, I was just looking for directions." There's nothing they can really do.'

Nevertheless, as I was speaking to Ann, Emma and Clare the three split up quickly when a Garda car containing two female gardaí pulled up. Once they had ascertained that I was not kerb-crawling they moved on, and the women came back.

'If it's a woman garda we're far more likely to get done,' said Emma. 'You can have a bit of a banter with the men, but the women really go to town.'

While it cannot be doubted that the gardaí circling the streets are working hard to protect the women, one has to question whether there are enough patrols on the streets, and whether they are active enough in driving the problem away. The gardaí will walk or drive up to the women, will speak to them, and drive away. Rarely do the women leave the scene.

Whether it means taking a tougher and more uncompromising stance with prostitutes or whether it means making more of an effort to catch the men, it seems that something really needs to be done as soon as possible. This is especially so because every night they are out the women's lives are in serious danger.

———

The lethal nature of prostitution was brought into sharp focus in England with the murder of five prostitutes in Suffolk in 2006. Even when the killer was still at large, prostitutes there continued to take to the streets, because they needed money to support their drug habit. Tania Nicol, Gemma Adams, Annette Nicholls, Paula Clennell and Anneli Alderton were all prostitutes, all had experienced drug problems, and all met their death at the hands of Steve Wright. The remains of the five women were found in isolated spots near Ipswich during the ten days before Christmas.

Each of the women was in the circumstances she was in because of the tight control drugs had upon her. All of them knew the risks, but their addiction drove them to take greater risks. Even when the first two women disappeared, Paula Clennell still went out on the street. On the 5th of December she gave an interview to a local reporter in which she said that the murder of Gemma Adams and the disappearance of Tania Nicol had made her 'wary' of going out, but she needed the money. She had even given a statement to the police after her friend Tania Nicol vanished, in which she described last seeing her being driven away by a customer. One week later, her naked corpse was found.

Unlike the other women, Annette Nichols had been using drugs for only a short period before she disappeared. But her relatively late access to heroin did not make her habit any less consuming: in fact before she died she had gained a reputation as one of the most desperate of the women on the streets. She would regularly steal from punters, even stealing a mobile phone and selling it to get money for drugs. Two months before her death she told the police she had been dragged into an alleyway and raped. Ironically, because she was dead the case against the man arrested in connection with that attack had to be dropped.

The facts that emerged in the case against Steve Wright were harrowing. He had 'systematically selected and murdered' his victims over a period of six-and-a-half weeks. The prosecutors said he had stalked the red-light district near his home while his 59-year-old partner, Pam Wright, was working night shifts at a call centre.

Wright pleaded not guilty to murder but when arrested admitted picking up all the women on the nights they disappeared. In court he confirmed that he had sex with all of them, except Tania Nicol, but he denied any involvement in their deaths.

Tania Nicol and Gemma Adams were found in a stream. Anneli Alderton and Annette Nicholls had been laid out in the shape of a crucifix, with their hair carefully arranged above their head. The body of Paula Clennell was dumped near a road.

The jury heard that Wright's DNA was found on three of the women's bodies, blood from two of the women was found on one of his coats, and fibres from his home or car were found on all five. Wright told the court that Paula Clennell's blood had ended up on a work jacket after she had bitten her tongue.

Mr Justice Gross, at Ipswich Crown Court, ruled that Wright, a 49-year-old former fork-lift driver, should serve a whole life term and never be released.

It is right [that] you should spend your whole life in prison. This was a targeted campaign of murder. Drugs and prostitution meant they were at risk. But neither drugs nor prostitution killed them. You did. You killed them, stripped them and left them . . . Why you did it may never be known.

Two weeks after the last of the Ipswich bodies was discovered I spoke to 'Anna', a twenty-year-old prostitute whose regular haunt was the red-light district off Baggot Street, Dublin. Even though she had shot up only minutes earlier, the drugs had given her no Dutch courage. She was terrified, blending in behind a tree, apparently torn between needing to earn money and wanting to hide in the shadows.

Anna was relatively new to the streets, professing that she was determined to get out of it as soon as she could get the better of her habit. She said she had been having nightmares after learning of what had happened in Ipswich.

As the cars pull up I've found myself looking closer at the punter. I've walked away a couple of times, 'cause I got this bad feeling. At the end of the day, though, I will just get into another car.

While there has not been a serial killing of prostitutes in Ireland, that is not to say that women have not been murdered. While the more famous killings have been indoors, such as that of Belinda Pereira (see chapter 5), one killing that hit the headlines was that of 24-year-old Layla Brennan, who was strangled and her body thrown into a ditch in the Wicklow Mountains.

Layla Brennan had been a dental receptionist but had become addicted to heroin and had lost her job as a result. She then turned to prostitution to pay for the addiction. On the night of her death in March 1999 she was walking along Nassau Street, Dublin, towards Baggot Street when her killer pulled up alongside and asked for directions.

Philip Colgan, then aged twenty-seven, had already served eight years in prison for the aggravated double rape of a 79-year-old woman and a young Spanish student. He had been released for a little over a year when he murdered Layla Brennan. He gave a signed statement to the Gardaí in which he admitted the murder. In it he said that he grabbed her by the throat. 'I knew if I let go I'd be going back to prison. I took off her bra and tightened it around her neck, and tightened it as tight as I could for 10, 15, 20 seconds. I knew she was dead.'

He had even told his wife that he had strangled a prostitute and had thrown her naked body into a ditch in the mountains. She had convinced him to dictate to her what he had done so that she could take notes. She read from her notes at her husband's trial:

I hit her the second time and knocked her out. When she woke up she was screaming. I couldn't stop her. I grabbed her by the throat and squeezed until she stopped moving. I put her in the boot of the car and drove to the Dublin mountains.

However, in spite of the evidence that he had admitted the killing both to the Gardaí and to his wife, Colgan dreamt up a fantastical story to explain what had happened. Firstly, before the case reached the court he retracted what he had told his wife. He told her his gay sexual partner forced him at knife-point to strangle the woman. Then in court he stuck to this theme but took it one step further. He said he had been driving his car on the night in question with another man, who he did not identify, and that this man spotted the young prostitute walking along Dame Street. He said they let the woman into the car and drove off towards Donnybrook.

> There was an understanding between us, because she owed him money. I asked him did she owe enough for the both of us, and we'd both be able to have sex with her [and] he said yes.

He said he got out of the car while the other man had sex with the woman, but when he came back to the car he saw her lying face down in the back, with her bra tied around her throat. He said the other man told him she tried to rob him, and so he had tried to 'shut her up.'

Colgan, of Crannagh Castle, Rathfarnham, claimed that the two men put her in the boot of the car and drove to a lay-by in the mountains, where they dragged her for a distance into the undergrowth and dumped her in a ditch. He said the other man then hit her with a wheel brace.

> I was nervous. The reason I stopped in that lay-by was because I was afraid for my own safety. I had been nervous in the first place going any further into the mountains with him. When he came around the back of the car I grabbed him. I felt if I didn't I was going to end up getting hit with the wheel brace.

He said they had a pretty violent struggle, which left the other man unconscious. He then put this man into the back of the car and drove him further into the mountains before dumping him, not knowing whether he was alive or dead.

Prosecution counsel, on the other hand, said that Colgan was a 'cold, dispassionate, calculating and clever liar, who had employed a "Halloween story, a film script from a horror story," in trying to dupe the jury.' The jury evidently agreed and found him guilty of murder. He was sentenced to life imprisonment.

———

Not far from where Layla Brennan's body was dumped, another Dublin woman nearly met a similar fate in September 2000. The young woman was working as a prostitute in the Baggot Street area when the nightmare began at about 2:45 a.m.

She was approached by a man driving a large wine-coloured car who propositioned her. When she got into the car he drove her a short distance to Greenore Terrace, off Macken Street, between the Grand Canal and the Liffey, where he picked up two other men. She was overpowered and handcuffed, and a bag was put over her head. Her captors drove her thirty miles to the Devil's Glen, an isolated wooded area a few miles off the main road outside Ashford, Co. Wicklow. There she was repeatedly forced to carry out sexual acts with the men, who also raped her. She claimed that at least two of the men had knives. When they had finished assaulting her they left her handcuffed to a tree, bleeding, bruised, and terrified.

She managed to muster the strength to call for help, and eventually at 5:30 a.m. a local person heard her cries and called the Gardaí. She was brought by ambulance to the Rotunda Hospital, where she was treated in the Sexual Assault Unit.

It later emerged that this was the second time this woman, who was working as a prostitute to feed her heroin habit, had been held against her will. Three months previously she had been rescued by the Gardaí in a house in south Dublin where she was held captive by a customer.

———

In the same year, one attacker tried to escape capture by hiding his identity by wearing a motorcycle helmet throughout. The 27-year-old woman was working in Benburb Street, Dublin, when she was approached by a man on a motorbike. They agreed a price, and he gave her a helmet and said he would bring her to a place where they could have sex. However, when they got to their destination, a house in Rathfarnham, he turned nasty when she asked him to pay her in advance. Producing a knife, he told her in no uncertain terms that she would not be getting any money. 'I'm twenty-seven years old, and I've never paid for sex,' he told her before ordering her to strip. He then forced her to perform oral sex and raped her. He kept the helmet on throughout, and when he was finished he put her back on the motorbike and brought her back to Benburb Street.

The woman was brave, and even though he told her he would kill her if she reported what he had done, she told the first garda she saw.

Though she had a heroin habit (defence counsel at the trial made much of the fact that she needed to take up to twelve bags of heroin a day) she was able to identify the house where the attack occurred. Nevertheless, it seemed for a while that her attacker might get away with his crime, as she was unable to identify him because he had been wearing the helmet.

Not surprisingly, when 31-year-old Stephen Doherty of St Mark's Drive, Clondalkin, was arrested he denied all knowledge of the attack. However, he was forced to admit he was the culprit when the Gardaí were able to produce DNA evidence gathered from a curtain on which he had wiped himself after the oral rape. He was convicted of false imprisonment and three further charges of rape, oral rape, and threatening to kill his victim. Judge Paul Carney said that Doherty had clearly planned the offence and sentenced him to ten years' imprisonment for the rape, three years for false imprisonment, and five years for the threat to kill the woman.

——

In 2008 a convicted armed robber was jailed for three years in Dublin Circuit Criminal Court for slashing a heavily pregnant prostitute across the face and upper body with a knife in a laneway. 41-year-old Darren Geoghegan, who had previously served a nine-year sentence for armed robbery, was found guilty of the vicious attack after a two-day trial in which the jury heard that blood samples taken from the knife found on him matched that of the victim. The woman was six months pregnant at the time.

Gardaí gave evidence that on the summer night in August 2004 he approached the woman in Fitzwilliam Place. When she brought him to Pembroke Lane, where she took clients for sex, he produced the knife in order to steal her handbag, then punched her hard and cut her face and body.

The woman took refuge in a restaurant and was able to identify Geoghegan to the staff as he passed the premises seconds afterwards. An English diner, joined by another man who had seen Geoghegan chase the woman from Pembroke Lane, followed him to Mercer Street as the Gardaí were called.

Even while in custody Geoghegan, of Pearse Street, Dublin, tried to get rid of the knife, but it was confiscated and sent for DNA analysis, which showed that it was the weapon used in the attack.

The then 41-year-old claimed that he couldn't remember assault-ing the woman, who sustained cuts above and below both eyes, puncture wounds on her right arm and left breast, and repeated punches to her face and abdomen. Even when he appeared in court four years later, witnesses said the woman's facial scars, though well healed, were still visible.

The violence that all these women experienced is terrifying. But it is not just the violence that leaves the women scarred. Even those who escape the stabbings, the rapes and the beatings face hardship at every turn when they are on the street.

——

The story of 26-year-old Louise emerged in 2007. Addicted to heroin, she turned to prostitution to support her habit and ended up sleeping in a tent in the Phoenix Park along with her young child. Park keepers, realising that she was staying there regularly, moved her on. She was forced to move the tent to the banks of the Grand Canal, near where she worked the streets. For the few hours when she managed to seek refuge there each night she would regularly be woken by brave young men attacking the tent with bottles and stones.

Her plight emerged on the RTE radio programme 'Liveline', on which she admitted that both she and her partner had contracted HIV. Her heart-rending story affected many people; and, on one of the few occasions in the world of prostitution on which there was if not a happy ending certainly a more uplifting one, a listener rang in to say she could offer the young woman a mobile home, where at least she would be warmer and safer at night.

————

In a similar vein, and equally harrowing, is the story of a girl who came to the attention of the authorities in 2004.

A very young heroin addict, she would go out on the streets every night to sell her body—with her mother and her six-year old sister in tow. When she came to the attention of the Gardaí she was having sex with a fifty-year-old man in a laneway, with her mother and sister close by. During frequent court appearances the girl would say that her mother was there to look after her and to prevent her getting pregnant.

The unfortunate girl could not keep herself out of trouble. Granted bail at her first court appearance, she breached a curfew that was part of her bail conditions. Gardaí called to her home and were told by her mother that she had popped out to buy drugs. She failed to turn up to a later appearance and the court was told she had left the care facility in which she had been placed and had disappeared with her mother. Eventually the authorities managed to get her back into care, where, according to her last court appearance as a juvenile, she had finally begun to kick her habit and to rebuild her life.

——

Numerous studies have been undertaken on street prostitutes, particularly of the risks they fall into and the addictions that usually motivate their actions. Researchers at the University of Ulster carried out an investigation into the life, risk behaviour and health-care needs of street prostitutes in Belfast in 2004. The findings were predictable but shocking.

> This study supports the well-documented findings from previous studies that childhood sexual abuse (incest) is an antecedent to prostitution. Two-fifths (40%), have had their first sexual experience before the age of 10 years, with half the women (50%) sexually abused by perpetrators who were family members in a position of trust. They were regularly exposed to serious health risk factors including psychological responses to traumatic events resulting in post traumatic stress disorder (PTSD), violence, drug abuse, and severe depression that put them at risk for acute illness, injury, and eventual suicide.
>
> None of the women accessed medical attention and [they] frequently commented on the attitudes of healthcare professionals towards them and the sense of shame that they had experienced. Whilst struggling to survive, these women live chaotic lives and dwell in a 'here and now and tomorrow will take care of itself' philosophy. They barely focus on the day-to-day requirements of a 'normal' living and evidently, are not receiving care appropriate to their vulnerable circumstances and high-risk status.

These findings are mirrored by a survey by O'Neill and O'Connor (1999) who looked at seventy-seven women involved in street prostitution in Dublin who were also drug-users. Most of the women had one or two children; 45 per cent of the women were homeless at the time of the interview. The study found that the women had been subjected to high levels of violence and sexual assault and had a wide range of health-related problems: 38 per cent had attempted suicide, 35 per cent had hepatitis C, and 11 per cent were HIV-positive. The report found that at the time of the research, in the late 1990s, the Gardaí estimated that there were four hundred intravenous drug-users in prostitution in Dublin.

That leaves a lot of work for Ruhama's support van. It is a fairly constant presence on the streets, offering moral support to the women. Nonetheless, not all appreciate the services it provides. According to Paula,

> We are being portrayed in a very bad light by Ruhama. A lot of us have stopped talking to them. They have done us a lot of damage, they really have. They portray us like we are drug addicts and alcoholics. They say we have all been sexually abused and we have no intelligence.

Over the Christmas holiday period, workers in and around the red-light districts of Dublin report huge numbers lining the streets to make the most of the high spending before the January slump. They will be there all year round, hail, rain, or shine, because it is the only way to satisfy the gnawing craving.

There are three districts of Dublin where the level of prostitution is particularly high, as one crudely named web site, *Brassers.com*, demonstrated for some years. The site offered reviews of fifteen areas in the city, written by those who had availed of the women's services. Those who offered sexual services without a condom seemed to get the most attention.

Arbour Hill was given seventeen reviews and had an average of two stars. The reviewers described encounters they had, in particular with an eastern European woman. She received rave reviews because of her willingness to offer all types of sex without a condom. In a rare moment of candour on the site, one reviewer asked, 'Is it not a bit dangerous to not use protection?'

Baggot Street received one star from its five reviewers. One complained:

> Where are all the street walkers gone? A few years ago, there was never any problem finding one around the Leeson Street, Baggot Street, canal area, or around Benburb Street. True, many of them were junkies. But certainly not all of them . . . I get the feeling that, especially in the last few months, the guards have killed off the Southside scene . . . Surely at least the junkies have to go somewhere to earn their money? Is there a new location?

Benburb Street received two stars from its eleven reviewers. Again the Garda presence and the availability of unprotected sex were evident. However, crank advertisements and phone numbers pointed to the fact that children had gained access to the site and had used it to play pranks on their friends.

The eleven reviewers of Burlington Road, which got a two-star average, were lambasted by a woman who called herself Linda and claimed to work in the red-light district. She said she was disgusted that a web site has been made about the women.

The area that got the best rating was Fitzwilliam Square, with the women complimented for being 'up front, old style'.

Before much of the web site seemed to close down in the last number of months, its creators explained its rationale by saying:

> Despite the ever-increasing popularity of high-class whoring in Dublin, some punters still like Dublin prostitution as it used to be—on the streets. Some punters want it as cheap as they can get it, others get a thrill out of the danger element of kerb crawling. The streets are really where the 'world's oldest profession' is at for some punters.

Even the 'escort' web sites, supposedly offering the more expensive indoor women, include sections on street prostitution on their message boards. Given the economic crisis, these sections have become more and more popular. Inexperienced punters seeking advice on where best to pick up a street prostitute were not left short of advice by men who had turned to street women when their savings did not allow them to exclusively use the indoor equivalents.

Both in Dublin and elsewhere in the country, street prostitution definitely appears to be in decline, with demand moving more to the indoor market—though the economic crisis could reverse that trend. According to the Immigrant Council of Ireland, approximately 100 women are engaged in street prostitution, compared with the 400 the Gardaí referred to in the 1999 report by O'Neill and O'Connor.

> Figures are difficult to estimate outside of Dublin. Key informants in Cork city estimate that there are as few as five women in prostitution on any one night and possibly less than 40 over the period of a year. The estimate for Waterford city is approximately 30. The vast majority of women engaging in street prostitution are Irish, with a small number of women rotating between Britain and Ireland.

Given the smaller number of women available, commensurately fewer court cases are taken against the punters or the women. However, one self-appointed 'owner' of Cork's prostitution scene made headlines on a number of occasions in the early half of this decade in a long-drawn-out court process. He achieved his unwanted fame after he threatened to cut a prostitute up if she did not pay money to him every week.

The middle-aged woman had come to Cork from Dublin in 1999 to work in the Morrison's Island area of the city. On her first night in the area she was approached by a local man, Christopher Aherne, of Ferndale Villas, Lough Road, who told her she had two choices: pay money to him regularly or get out, because Cork was his town.

The following night he came and told her he wanted his money, but she said she would not give him any. He then told her he would 'put blades' on her. Fearing for her safety, she began paying him £240 per week for up to six months. That left her so short of money that she could not afford to get enough food. Eventually she had no choice but to report what was happening to the Gardaí, who set up a trap. One day in August she arranged to meet the man at Cork Opera House to pay him the money. The Gardaí had photocopied the notes, and shortly after the woman handed over the money Aherne was stopped with the copied notes. He also had a Stanley knife on him, which he claimed he had been using for gardening.

On Aherne's first appearance in court, on 15 February 2001, he was sentenced to ten years in prison. He appealed to the Court of Criminal Appeal, and a retrial was ordered. Then, in November 2004, he confessed to his crimes. The following May he was sentenced to six years' imprisonment, with the time already served, two years and eight months, to be taken into account. Now at liberty, his connection with the sex trade appears to have ended.

————

Street prostitution has taken on a particularly horrifying aspect in Limerick, especially in the the past few years. In 2006 the Gardaí launched an investigation amid claims that the children of eastern European asylum-seekers were being forced into the street sex trade by their parents. Children as young as fourteen were offering to perform sexual acts for as little as €80, and a Dublin journalist reported that he was offered 'threesome' sex for €120.

The children were operating at night in the Glentworth Street and Davis Street areas, near Colbert Station. One particular girl was repeatedly seen getting into various cars between 10 and 11:40 p.m.

The children were brazen. Cars that were stopping would be approached and sexual services would be offered without any indication that the men had been seeking them. If rebuffed, the children were undeterred and would simply move on to the next vehicle.

One prostitute in Limerick who was equally brazen and in early 2009 was still operating there was Lorna, also known as 'pussand-boots'. This woman seems to be an amalgam of street and indoor prostitute, in that she lists her services on the internet through the message board of one of the 'escort' web sites but also works both out-calls and what she calls 'car-calls'. Essentially, punters in the Limerick area ring her after 9:30 p.m. and she will meet them to offer her services in a car—the same services that most street prostitutes offer in the same environment.

She seems to have her system well organised. Punters must first ring her before she will meet them in an appointed place, always after 9:30 p.m.—probably to make sure it is dark when she brings them to whatever secluded spot she uses. As she does not accept calls from blocked numbers, she already has some information about her prospective client—an extra security measure. Also, she does not need to hang around a street corner, exposed to the elements and to any unknown dangers that passers-by could pose.

However, in April 2009 she incurred the wrath of an escort site for repeatedly publishing her number, without the web site making any money from her. The web site wrote:

> We don't let non-advertisers post phone numbers here for various reasons as explained in our rules. This lady kept posting phone numbers in violation of this rule. She was warned three times to stop, but she kept doing it so she was banned. If she'd wanted to stay around she could have heeded any of the three warnings she got and stopped posting her number. We'd have let her be if she'd only posted an email address, but rules are rules and it is not one set for her and another for everybody else, so she had to go once we realised she was refusing to comply with the rules. If I recall correctly, I only banned her for a week or a fortnight, to try to get her attention, so she may be back soon, though she will be banned again and permanently if she comes back intent on continuing to break the rules.

05 | SLEEPING WITH THE ENEMY

Billy Keogh was a Waterford businessman, a 46-year-old married man with six children, who had never been in trouble with the Gardaí. What his loving family didn't know was that Keogh had a passion for 'vigorous' sex, which he had with a string of prostitutes over a number of years. He also had scant regard for the sexual health of the women or of himself, willing to pay extra if he was allowed to forgo the use of a condom.

He pushed his luck with a Croatian prostitute in 2006, and paid for it with his freedom. With his actions, either he or the woman could have paid for it with their lives.

On 21 May 2006 Keogh, of Wilder, Kilmeaden, went to the Tower Hotel in Waterford, where the prostitute had checked in some days earlier. He was just one of a number of clients sent to her room by the Red Velvet 'escort agency'. When Keogh arrived he agreed to pay €150 for half an hour of 'regular sex with a condom, no kissing, no licking.' The 26-year-old woman thought this was just another Irish punter. She had been in Ireland for only four days of her current tour but had worked here on a number of other stints, amounting to approximately two months. On some days she admitted she was seeing ten customers a day, but on this particular day she had seen only one man before Keogh. It was not long before she was very much regretting her return visit to Ireland.

First he tried to kiss her, even though she had clearly specified that the fee excluded it. Then she said he became agitated and aggressive and began to choke her, demanding that she take off the condom she had put on him. When she refused he ripped it off himself, then continued in what had now become rape. When she struggled he threatened to throw her out the window of the hotel.

The prostitute claimed that when Keogh finished he dressed and went through her bag, taking €1,050 along with the €150 he had given her. She claimed that before he left he told her: 'I am the Guards. You're fucked up.' The woman locked the hotel room door and phoned the Red Velvet agency in Cork.

The receptionist who answered the call was all too familiar with Keogh: when she had been a 'working girl' herself he had used her up to ten times. The Croatian woman told her she had been raped in the hotel and was afraid that he was going to come back. The receptionist phoned Keogh and told him, 'You were in the hotel and you raped a girl,' before she rang the Gardaí.

The Gardaí described the woman as being 'extremely upset and in fear.' A book of video stills was taken from the hotel's CCTV camera for the court case that was to follow. The woman was taken to the Sexual Assault Treatment Unit in Waterford, where doctors found six small bruises to her face and shoulder 'consistent with trauma to her body.'

At the ensuing trial it was put to the woman that when Keogh told her he wanted to have sex without a condom she told him it would be 'another three or four hundred.' She denied this, saying there was no such discussion. She said she would never have sex without a condom, because 'I am too scared of diseases and pregnancy.' She said that while some escort workers had a 'menu', and customers could pay extra for things such as not using a condom or for allowing kissing, no such concessions were available from her.

Keogh, however, insisted in his evidence that the woman suggested a price of €300 to €400 for not using a condom but that he had offered €100 and she accepted that.

His opinion of prostitutes, whom he had used on so many occasions in the past, was made clear by his next comment. He told the court: 'If the girl was good-looking I'd have no problem with having sex with a condom, but this girl wasn't great-looking.' He admitted that he 'went at it vigorously' but claimed that when he gave the woman the €100 she became upset and demanded more money from him and threw a hairbrush at him. He claimed he threw the money on the bed and left.

> I wish to add that I am a respected businessman in Waterford city. I have never been in trouble with the police. I have never hurt anyone, man or woman.

The jury cleared Keogh of taking the woman's money. However, after six hours of deliberation and a night in a hotel, by a majority of 10 to 2 they found him guilty of rape.

Before he was sentenced there was another twist in the tale. After the guilty verdict, Keogh's defence counsel said he was willing to pay the woman compensation. Over the following days she replied from Croatia that she was not interested in 'voluntarily accepting' Keogh's money and that she had begun a new job there. However, she claimed that she had been approached by two Albanian men in her own country who offered her money to withdraw her evidence. The fresh allegation was never dealt with in court, as she was unwilling to come back to Ireland to give evidence. Therefore the sentencing went ahead in accordance with the jury's verdict; and what was handed down was galling for the victim and for women's groups.

Billy Keogh's name was placed on the sex offenders' register, and he was sentenced to five years' imprisonment, though three of those years were suspended, meaning that he would spend a maximum of two years in prison, and even less if he behaved himself.

It was not only the sentence but also the summary by Mr Justice Barry White that caused offence. Sentencing Keogh, he told him: 'It is quite clear to me that you are a man of good character and that you have brought shame and disgrace on yourself and shame and disgrace on your wife and children.' He suspended the last three years of the sentence, saying he was impressed by how Keogh re-established himself after losing his business in 2004 and that he also had an elderly dependent mother and seven employees to support.

Could Keogh be described as a 'man of good character,' considering the fact that, unknown to his family, he had a passion for 'vigorous sex' with a string of prostitutes over several years? Could he be described as a man of good character when he had such scant regard for the sexual health of the women or of himself that he was willing to pay extra if he was allowed to forgo the use of a condom? Could he be described as a man of good character when, as the court was told, after he raped the woman he told her he was a garda, possibly in an attempt to dissuade her from reporting his crime?

Ruhama said it feared that raped prostitutes would no longer report their attackers, and that men would feel that crimes against sex workers would be taken less seriously.

The five-year sentence is the minimum which should be imposed for such a crime and we are somewhat surprised that three years of this was suspended. We hear reports of rape of women involved in prostitution almost on a weekly basis.

Our judicial system needs to give the women the confidence to come forward and seek justice. Rape, no matter where it happens or to whom, has a longstanding impact on the victim. Sentences need to reflect this and act as a clear deterrent.

The major outcome to emerge from this court case is the fact that a woman was abused and raped. This woman was clearly vulnerable and exploited. We are well aware in our work that this is not an isolated case of sexual violence towards women in prostitution, what's unusual about this case is that the woman reported the incident to the gardaí. This case demonstrates the dangers for women involved in the sex industry and challenges the myth that indoor prostitution is 'high-class' and safer for women. The agency which the woman was attached to is illegal and it's a matter for the gardaí to investigate. There is clearly a gap in legislation when such agencies can operate with impunity.

Rape Crisis Network Ireland said it was very concerned at the minimising of the serial use of prostitution.

This man clearly demonstrated a level of casual use of violence against prostitution. To deem that person of good character is to minimise the whole practice of buying prostitution and buying sex.

The attack on the Croatian woman, though clearly terrifying, did not act as a deterrent to the women putting themselves at risk by operating on their own in hotels. And it was only a matter of time before another attack made the news.

This time it was a Russian prostitute describing herself as 'Beauty Brenda'. On 20 August 2008 she was hired to meet a man in a Galway hotel room. She claimed that he demanded her money and that when she did not give him any he beat her about the head. The young woman was admitted to hospital but was able to give a statement to the Gardaí, though her attacker was never brought to account.

However, her experience did not deter her from carrying on with the work that nearly got her killed. She even continued to take clients in the same area where the attack happened, and within days she was advertising tours of Galway, Athlone, Sligo, and Castlebar.

———

Two years earlier another prostitute, a native of Cork, was lucky to escape with her life after a punter with a penchant for violence decided he wanted more than sex. 28-year-old Wayne Keogh of Kiltalawn Way, Tallaght, met the woman in a bedroom in the Herbert Park Hotel in Anglesey Road, Dublin, in September 2006. He had made a booking over the phone for a session at €200 per hour. However, after availing of her services for only twenty minutes he suddenly, according to the woman, began 'talking nonsense about drugs' before disappearing into the bathroom.

Suddenly the woman heard the sound of glass shattering. Keogh came back into the room brandishing a shard. At Dublin Circuit Criminal Court gardaí told how he threatened the woman before taking two mobile phones and demanding access to her safe with the warning 'Give me the code or I'll glass you.' He took €350 in cash that was lying on top of the wardrobe, €40 from the woman's pocket, and €30 from the safe after she bartered her mobile phones for the code.

In court it emerged that Keogh had been on alcohol and cocaine that day, but apparently it had not diminished his wits too much. He knew the woman had been working in Dublin for a number of days previously, and demanded the proceeds. She told him she had already been to the bank that morning and had deposited the money. The Gardaí testified that when taken into custody Keogh claimed he had no intention of harming the woman but had 'decided on impulse' to rob her.

Judge Martin Nolan acknowledged that the defendant was remorseful, and that he had spent a considerable amount of his youth in custody. He sentenced him to eighteen months' imprisonment for the robbery.

Billy Keogh's case, Beauty Brenda's assault and the Cork prostitute's lucky escape in Dublin encapsulate two problems faced by victims in Ireland's prostitution trade: that of the women whose lives are in danger while working as prostitutes, and that of the women who are unlucky enough to come across the punter next.

Beauty Brenda was alone in her hotel room. For the sake of €350 she could easily have been killed if her attacker had had any weapon. She put details of the attack on the message board at *escort-ireland.com*, and even the punters there questioned whether it was worth the risk. Billy Keogh could have picked up a sexually transmitted disease from that prostitute if she was infected. Sex without a condom with a prostitute who has sex with hundreds of other men has obvious risks.

While it emerged in court that the Croatian woman was especially careful and refused to have sex without protection, many more, anxious to make an extra few euros, would not be nearly so careful. Billy Keogh could not have known of her self-preserving and diligent nature. What if her carefulness had been only newly founded and he was raping a woman who had been infected with HIV? In five or perhaps ten years Keogh might have found himself feeling slightly unwell, and tests could have led him to the dreaded conclusion that he was HIV-positive.

Many people might say that, having attacked and degraded a woman, he deserved such a comeuppance. However, did the wife who had borne his six children deserve the death sentence he might have passed on to her? As we have already seen, a very large proportion of the men having sex regularly with prostitutes are either married or in a relationship.

At the end of 2006 there were 4,419 reported cases of HIV infection in Ireland. Many more went unreported. Of the 337 newly diagnosed cases reported that year, half were heterosexually acquired. It follows that the risk of acquiring HIV from having sex with a person who has multiple partners is drastically increased. Yet many men are willing to risk their own and their partners' lives because they are not willing to have a loss of sensation by wearing a condom. They clamour for more information when they read reviews about a woman who dispenses with protection when she is providing certain sexual activity

This careless approach makes the web site *www.adultwork.com* popular with a number of punters. On this site two women who described themselves as escorts working in Ireland said they were willing to have sex without a condom. Even on the established *escort-ireland.com* site a group of women published their intention of coming to Ireland and having dangerous sex with men if they so desired. They referred to themselves as 'bareback girls'.

We are six english girls (middle 20s) and we have just arrived on your lovely shores today. We are sorting out our accommodation in a discreet apartment in Cork, but will be traveling

around as we hope to stay in Ireland until May. We will be
ready to offer you our every-thing-available service in a few
days. We will get an irish sim card tomorrow. We hope to get
our profiles up on this site in a few days. In the meantime, if
you want more information, pics, a sample video of us all
having a pint in Cork airport please email us.

Anyone who emailed them was greeted with a confirmation that
they would be offering sex without a condom, and that they were
in the process of organising a five-bed apartment.

To be fair to the operators of *escort-ireland.com*, they did
remove these women's details from the message board as soon as
it was brought to their attention. However, before they could react
at least two men had expressed an interest in the women's service.

The dangers posed by using prostitutes was brought into sharp
focus in Galway in July 2008 when one woman was forced to contact the web site advertising her services and ask them to put up a
notice saying that she had contracted gonorrhoea from a client
there. Given the numbers of men she had seen in Galway, she had
the decency to ask the owners of *irishindependentescorts.com* to put
an alert on the site for men who might have visited her while she
was on her seven-day tour of Galway. It was arranged that a text
message would be sent to all the men who had used her services,
saying 'What time is the match on?' with the men receiving the text
to take it as their cue to get themselves to a doctor for testing.

Punters on the rival site *escort-ireland.com* were quick to seize
the moral high ground. One enterprising contributor ran a hastily
put-together poll of his fellow-users of the site and found that
56 per cent regularly had a check-up. The fact that this referred to
only ten men did not lend much authority to the poll.

Prostitutes themselves saw the slip-up in Galway as an opportunity to publish a bit of self-promotion. 'Sexy Naomi' wrote on
the message board:

I went to do my full STD [test for sexually transmitted disease]
about 10 days, two weeks this thursday coming so I will have to

go to get my results. They will give me a card were all the details of my STD are printed so if I don't show you, welcome to ask me to do so.

In 2006 the Joint United Nations Programme on HIV and AIDS published a report on the risk of such diseases in eastern Europe and Asia, two of the main sources of non-national prostitutes in Ireland. It said:

> In almost a decade, the rise in numbers of HIV- and AIDS-affected people in Eastern Europe and Central Asia has grown and is affecting ever-larger regions on these continents. The number of people living with HIV in this region reached an estimated 1.6 million in 2005—an increase of almost 20-fold in less than 10 years. With the collapse of the former Soviet Union in the 1990s, a sharp increase in the incidence of substance abuse, prostitution, HIV and other sexually transmitted infections resulted.
>
> Increasing numbers of women are acquiring HIV from male partners who have become infected when injecting drugs. Despite this initial concentration among injecting drug users, the epidemic has now found additional momentum among sex workers and their clients. Furthermore, condom use is generally low among young people, including sex workers and injecting drug users—who are at highest risk of HIV transmission.
>
> This best practice publication describes the experiences of, and challenges faced by, five organisations in Eastern Europe and Central Asia, which developed effective practices and implemented HIV/sexually transmitted infection prevention programmes for sex workers. These organisations operate in low resource settings with little or no support from local and national governments. The experiences drawn from these programmes can be helpful in initiating and moving forward similar projects, thus contributing to greater coverage of sex work populations and improved quality of existing projects.

In the Russian Federation, HIV prevalence of approximately 15% has been detected among sex workers in Ekatarinaburg [Sverdlovsk] and 14% in Moscow. Through the exchange of sex for drugs, or the use of sex to support drug habits, the two pathways of HIV transmission are being linked.

Closer to home, in 2007 researchers published the results of a survey entitled 'Sexually Transmitted Infections among UK Street-Based Sex Workers.' They believed that reports of a declining incidence of sexually transmitted infections among prostitutes were inaccurate, and their research supported that hypothesis.

They carried out an observational study of street prostitutes attending a GU (genitourinary) clinic in London between July 2006 and January 2007. The local sex worker outreach project had developed a weekly drop-in centre. From here the prostitutes were 'fast-tracked' to a range of specialist health services, including the GU clinic.

The team made contact with 120 prostitutes in the district. Of these, forty attended the drop-in centre and twenty-five attended the GU clinic. There were frequent reports of recent drug use, unprotected sex with clients, and no reliable contraception. Of those surveyed, 6 were HIV-positive, 7 were pregnant, 8 had TB, and 12 had syphilis; a further 17 sexually transmitted infections were identified.

The services that prostitutes in Ireland are offering are increasingly diverse, and increasingly risky. While the prostitutes' looks are obviously a factor, the men are increasingly choosing women according to whether they will provide a service that the men cannot get elsewhere. This means that oral sex without a condom is almost *de rigueur*. Such services are not restricted to street prostitutes, whose willingness to provide any service is made necessary by the need for money to sustain a drug habit: increasingly these services are being offered by women who operate in the supposedly more upmarket indoor trade.

Of the 539 women listed on *escort-ireland.com* on 20 April 2009, 309 were willing to offer oral sex without a condom, according to their listings, and 154 were willing to let the client ejaculate in their mouth. This practice has the potential to transmit herpes, genital warts, gonorrhoea, chlamydia, syphilis, and hepatitis B, all of which are eminently spreadable and can lead to serious health complications. Even HIV can be passed on in this manner.

The Croatian woman in the Keogh case was one who refused to offer any sexual service without a condom. However, that constraint did nothing for her on that day in 2006. She endured a terrifying ordeal at the hands of her attacker, and now she must not only live with the memory of the act itself but also with the psychological scars it will inevitably have inflicted. The agency for which she was working closed down as a result of the incident, the receptionist who gave evidence fearful that she might face some sort of recrimination.

———

This woman was not the first to be put in such a terrifying position because she demanded that at least some protection be used. In 2005 a prostitute endured hours of rape and violence at the hands of a 38-year-old Dublin man in a disused railway carriage at Heuston Station. Throughout the ordeal she begged that at the very least he use a condom, but to no avail.

According to the evidence given in court, Martin Stafford, of Cork Street, Dublin, stole a car some days before the attack. On 10 March 2005 he took the car to pick up the prostitute, who was working in the Baggot Street area of Dublin. They agreed a fee before Stafford drove her to Heuston Station. They went into a disused carriage, which, unknown to the station authorities, he was using as a home. To avoid being identified he would often wear a fluorescent orange jacket similar to those worn by Iarnród Éireann workers.

That night was not the first time the two had met. On two occasions earlier in the week the woman had agreed to sex with him for the fee of €100. When she met him again on 10 March, therefore, she had no idea that she was in danger. That was until he locked the door of the carriage from the inside, took her bag from her, and switched off her mobile phone. He then told her: 'Tonight you're going to get fuck-all money. You stay until I tell you to go, and you're going to have sex with me the way I like it, and you're to strip off everything.'

He grabbed her and pushed her down on the bed. He picked up a hammer and threatened to smash her face. He then took off her clothes and demanded that she perform oral sex. She begged him to use a condom, but he refused. He then raped her. Afterwards he told her that they were going to have sex all night, and that he would not let her go until he was finished.

The woman later pretended to be asleep while Stafford drank alcohol and smoked cannabis. After about an hour he forced her again to have oral sex with him, before he raped her again. Afterwards she managed to grab the hammer and hit him around the side of the head. She tried to get out of the carriage, but he grabbed her and pushed her back in. He told her she would be punished and that she was going to stay there to satisfy his needs. At that point it was claimed that he gave her a choice between oral and anal sex. She opted for the former. He then had sex with her and made her perform oral sex. During this attack, scissors were held to her throat. During the woman's ordeal Stafford allowed her to go to the toilet on one or two occasions in what was in effect a cardboard box.

A number of hours after the first attack, Stafford fell asleep. The woman managed to get hold of her mobile phone and to ring for help. The Gardaí could not hear her in the first call, as she was whispering. In a second call, however, she managed to tell them where she was, and they told her to make a noise so that they could find her. She turned on a radio at full volume, and while it woke Stafford it also enabled the gardaí to find her.

At Stafford's trial his defence counsel said he was 'very remorseful' for his actions but that he had come from a dysfunctional background. His mother died when he was fourteen, after which he became a chronic drug abuser. However, it also emerged that he had twenty-three previous convictions, including a seven-year sentence in 1997 for false imprisonment of a woman who he forced at knife point to perform a sexual act.

He was sentenced to nine years' imprisonment, but this was felt to be too lenient, and the Director of Public Prosecutions appealed to the Court of Criminal Appeal. The DPP argued that the trial judge had not given enough weight to such factors as the victim being subjected to ten hours of false imprisonment, the fact that Stafford's actions were premeditated, and that he had previous convictions for false imprisonment and indecent assault.

However, while the Court of Criminal Appeal agreed that 'by any standard' the crime was 'horrific' and that 'a substantial custodial sentence was warranted,' it said that the nine-year sentence should stand. There was 'concrete evidence' that Stafford was making genuine attempts at self-rehabilitation regarding his drug problem.

———

The woman who suffered at Stafford's hands was lucky to come away from the situation alive. Others have not been so lucky. On 29 December 1996 the body of Belinda Pereira, a 27-year-old Englishwoman of Sri Lankan extraction, was discovered in a flat at Mellor Court in Lower Liffey Street, Dublin. She had suffered massive head injuries. The investigators found no defensive wounds on her body, nor signs of forced entry to her flat, which led them to believe that the killer or killers were either known to the woman or had portrayed themselves as punters.

In the immediate aftermath of Belinda Pereira's murder, and before it was known that she was a prostitute, there was a high level of public sympathy for the woman. However, that sympathy tailed off when her occupation emerged.

She was one of a number of women travelling to Ireland from Britain to work as prostitutes for short periods. She had flown to Dublin on Christmas Eve and had planned to work until New Year's Eve before returning to England. It was not the first time she had worked in Ireland. This time she arrived after contacting an Irish pimp through an advertisement in a London event guide, and she was contacted by clients through a mobile phone number advertised in a Dublin magazine.

Knowing her to have been alive at 10 p.m. on 28 December, detectives based their investigation on 438 calls made to her mobile phone since 8 December. They issued a picture of her, and approximately four hundred people were interviewed in the nineteen months between her murder and the inquest. As her killer carried the murder weapon to and from the apartment, the attack appeared to have been premeditated, and for some time the Gardaí were satisfied that she was killed by a client. Despite extensive searches in the apartment block and in neighbouring streets, as well as the River Liffey, no murder weapon was found, although the ferocity of the blows to her head suggested that a lump hammer or similar instrument was used.

A number of blood samples were taken for DNA profiling, and fingerprints were compared with those found in the apartment.

At the inquest the State Pathologist, Professor John Harbison, reported that Pereira had died of lacerations and contusions of the brain, subdural haemorrhage and fracturing of the skull caused by multiple blows with a blunt instrument. A verdict of unlawful killing was returned.

Members of Belinda Pereira's family believed she had a well-paid office job and that she was working to finance her mother's return to Sri Lanka after her parents' marriage broke down. When contacted through Interpol, they came from Sri Lanka to Dublin, where Hubert Pereira identified the body of his daughter at the City Morgue on 4 January.

The investigating gardaí said that Pereira's was 'one of the saddest murders.' One garda commented: 'The only thing these women see of Dublin is the airport, a taxi to the apartment and back. She was there in that little rabbit-hutch of an apartment for a week on her own.'

The investigators were also told of a severe beating given to another prostitute by a man known to have been associated with

Belinda Pereira. This man was described as a pimp and a minor criminal with drug connections, and was known to have demanded sexual favours from prostitutes whom he placed in city-centre apartments. He had not previously come to the attention of the Gardaí for any serious crime, however, and no charges were made. In his book *Sex in the City*, Paul Reynolds, RTE crime correspondent, writes that the prime suspects are two pimps from Co. Monaghan, 'but there's not enough evidence to bring a prosecution against them.'

————

In September 2006 the *Irish Independent* reported on the terrifying sexual assault of a prostitute in Dublin. The Gardaí launched a hunt for two men who raped the woman, who was working in a plush apartment in the Financial Services Centre at Custom House Dock. The woman had been operating with a friend in the apartment for several months and had built up a regular clientele. On the day in question, when she opened the door to what she thought was a potential client she was rushed by the two attackers. She told the Gardaí she was assaulted by both men and was left badly beaten before they robbed her and left. The Gardaí said the assault was extremely brutal and that the woman was lucky to have survived.

This level of violence and intimidation is so prevalent that a group of independent and former 'escorts' have launched a web site entitled *escort-watch.com*. Describing itself as an independent on-line information resource for those involved in the escort industry in Ireland, it claims that its first concern is the well-being of Irish escorts and their clients. It compiles reports on a number of topics, including bad clients and bad escorts.

Since 2005 it has reported on at least ten cases of women being attacked. Obviously the attacks are not verifiable, and the outcome of legal actions is not published, as in many cases the incident is not reported. Essentially the web site is a warning to women when a particularly violent client strikes. One such case was published on the site on 28 April 2005.

> All ladies working in Ireland, please read this story and please pass it on too. I have this morning been made aware of an extremely dangerous client who could well strike again anywhere in Ireland anytime. An independent lady who works in Ireland and the UK is the source of this story. However, the lady is remaining anonymous. The lady was recently touring in Cork and that is where this incident happened. The lady was visited by a client at her place. She doesn't have a phone number for the client as she had unfortunately given her incall details to numerous potential clients that had called her earlier in the day. He attacked the lady very seriously once he got into her place. He got a towel and attempted to strangle her with it and threw her up against a wall causing a gash in her head. Eventually she managed to run out of her place screaming, beaten, but alive thankfully, and the police did arrive at the scene. The man gave the lady the name [. . .], but, he gave the police the name [. . .]. The lady also said he was saying to her throughout her ordeal that he had killed, so killing her would be no problem to him.

The next section is typical of the fear women have of reporting crimes against them.

> The lady did not feel able to press charges with the police against this client. Like many in this business, she has friends and family that don't know what she does and she is very concerned about her privacy. She has asked me to let as many escorts in Ireland as possible know about this highly dangerous individual. Please take this report very seriously. It is clear that the lady that has already been attacked by this client is lucky to be alive and the client does represent an ongoing threat to all ladies working in Ireland. Thank you very much to the lady for sharing this information with us. You are very brave and our thoughts are with you.

Three years later, *escort-watch.com* reported another attack, this time in Dublin.

A new client who had never visited her before rang her number and arrived as normal clients do. When he entered her apartment he asked if she was here alone and if she worked alone. He then opened every door and looked in every room to make sure that she was alone. When he knew she was, he said he would stay for half an hour and they went to the bedroom. As usual she asked for her money at the start of the appointment, then he took out a pair of industrial scissors and held them to her neck and said he was going to kill her.

She does know a bit of self-defence and was able to defend herself, but he did cut her hand badly that she needed to go to the hospital. This struggle lasted about 2 or 3 minutes. She says that he was strong and used much force but thinks her own strength and self-defence frightened him and she managed to get him out the door when he then ran away.

This man looked normal, average build, between 167cm and 170cm high, grey/white hair and in his mid to late 50s

The phone number he used is 085-*******. This man is dangerous and may attack other escorts.

In 1999 the case of one of the most frightening attacks on prostitutes reached the courts. If one man illustrates the dangers that women face it is Robert Melia, of Kilmore Road, Coolock. Then thirty-five years old, he kidnapped four women, including three prostitutes, and sexually assaulted three of them after posing on different occasions as an English visitor and as a football fan in Dublin for an all-Ireland semi-final. He duped the prostitutes into believing he simply wanted to have sex with them; however, once he had them in a quiet spot his demeanour changed completely. He tied them up tightly, threw them to the ground and, while holding them face down, sexually assaulted them. If his hatred for the women was not evident enough, he would tell his victims that he hated prostitutes.

With his first victim Melia posed as a football supporter when he approached her and went with her on foot to Misery Hill, off Pearse Street, Dublin. Once he had her alone he used the straps of her handbag to bind her hands and legs together. Holding a knife to her, he forced her to the ground and pushed her face in the mud before sitting on her back. Then he sexually assaulted her before robbing her of £70.

He took £50 from the other woman he sexually assaulted while posing as an English visitor. He was not a good actor, however, and she noticed that his accent had a tendency to slip. In this incident he took his sick fantasy a step further by urinating on the woman after forcing her to crawl under a car.

With the third victim he again pretended to be an English tourist. Again he used a knife, a Stanley blade, with which he threatened to kill the woman, then sexually assaulted her, and again he stole from her. This time he did cut the victim with the knife.

With the numerous cases appearing to the Gardaí to be linked, they began to monitor Dublin's red-light districts very closely, and Melia was arrested when he was found with a Stanley knife on 21 November 1997. A number of items belonging to the women were found in his home. Subsequently the Gardaí linked him to another woman who he attacked and forced into her car. He ordered her to drive to Swords, where he tied her to the seat of the car and pushed something into her side, which she believed was a knife. Luckily for her, given this man's record, she managed to sound the car horn, and Melia ran off.

For these crimes Robert Melia, from Coolock, Dublin, was jailed at the Central Criminal Court for nine years. When he was sentenced one of the women who had given evidence cried: 'Yes, this is what I wanted!' It emerged after the sentencing that he had previously been jailed in 1991 for six years for rape and was also serving concurrent five-year and four-year sentences for robbery, imposed in October 1998.

The Director of Public Prosecutions appealed the period of imprisonment handed down, arguing that it was unduly lenient.

The judges in the Court of Criminal Appeal said 'it was beyond argument' that each of the offences of aggravated sexual assault committed by Melia was extremely serious. They said the prostitute victims were in a particularly vulnerable position and were subjected to a frightening and degrading experience, accompanied by the infliction of violence or the threat of violence, which had a traumatic effect on them. While the fourth woman was not sexually assaulted, the court argued that she had suffered a horrifying experience and that, not surprisingly, it had had a serious effect on her life. The judges concluded that if Melia was being sentenced in respect of only one of those offences he would inevitably have received a reasonably significant custodial sentence. A further three years were added to his sentence.

In a similar vein was David Power of Brittas, Thurles, another man who clearly hated women, who became notorious several years after his attack on a prostitute. At the time of the attack, in June 2000, he was twenty years old and was in the army. He approached a prostitute in Fitton Street, Cork, and agreed with her that she would masturbate him for £40. She took him to a nearby car park attached to a hotel. As they walked through the gate he grabbed her by the back of the head and pushed her to the ground. She fell on her face, and Power pulled down her clothes. He twisted her right arm behind her, knelt on her back, and grabbed her throat when she tried to scream. However, she managed to elbow him in the chest and knock him backwards. She ran away but noticed that he was following her, and she began screaming again. Some men nearby and workers from a hotel heard her and came to her assistance. Power ran off when he saw them.

The Gardaí were called, and they went to inspect the car park. While they were there Power returned, looking for his jacket. The gardaí identified him from the woman's description, and arrested him. Two years later Mr Justice Paul Carney sentenced him to three years in prison but suspended the last year, taking into account Power's guilty plea.

Three months after the first attack, and again in Cork, the same man had launched an unprovoked attack on a woman as she walked home from work. He forced her to the ground, tore her clothes off, and attempted to rape her. He slapped her across the face so hard that her head banged off the ground, and when she tried to scream he shoved his hands down her throat. Again it was only the intervention of passers-by that prevented her being raped.

Again the judge was Paul Carney, and this time he imposed a five-year prison sentence. He said the sentence was high because of the evidence of the victim. She reported that the attack had left her so traumatised that she now suffered from depression and could not continue with her career. She felt that her attacker should be sent to prison for ever. Unfortunately for another young woman, he wasn't.

When Power emerged from prison after serving the two sentences it took only a couple of years for him to attack again. This time the victim was on her way home from a nightclub in Nenagh with her boy-friend when she needed to use a toilet. They stopped at a restaurant, and she went upstairs to the women's toilet while he waited outside. She later told the court that as she opened the door of the cubicle she was pushed inside by Power. Her cries for help were drowned out by loud music in the toilets. Power put his two hands around her neck before pulling down her clothes and raping her. She managed to scrape his face.

The woman's boy-friend became concerned at how long it took for her to return and asked a girl to go into the toilets to call out her name. When the victim shouted out 'Yes,' Power stopped his assault and left.

When the young woman was examined it was found that he had strangled her so hard that the whites of her eyes were red. When gardaí examined CCTV footage it showed Power entering and leaving the women's toilets that night.

The court was told that Power had drunk fifteen pints and six shots of spirits and had taken a cocktail of ecstasy and speed (amphetamines) before carrying out the attack.

Again the judge was Paul Carney. This time he was determined that Power would be kept away from further potential victims for as long as possible. He sentenced him to life imprisonment, commenting that he had tried to help him in the past when he had imposed what might now be considered moderate sentences.

———

Obviously Ireland is not alone in having prostitutes experience extreme violence, but whereas here they usually suffer in silence, in other countries they have banded together to take a stand.

One such woman is Fiona Broadfoot, who describes herself as a survivor, having worked as a prostitute in London and Edinburgh, both with and without a pimp. She is now a renowned campaigner who has worked to help young women get out of the sex trade. She spoke out about her experience at a recent conference of the European Women's Lobby under the title 'Not for Sale'. Of her pimp she said:

> He put me on a street corner and gave me some condoms. I was immediately at risk of the most horrendous violence and abuse. I was raped, I was buggered, I was beaten, I was spat at, I had urine thrown at me by residents in communities that I worked in.

Fiona Broadfoot entered prostitution in her mid-teens and spent eleven years either on the street or in saunas and 'escort agencies' in Leeds and London, where she was forced to work seven days a week. She was regularly robbed and beaten by punters, but, like so many other women, she also suffered at the hands of the man who put her there. Her pimp would beat her up if she did not make enough money. He would cut her hair as a punishment and lash her with a flex. On one occasion she claimed that a pimp beat her so hard that he almost killed her and left her for dead in his flat. She woke up in hospital, where she stayed for three months, suffering from 'mental and physical breakdown'.

The 'wake-up call' that made her escape was very sudden and very brutal, as she explained to the 'Not for Sale' campaign.

> In 1995 it all came to a very sudden end when I turned on the local news on television and my beautiful little cousin's face came up. It was obvious she was on heroin. It said: 'prostitute found dead in house'. She was 17. The last time I had seen her was at a family wedding when she was six. Unfortunately she fell into the arms of a pimp at the age of 14 and was murdered brutally at the age of 17. That gave me the strength to exit prostitution. It shook me into a very harsh reality and it is now 10 years since I exited.

Another speaker at the conference, Vednita Cartner, a former prostitute and founder of the American organisation 'Breaking Free', reinforced the point.

> The 'john', the trick, these individuals are usually men who pay for the right to do whatever they desire to the supply. The guy is usually the guy next door, he is someone's husband, brother, uncle. He may be a doctor, own his own business, be a painter, a carpenter.
>
> The 'john' may desire to tie a woman or a girl up, he may demand not to use a condom, he may want to rape the supply over and over until his desire is met. When he is finished with the supply, he gives her or the pimp trafficker the agreed upon money, puts his suit back on, goes home, tells his wife or girlfriend he loves her kisses his daughter goodnight and goes to bed as if nothing has happened. He feels justified for what he just did and never thinks about how the supply feels. He paid for what he did.

As the experience of both these women shows, the dangers posed to prostitutes come not only from men posing as punters and from opportunist thieves but also from within the ranks of the 'sex industry'. Several Irish 'escort' web sites have reported details of intimidation by brothel and site owners of women working either for them or in rival organisations.

There are several references to a particular set of pimps who, it was alleged, attracted women to Ireland for tours and proceeded to take most of the money they made. Two such women, who were friends, claimed they had been held in separate apartments where two 'heavies' would arrive twice daily to take money from them. It was claimed that one woman escaped only when the apartment she was in was raided, and she warned her friend. Both were able to get to the airport and back to Britain. The *escort-watch.com* site warned:

> There are agencies in Ireland that treat their ladies well, but, as this report highlights, there are also those that treat their ladies very badly. If you are planning to tour Ireland with an agency, make proper checks on the agency before you do anything else. Good Irish escort agencies that invite touring ladies should have lots of escorts that have toured with them previously willing to recommend them.

In 1998 rivalry between two agencies led to the intimidation and robbery of two agency prostitutes from Dublin working in Cork. Two men posing as clients visited the women at their luxury flat in Douglas and threatened them over their activities. The women told gardaí that the men stole about £500 in takings and warned them that they must return to Dublin and stop coming to Cork and taking business from local prostitution rackets. It was claimed that the agency was offering a more 'upmarket' service than that being offered locally, and it was beginning to affect business in several Cork brothels.

So far, the women working in prostitution have largely been portrayed as victims of crime. However, it must not be forgotten that there have been numerous instances in which the women have been the perpetrators. They realise that the men they rob are likely to be stigmatised if they take the matter to the Gardaí and risk being exposed as users of prostitutes. Cork has seen its fair share of such opportunistic robbers.

In 2004, in a case brought before Cork District Court but dropped by the Director of Public Prosecutions and therefore never proved, a woman was allegedly picked up as a prostitute but then robbed the man at knifepoint and forced him to get cash from a bank machine. The case was dropped because the alleged victim was very ill and under stress and was unwilling to go through with the case.

He had claimed he picked the woman up in January 2004 at Lapp's Quay, in the city centre. This area is regarded as the red-light district of Cork. He claimed he drove to the car park by Cork School of Music and parked in the far corner, away from the road. He told the Gardaí it was there that they were going to have sex but that the woman first asked him if she could use his mobile phone.

After she made a couple of calls he said she pulled a knife on him and demanded money, and then demanded to be driven towards her home. The alleged victim also said she forced him to use his bank card to withdraw cash from a cash machine. The man had been expected to claim that she stole his car as well as €220 in cash and the mobile phone and bank cards. The woman had expressed her intention of contesting the charge.

Again in Cork it was reported that a Polish woman working the streets was bringing men to a spot where the money was handed over and then running off. A heavily built man driving a red car would wait for her and whisk her away.

Few cases of men who have fallen victim to robbery by prostitutes will ever be reported to the Gardaí. The loss of a couple of hundred euros is seen as nothing compared with having to go to a Garda station, possibly being obliged to go to court to testify against the woman if she is caught, and then having the ignominy of their name being published in the newspapers as a user of the women's services. Nevertheless, some of the thieves have had to face the rigours of the law.

Lisa Healy, a 24-year-old Dubliner from Esker Road, Lucan, robbed a supermarket security guard of €100 after he propositioned her on his way home from work. It emerged in court that she had hepatitis C, was HIV-positive, and had 'life-threatening' blood clots.

She met her victim in Baggot Street, Dublin, on 4 February 2005. The two fell into conversation, during which she told him she was an office employee but was working as a prostitute because her pay was poor. They were captured on CCTV going into the Spar shop in Lower Rathmines Road together to get condoms before agreeing that they would use an apartment in which to have sex. They never reached the building. The man was attacked by another man and was forced to hand over €100 to the young woman.

Unlike many men duped in this way, the victim was willing to testify, and the Gardaí had the CCTV evidence. Despite her starting to cry loudly as her sentence was pronounced, the woman was sent to prison for a year.

06 | IT TAKES TWO

> **M**yths that surround the perpetrators of prostitution rationalise or excuse male behavior. We've all heard such remarks as 'They are basically decent men looking for a bit of harmless fun;' 'It's the inevitable result of natural male instincts;' 'Prostitution protects "good" women against rape;' 'Men need to release tension;' 'Male biology is different from female biology and requires multiple women for sexual satisfaction;' 'It's a way of initiating boys and men into sexual activity;' and 'Men are giving these women the means to make a living.' These are fictions, not facts. The sex industry promotes these myths to justify its existence and to promote its 'products.' Unfortunately, many men who use and abuse women in prostitution rationalise their behavior on the basis of such myths.—Ilvi Jõe-Cannon and the Coalition Against Trafficking in Women, *Primer on the Male Demand for Prostitution* (2006).

How many Irish men have paid for sex from a prostitute? A straw poll would obviously yield very inaccurate figures, as few are prepared to admit that they would do such a thing. However, with an assessment of the usage in other western European countries it is possible to gauge the psychological drivers that apply to a cross-section of men, though obviously it is dependent on the legality of prostitution in each country.

Internationally it is estimated that in a 'First World' society as many as one out of every ten men has had sex with a prostitute at least once. In fact that would appear to be a conservative estimate. According to the Coalition Against Trafficking in Women, data published by the Swedish Ministry of Industry in 2003 showed that one out of every eight men uses women or children in prostitution. A study in Sweden showed that men who have had many sexual partners are the most common buyers of prostituted women, thus dispelling the myth that the buyer is a lonely, sexually unattractive man with no other option than to buy sex from prostitutes.

In Italy it has been estimated that one out of every six men has visited a prostitute, while in Germany, where prostitution is for the most part tolerated, psychologists claim that 18 per cent of men regularly pay for sex.

In Britain a survey of 11,000 adults taken in 1990 and again in 2000 found that the rate had increased from one in every twenty men to almost one in ten over that period. The report, published in the journal *Sexually Transmitted Infections*, linked the rise to increasing use of the internet to advertise sex, a higher divorce rate, and more sex tourism. One of the joint authors, Dr Helen Ward of Imperial College, London, told the *Guardian*: 'I was surprised by how quickly the figure had gone up, though there are more men in the potential user groups now.' She noted that the study found the most frequent visitors to prostitutes to be single men aged between twenty-five and thirty-four, men who had previously been married and were now divorced or widowed, and men who lived in London. She also suggested that the increasing popularity of foreign travel—for business, for pleasure, and for stag weekends—meant that many men might pay for sex abroad.

The *Observer* published a survey of British people's attitudes to sex, including questions regarding prostitution. It found that 18 per cent of British men had visited prostitutes. This was an increase of 3 per cent since 2002. The use of prostitutes was highest among men aged between thirty-five and fifty-four, and 14 per cent of married men had also visited a prostitute. 6 per cent of those who had not done so would consider paying for sex in the future. In total, 27 per cent of British men had either visited a prostitute or would consider doing so in the future. Fewer than 1 per cent of women had used prostitutes, though 2 per cent would at least consider the possibility.

Here in Ireland the Irish Study of Sexual Health and Relationships interviewed 7,441 adults in 2004–05 and found that an estimated one in every fifteen men has had sex with a female prostitute. The survey found that older men in professional jobs were far more likely to have paid for sex than any other category. It did not look at men who used gay prostitutes, but among those who had paid women for sex, age was a significant factor. 'Compared with men aged 18–24, men aged 25–54 were over two-and-a-half times more likely to have paid for sex, while men aged 55–64 were over four-and-a-half times more likely.' Among those who said they had been with a prostitute, 10 per cent never used a condom, while 82 per cent always did. It did not find any trends in the reasons why men used prostitutes according to relationship status, social class, or where the men live. However, after analysing all the variables, the authors reported that married men were the least likely to have had paid for sex, compared with men in a casual relationship. Among men aged 55 to 64, 8½ per cent said they had been with a prostitute at some point in their life, though fewer than 1 per cent had in the previous five years.

Certainly Dublin would seem to be no different from any other cosmopolitan city. Indeed it is well known that at any given lunchtime in the city there is a weekday rush as men flock to the myriad escort agencies to have a very expensive repast. Gardaí carrying out surveillance of known brothels in the city have been astounded by the number of well-heeled executives shuffling into apartment doorways, furtively glancing around to see if they have been noticed before slipping inside, only to emerge up to two hours later. What is certain is that the reasons why Irish men use the services of prostitutes are the same as those in any other society.

Can visiting a prostitute be only about the sex and not about friendship, ego, admiration, or conquest? Is it merely a cold and emotionless business transaction brought about by a man's instinctive urges? There are a number of basic headings under which the reasons for the use of prostitutes can be classed.

POWER

There is no doubt that power is an aphrodisiac for many men, not least those who do not enjoy this feeling in other aspects of their lives. They come from their nine-to-five jobs, where they are slaves to the clock or to a demanding boss. In the arms of the prostitute they are suddenly the ones calling the shots. They know that they hold the financial reward the woman is looking for, and therefore for those thirty or sixty minutes they can tell the woman exactly what she must do. These men have the power to demand whatever service they want, not what they can persuade a wife or partner to do. They know they will not be rejected and that if this woman wants that money she will have to comply. According to the Coalition Against Trafficking in Women,

> There is a gross power imbalance between a prostituted human being and the buyer. Prostitution is inequality made sexy. This power imbalance is clear in the way that buyers decide who they will buy in prostitution whereas prostitutes can rarely if ever refuse a 'customer', no matter how disgusting his smell, ugly his looks or foul his temper.

However, it would be naïve to think that all men enter the situation with a prostitute looking for sex that they control. The level of power seems to be commensurate with the particular man's level of confidence. One punter admitted the guilt and shame that plagued him as he went through the door of the brothel every time, the addiction to the services within meaning that he was always, as he put it, a 'bumbling mess.'

I hate the whole experience when I am there. I just let the woman tell me what to do and wish it would all be over. Yet a few weeks later I will go back again.

For some men, the ability to have sex with a beautiful woman does fill them with confidence. Conveniently forgetting that they are paying her to be there, they pretend she is enjoying his company and enjoying having sex with them.

FANTASY

Michael wants to be able to experiment with his sex life. He loves his wife but she is only willing to do old-school sex in the bedroom. He has watched pornography, he knows what else is out there, and he wants it. The women on the internet offer the sort of services he craves.

This is a frequently used reason offered by men for visiting a prostitute. It is certainly true that as the women offer a bewildering range of services, any particular fantasy a man has can in general be fulfilled, simply by searching around. Sex without a condom, though frowned on even within the sex industry, given its inherent risks, is available if the man looks carefully enough. The fantasy element is a common reason given by men for using the services of prostitutes, in particular with regard to oral sex, which the men claim they want but their partner is unwilling to provide.

One user, Guy, admitted that it was the simple fact that it meant he could have sex with a different woman from the one he was married to. He felt that it did not constitute cheating because he had no romantic feelings towards the woman, only a sexual attraction, which could be taken in isolation.

In a paper entitled 'The practices of male "clients" of prostitution: Influences and orientations for social work' by Sven-Axel Månsson of the University of Göteborg, the author gives the example of the fantasy of the 'dirty whore'.

For certain clients, in a distinct and immediate manner, the image of the 'whore' is sexually exciting. The 'whore' is perceived as a sexual animal, for violent desire and urgency, sexual desire which here is often tied to secrecy and guilt . . . 'the whore' seems at the same time more accessible as a source of dreams and erotic fantasies. Many men are motivated by curiosity to have contact at least once in their life with a 'whore,' to look at her, to experiment with this type of sexual relation. Also, the environment of prostitution provokes curiosity and excitement. In red-light districts or other places where the sex industry exists, the environment of prostitution functions like an 'invitation' to sex. This is made obvious by the pornographic framework, for example in sex clubs and porn boutiques which line the 'promenades' of large cities, or porn ads on Internet Websites. In no other place do we find women who so openly display themselves sexually.

DETACHMENT

Foreign women make it easier to participate in prostitution because they are foreign: it is easier not to see them as your sister. It is easier to objectify and therefore remove yourself from responsibility.

So said Trish Murphy, a psychotherapist, speaking on the RTE television programme 'Prime Time' in 2006.

There is no doubt that men can and do detach themselves from the reality of what they are doing. In general they discount the background, the feelings and the motivation of the woman they are with. They selfishly seek their fulfilment, justifying the detachment by telling themselves they are paying significant amounts of money to avail of the woman's services. It is this isolation from reality that makes it rare for men to act if they believe the woman they encounter may be trafficked.

SKEWED LOYALTY

One of the most common justifications offered by men who are married or in a long-term relationship for their repeated indiscretions is that they do not want to have an affair. They barely class what they are doing as cheating, because, unlike an affair, the interaction is not based on love, merely on sex. They manage to divorce themselves from the reality that the level of intimacy could rarely if ever be considered anything other than cheating by their partner. That could be because, as has frequently been claimed by psychologists, men can separate sex from love, while most women cannot. Some men even claim that the act brings them closer to their wife or partner, because the sexual frustration they had felt is removed from the relationship and they are able to enjoy a more harmonious relationship.

LAZINESS

A small but significant number of men use the women because they do not have the time or are unwilling to put in the hours and the effort necessary to seeking out or sustaining a relationship.

It is these men who are most habitual in their use of prostitutes. They see the women as a simple way to attain a specific result: satisfying their sexual desires. In many instance these men find it difficult to relate to women in an emotional way, or are poor in social situations. In the real world there are always emotional obligations attached, no matter how casual the encounter. By avoiding such situations, these men's dependence on prostitutes for sexual gratification grows.

Another aspect of laziness is that the man does not have to make much effort to have a good time. The women they are visiting are well practised: therefore they tend to have better sexual prowess than other women and can arouse the men easily.

LONELINESS

When prostitutes advertise their list of services on the internet, one of the most common services is 'GFE', or 'girl-friend experience'. This is widely demanded by men, and often comes at an extra cost, as the women know that the men are willing to pay that little bit extra. It is sought by those who want the feeling that the woman they are with will be romantic, open to communication, and will want mutual sexual fulfilment. The web site *sexwork.com* gives the following description:

What it means to each person is a little different, but to most guys it means a provider that makes the experience seem unrushed, enjoyable, fun, relaxing and more like a 'real date' than a quick commercial encounter . . . it involves . . . the illusion or reality of passion on the part of the provider. Most of all its about being a sincere mutually desired human interaction. It is the opposite of the women being treated like a sex toy and the man an ATM machine.

The fact that 'GFE' is so often demanded illustrates the reality that, despite the sentiments claimed in 'skewed reality', many men do look for more from the transaction than mere sex.

One of the frequent comments of prostitutes is that a large proportion of their regular clients want to talk, to find out more about the woman, and to build a rapport or a relationship with them.

In tandem with the condemnation of anti-prostitution campaigners, for reasons that are well documented in this book, there must also be an acknowledgement of the reality that, for some men at least, sex with a woman may not be achievable for a number of reasons, whether it be looks or other personal circumstance, such as a disability. These men still have sexual urges but have no access to the touch of a woman, and so they seek out the attentions of a prostitute. They pay extra for 'GFE' to give themselves the illusion that the woman wants to be there with them. It gives them a vindication that otherwise eludes them.

BECAUSE THEY CAN

At the end of 2008 the Vatican announced its intention to make seminary candidates undergo a 'psychological evaluation', and part of this was an evaluation of the ability to live a celibate life. Undoubtedly the amount of homosexual abuse in the Catholic Church, as well as the number of clerics found to be having secret trysts with women, was one reason for the introduction of the tests; but it is a symptom too of what cannot be ignored: men and women are sexual beings, and the simple truth is that the majority of women can control their urge much more.

Society sexualises the female form through advertising, through television programmes, and through fashion. Sex sells to men. Through prostitution there is just an unreserved tap of sexual availability. It is for this reason that prostitution will, more than probably, never end in our or any other society.

Michael Bader is a psychotherapist in San Francisco who has treated dozens of men who have told him they find prostitutes irresistible.

> I have found that for the overwhelming majority of them, the appeal lies in the fact that, after payment is made, the woman is experienced as completely devoted to the man—to his pleasure, his satisfaction, his care, his happiness. The man doesn't have to please a prostitute, doesn't have to make her happy, doesn't have to worry about her emotional needs or demands. He can give or take without the burden of reciprocity. He can be entirely selfish. He can be especially aggressive or especially passive, and not only is the woman not upset, she acts aroused. He is not responsible for her in any way. She is entirely focused on him. He is the centre of the world. Now, of course, these interactions are scripted. The prostitute is acting. But it doesn't matter. For men who like to go to prostitutes, the illusion of authenticity is enough.

A question was posed on one of the Irish 'escort' web sites: 'Why do men pay for sex?' Below are some of the responses, which show a wide gamut of reasons. From 'Cooperfield':

> We pay for it because its like any other craving that needs to be satisfied like when people try to quit smoking and all of a sudden that cigarette looks like the most delicious thing in the world and after you smoke it you find that its just another plain old cigarette.same thing with the sex thing if i haven´t got my end away for good while i can dig out the porn for a good old reliable tug but if i have the money and i remember that some sex with a woman who looks like the porntars on my televsion is just a phonecall away wild horses won´t drag me

away from satisfying my sexual urges.But of course afterwards, after my craving has been satisfied the guilt automatically comes,this isn´t the case with every man but i´d say its there with a good few of us.Is this good old reliable catholic guilt or that its short term meaningless cold sexual gratification i don't know,all i know is that these thoughts aren't going thru my head when i´m on the hunt only after so that might be my problem or maybe thers something niggling at the back of my mind saying i should be having sex with someone i love(idealistically)or at least just a girlfriend.But on the plus side and the other way of looking at things would be the view that its a very healthy endeavor when you look at the social scene in Dublin on the weekends,people having to get pissed drunk to work up the confidence to talk to each other. The thing that would make you feel better about paying for sex is knowing that you don´t have to go out get pissed drunk and try all night to negotiate sex from some scanger that isn´t even worth two seconds of conversation and still theres the risk that you still mightn´t be getting any at the end of the night so on the other side of things the escort set up is perfect in that thers a simple understanding between two people you are there simply for sex and she is there to recieve money for sex so no bullshit games and acting has to take place.

'Violette', one of the prostitutes, surmised:

The reason men pay for sex, or seek it out for free in pubs, is a simple as our biology! Men's evolutionary prime directive is to spreed as much of his sperm around as possible, the more and different partners the better! But society and its totally artificial constructs have tried to inflict a boundary on the randy nature of the beast, of course to absolutely no avail! So, by going out and wanting to screw different ladies, perfectly natural, the guilt is UNnatutal.

Just incase you want to know what the female's prime directive is, it is to select the best mate for our future off-spring, in other words we are ALL natural born Gold Diggers! A match made in heaven!

'Roryman' took on a rather sarcastic tone in his response:

Because . . . Sex, sex, sex is everywhere—on the tele, billboards, 'bottom' shelf mags, hell even on the radio. My laberdor is losing her good looks and all the sheep run away from me! Theres never anything on the tele (except sex) Like all men, I cant help it, I am genetically programmed to always want it. Call me warped, but I just like being in the company of good looking women with great bodies and it only costs me 150 notes—thats the same money as paying a gas man to look at my old boiler!

The response of 'Flypan' was much more straightforward.

Why do we pay for sex?? because when you are done with it you don't need to think on what you owe her anymore, cause you have already paid her. Instead, if you got a girlfriend, it's like you are owing her something all the time . . . so people need to feel liberated once in a while, and so go for it!! Of course, there are lots of other reasons, but the best one is the one that applies to yourself, so try to find out by yourself why would you go to visit an escort . . .

There were a number of honest responses that revealed that some men really were not happy about what they were doing. 'Wilko88' said:

I can only tell you why i ever paid for sex.my first ever punt was out of sheer intregue as it was something i always said i would try. i had no idea what to expect, and it was definetly a good buzz. it was also very weird if i'm honest,and slightly soul destroying. theres a balance involved for me, if you enjoy the sex enough not to feel too bad about yourself or the escort after,then you're laughing. i've had a handful of punts over the last 6months and the balance is going the wrong way for me.i've decided not to punt anymore and so came on to give the escort the glowing review she deserved. after all its not her fault my conscience won the battle.lol.was a good laugh while it lasted . . .

P.S. i was raging i never got to see English Rebecca,shes seems like a bit of a treat, but as far as the girls i experienced, Sara in Galway is in a different class. Out of this world!

Thanks to all concerned xxx

On the *irishindependentescorts.com* message board another punter, 'Waterford Guy', was put straight on a couple of points by one of his fellow-commentators.

Ive been with escorts before when ive been single, the reason is obvious, I want a ride from a good looking woman.

And I've been with them when I was with my ex-girlfriend, who was actually good looking, reason being I wanted a ride without any nagging.

But recently I'm with a new woman who I think is great. Checks all the boxes for me, sexy, kinky, fun etc etc. Everything I want, so I figured when I got with her I wouldn't be seeing any more escorts. I was wrong! I still got the urge to go see one the other day, now I think the reason is the thrill of it all, sneaking around doing something 'taboo,' the rush of walking into the hotel and trying to get through the lobby without looking obvious.

Does anybody else get nearly as much of a kick from this side of the whole experience as from the ride itself . . . or am I just a freak who will habitually cheat on his partner!!?

'Sex on Wheels' agreed. It's the whole build up, from seeing who's going to be in your town, to choosing who you want to see, to the drive down the road wondering what it's going to be like, wondering if you're going to get caught, wondering if she's going to look like her pics, wondering if you'll get spotted by someone you know in the hotel, but the best for me is going up in the lift and going down the corridor to the hotel room, my heart does be pounding and I'm as nervous as feck, what a thrill, I'm buzzing at this stage, its like a drug, and then there's the knock on the door. Jesus man even here thinking about it now just gives me a massive thrill. The build up sometimes can be better than the actual physical end of things I find, and I also find punting often can make you loose the excitement, better leaving it for as long as you can otherwise it just becomes like everything else if you do it a lot, boring.

However, '1210' pointed out the gaping hole the other man appeared about to fall into.

i was like waterford guy, had the wife, kids all the trappings. My ex-wife is stunningly beautiful, kinky, fit especially after having kids and could in general give most escorts a run for there money. However, i still went to escorts, i have done it for most of my adult life and as described perfectly it was the thrill, the hotel etc. Usually the punt was never as good as the expectation even if the girl was really good looking. So eventually i was found out and kicked out, my entire wages goes to my ex who rightly, shows no mercy. I went to therapy as i thought i was going insane, why go to a working girl when i have the women i love and lust after at home? Simple, i was diagnosed as an addict, someone mentioned it as a drug and while alcohol and drugs work for some mine was the thrill of going with an escort. All that was described before about the life etc is known as the pre-occupation, its the picking of the woman etc, then the acting out then followed by the guilt and shame. Going home to my family after behaving like an idiot and going to a girl was so shameful, i am/was so disgusted with myself. I now go to meetings to realise that going to escorts is pure fantasy, they want you in and out as quickly as possible, take the money and run type thing Basically, if you can't stop this then break up with her.

One of the men even had advice for one woman who went onto an 'escort' site and asked what it took to become an escort. 'Dreamon' wrote:

> Anyway, Want2playwithme, forgive the cynicism of an old guy. Advice; DONT DO IT. From your posts you have brains and wit enough to make a living another way. Escorting is like a tattoo, if you do it you will be stained forever. You will always be a prostitute or an ex-prostitute with all the implications that has for future relationships. You will not hear from the escorts here about how lonely and insecure the life of an escort is. Reality does not attract clients. You have heard all this before but it has to be said.
>
> If you want to make money out of sex, do not 'shit on your own doorstep'. Get a serious makeover and go join an agency in London, where you should make good money without the risk of running into someone you know. You will meet other girls and learn from them. when you have learned the business and how to cope with the difficult clients you can go 'independent'
>
> Do not start unless you have an exit plan. You are a bright enough girl to see from these boards that being in the business too long damages your mental health. You need to put yourself through some college course or set a goal of a certain amount of money to start a business. The escort business,or at least the money that it generates is as addictive as any drug. You have to control it and not let it contol you. Do not let it become your life. Be firm with yourself about about how much you spend and how much you put away. There will be fun times but be true to yourself and trust only yourself.

According to a survey by the web site *escortsurveys.com*, the average person who uses prostitutes is a young, educated professional earning an average wage, and 61 per cent of them are married or in a relationship.

They surveyed more than 250 men who paid for sex and were willing to fill out a detailed questionnaire on the reasons they visited prostitutes, the risks they were willing to take, and the social profile into which they fitted. It found that 74 per cent of the men had third-level education, 74 per cent were aged between 25 and 44, and most were earning between €30,000 and €50,000. Not surprisingly, given the number of women available, almost 40 per cent of the respondents were in Dublin, and 95 per cent were white and Irish.

One of the most damning statistics was that slightly more than 60 per cent of the men regularly using prostitutes were in a relationship, 43 per cent being married or with a long-term partner and 17 per cent going out with someone.

Most used a prostitute less frequently than monthly, but a significant 37 per cent also admitted that they had used a street prostitute in the past. Some 74 per cent said they obtained access to services from a home computer, and 59 per cent said they thought escort web sites had encouraged them to use these services more often.

Of the respondents, 27 per cent said they had been using the escorts for between one and three years, but a large number—16 per cent—had been using them for more than ten years.

One in four admitted they had met a woman they suspected was being forced to work in prostitution. A small percentage admitted that they had been offered sex with a girl who they believed was as young as fourteen. The youngest girl they admitted taking up the offer with was sixteen.

Some 26 per cent had been offered unprotected sexual inter-course, and 75 per cent had been offered unprotected oral sex. While most declined intercourse without a condom, 57 per cent agreed to oral sex without it.

Of the 252 respondents, 208 admitted that they had been sex tourists using services in other countries. Britain and the Netherlands were the most popular destinations.

A similar survey of the experiences of men who used women advertising on *escort-ireland.com* found that the average amount spent per visit was €327, with 81 per cent opting for 'in-calls' (in the prostitute's accommodation) as opposed to 'out-calls' (in the punter's home or a hotel room). The findings were based on 693 reviews from men who used the service.

The survey by *escortsurveys.com* and the reviews on *escort-ireland.com* revealed different attitudes. Among the comments submitted by punters were concern that there was an increasing number of foreign women in the industry, who may be the victims of exploitation or trafficking. On the other hand, many expressed a cavalier attitude, caring only about their own satisfaction. Some complained that the prostitute did not look as good as the woman in the photographs on the web site. Others complained that they were made to use a condom, contrary to the internet advertisement, or that the woman would not provide a service that was listed on the site. 'If I wanted sex this bad, I would have stayed at home with the wife,' said one.

One of the biggest gripes is the charge, with most saying that the women overcharged. However, even with that in mind, in the *escortsurveys.com* findings only three of the 252 men admitted that their spending on escorts had caused serious financial problems. One said: 'I think with the internet it has got too easy to access escort services. I have become addicted and am trying to give it up.'

———

One reason why men use prostitutes was not included in the surveys: sex tourism and its availability.

The journal *Sexually Transmitted Infections* surveyed more than 2,500 men at one sexual health clinic in Britain between October 2002 and February 2004. One of the most notable statistics in the report is that more than half said they had paid for sex while abroad. Worryingly for their partners past, present and future is the fact that unprotected vaginal sex was more common among those who paid for sex while abroad.

There is a certain escapism that business and holidaying tourists, particularly men, appear to embrace. The notion that they are not constrained by the normal restrictions that tether them while at home means they think they can get away with so much more when they are abroad.

The explosion of sex tourism from Ireland is nowhere better evidenced that in the stag-weekend craze. Thirty years ago—even ten years ago—men used to go out to the pub, get drunk, and, at worst, visit a lap-dancing club. The use of prostitutes to spice up the celebration, while undoubtedly occurring, was never flaunted. Now young men and their extended circle of friends are travelling far and wide to 'sow their wild oats' before they settle down. The only thing that constrains them is the cost, now estimated at an average of €395 per person per weekend. A number of them are simply going to a topless bar in Prague to swill beer and ogle women; but an increasing proportion are also paying to have sex with those women for knock-down prices.

Riga, the capital city of Latvia, has been one of the leading destinations for stag weekends for a number of years. A host of airlines offer weekend flights. With beer costing €3 or less and 'full massages' for €30, the attraction is obvious. On a Saturday night at almost every street corner two or three men are liberally distributing pictures of naked or scantily clad women who are working out of the nearby strip clubs. Many when asked will inform the punter whether the women are open to offering some 'additional services'.

The situation has developed so rapidly that young women going into Riga at night will be accosted by men who presume they will allow them to have sex if they pay them, or even if they buy them a drink.

While Riga's reputation is growing, it is still the Czech Republic that can 'boast' that it belongs among the top twenty sex-tourism destinations in the world, according to *sex-tourism.org*. Prague is now a paradise for tourists seeking prostitutes. The monthly income of the sex trade around Wenceslas Square is estimated at half a billion Czech crowns, or €19 million. The fact that in many of these countries the law regarding the sale of sex is so lax justifies to these men the claim that what they are doing can't be all that wrong.

The web site *sex-tourism.org* offers tips for the prospective traveller on where to find the best sex at the cheapest price. 'Latin America and East Asia have become the most popular,' it advises. 'Men enjoy visiting Asian countries where they find submissive, attentive women who have no problems and always smile.'

The Niall Mellon Township Trust is renowned for its charitable work, building houses for the underprivileged in South Africa. The work of the volunteers is lauded for its selflessness. However, in January 2009 the *Sunday Independent* drew attention to the sleazier side of what some of the tourists were getting up to. It told how a number of them, inhibitions dulled by cheap alcohol, were availing of the services offered by the dozens of prostitutes gathering in the hotel's foyer each night. One volunteer told the newspaper:

> A lot of lads were scared of getting the virus, but some lads were thick enough to go looking for a brothel and do their thing. Lads being lads, I wouldn't put it past them. We were warned not to take the risk of having sexual intercourse with any casual acquaintance, but this went out the window for some. The guys who are stupid enough to use prostitutes in a country like South Africa are the guys that are stupid and desperate enough to use them in Ireland. Being stupid and desperate is not a reason to bar anyone from going on a charity trip. Once they turned up for work the next day and worked as hard as everyone else, I have no problem with the retarded personal choices they make in their own time.

While I am not in any way insinuating that the people on the Niall Mellon project are engaging in child prostitution, it is in countries like South Africa that child-sex tourism is at its height and where children as young as four are being sold to carry out heinous sexual acts with western European tourists. Child-sex tourists come from all income brackets, with the perpetrators usually hailing from countries in western Europe and North America.

The organisation End Child Prostitution, Child Pornography, and the Trafficking of Children (ECPAT) is working around the clock to end the exploitation of children in sex tourism. Since the early 1990s it and many member-groups of its network around the world have worked with the tourism and travel industry to raise awareness and to take practical measures against children being sexually abused. Agreements have been established with hotels, tour operators and other sectors of the tourism industry for preventing the sexual exploitation of children; but they are fighting a tough battle.

According to ECPAT, child-sex tourism, with cash, clothes or even food being exchanged for sexual contact, is happening in brothels, red-light districts and even five-star hotels and beaches. It is also not confined to the headline areas in Asia. In Mexico it has been estimated that 20,000 minors are victims of prostitution; in Colombia the figure could be as high as 35,000. In Kenya, four coastal towns between them are estimated to have 15,000 under-age girls being exploited by tourists, and in the country as a whole an estimated 30,000 girls aged between twelve and fourteen are being used in hotels and private villas, according to research by UNICEF, the United Nations Children's Fund. This research showed that 32 per cent of the men using these girls are German or Italian.

Two countries formerly part of the Soviet Union, Russia and Estonia, are the most notorious for child-sex tourism. In Moscow it is estimated that up to thirty thousand children are being used for sex, with tourists travelling there to avail of their services after seeing the level of child pornography emanating from the city.

However, while nearly every country in the world has some level of child-sex tourism, it is in Asia that it is most prevalent by far. In the Philippines, for example, there are up to 100,000 victims of child prostitution, 20,000 in the Metropolitan Manila area alone.

There are 80,000 to 100,000 'sex workers' in Cambodia, 30 per cent of them under the age of eighteen. A survey of teenage Cambodian sex workers suggests that the average age of first sexual contact is eleven for girls and twelve-and-a-half for boys.

According to ECPAT, child-sex tourists come from all walks of life: they may be married or single, male or female, wealthy tourists or budget travellers. A frequent misconception is that all child-sex tourists are middle-aged or older men; in fact young tourists have been known to travel for the express purpose of sexually abusing children. Child-sex tourists may be foreigners but also local people travelling within their own country. Some child-sex tourists are looking specifically for children; most, however, are situational abusers who do not usually have a sexual preference for children but take advantage of a situation in which a child is made available to them. This type of exploitation can occur anywhere in the world, and no country or tourism destination is immune.

———

It would be naïve to think that Irish men are not engaging in this activity. Hundreds or thousands of Irish people visit Thailand every year. The majority are bound for the islands so as to enjoy the idyllic weather and scenery. Certainly large numbers want to engage in sex with adult women or with the renowned 'lady boys'. But a significant proportion are there with much more sinister intentions. For the most part, what they are looking for may not be possible in the cities, and they travel to smaller towns to see what is on offer. A large number will cross the border into Cambodia, where the trade in child sex is particularly prevalent.

In the Philippines the Irish child-sex tourist is so prevalent that Father Shay Cullen, joint founder of the People's Recovery, Empowerment and Development Assistance (PREDA) Foundation, has issued a public warning to them to stay away or he will have them jailed. He has devoted his life to rescuing abused children from Philippine vice dens. In an attempt to stem the ever-increasing numbers of Irish sex tourists pouring into the country, he has vowed to follow suspected perverts from the moment their plane lands until the second they leave.

It used to be American businessmen or soldiers. But now it's Irish men as well. They're coming in droves because it's so easy and cheap to buy child sex here.

He says he sees dozens of Irish sex tourists arrive every month, and he warns them:

They better watch out. I'm on their trail as soon as they touch down in the country.

According to PREDA, so frequently do Irish customers visit sex bars that the Philippine senate has identified Ireland as one of a handful of countries driving the boom in sex tourism. Together with the United States, Australia, Britain and Germany, Ireland has been found to be the origin of many of the men who travel to the Philippines to exploit under-age girls. Former child prostitutes have claimed that Irishmen were among the most numerous customers in the brothels and sex bars in which they worked.

Shay Cullen has warned that what happens on the faraway streets of a Philippine shanty-town will eventually affect small-town Ireland.

The abusers do not leave their habits and desires at the airport. These paedophiles come to whet their appetite, have their fill and return with their desires to molest children greater than ever.

In 2008 the United Nations accused India, Cambodia and Thailand of not doing enough to protect children from the risks associated with sex tourism, for fear of damaging their economies. The UN Special Rapporteur on the Rights of Children, Juan Miguel Petit, said there was a lot of pressure on governments to turn a blind eye to the problem of children's sexual exploitation for the benefit of tourists. He told the Associated Free Press:

Sometimes there are big pressures on governments, explicitly or implicitly, when there are enormous touristic activities going on, making millions of dollars. Some interests see the limitation on the sexual market as a limitation for their earning of money.

He said the police in those countries often appear unconcerned about the scale and gravity of the problem. 'They accept this kind of crime in a passive way, as if their job was only to chase bank robbers.'

In 2006 the Australian children's group Childwise carried out a detailed study of child-sex tourism in Cambodia. The authors, Dr Frederic Thomas and Leigh Matthews, said that Cambodia's growth as a sex-tourism destination could be attributed to its perceived reputation as a developing country with weak law enforcement, government corruption, and the low cost of travel to and within the country, as well as the cheap price of sex with a child.

Often there is no need to groom children as they are easily available in brothels or on the streets. One of the main reasons for the rapid growth in child-sex tourism is that in recent years child-sex offenders have come under greater scrutiny in their own countries. They travel to developing countries in an effort to escape Government crackdowns, tougher legislation and a heightened awareness of child abuse in their home country.

They found that organised child-sex tourists were even arriving in Cambodia in groups and taking sex tours that had been organised before they left their home country.

One of the most notorious destinations for child prostitution in Cambodia is Svay Pak, a village housing a Vietnamese community on the outskirts of the capital, Phnom Pénh. For more than twenty years child-sex tourists have swarmed to the group of ramshackle houses, knowing they would be able to find what they wanted. While girls of eleven or twelve would brazenly offer their services on the streets, even younger children would be made available inside the brothels. Children as young as eight would be able to tell the sex tourists that they offered 'boom-boom' (sexual inter-course) for $20 to $30 and 'yum-yum' (oral sex) for as little as $10.

Streetwise teenage boys would be enlisted by the pimps to meet tourists as they came into the village. These boys would bring the sex tourists on a tour of the village, showing them the brothels owned by the men paying them. They would fight with each other to get to the tourists. It was estimated that at its height several hundred girls, most of them trafficked from neighbouring Viet Nam, worked in Svay Pak.

Then, in January 2003, Cambodian police swarmed on the shanty village, closing dozens of brothels and ordering a halt to the trade. There had been a number of raids previously, but few had been so sweeping. Following the raid, a local police official said that Svay Pak was giving Phnom Pénh and Cambodia a bad name and was affecting normal tourism to the country. He vowed that this time the closures were permanent.

Yet three months later the authorities were raiding the shanty town again. This time they rescued at least thirty-six Vietnamese girls, some younger than ten. At least thirteen pimps and brothel-owners were arrested in the raid. The police said that at least twenty-two of the girls appeared to be younger than ten. According to reports, nine girls aged between six and nine were found in one house.

Since then there have been innumerable reports by aid agencies of the police supposedly closing down the sex trade in Svay Pak. In December 2004 the Phnom Pénh Municipality announced that a new shopping centre was to be constructed at Svay Pak, and that a new bridge was to be constructed nearby across the Tonlé Sap river, in an attempt to attract legitimate investment to the area. Nonetheless, within weeks sex tourists were being serviced there once more. Just as in the Philippines, Irish accents were frequently heard among the men looking for sex with children in Svay Pak.

One of the most unpleasant elements of child-sex tourism is the number of men who trek across the world looking for a child virgin. As we have seen, in the shanty brothels of the Philippines and Cambodia sex with a child is readily available, sometimes for as little as $10 or even less. A growing number of men are willing to pay fifty times that in order to find girls whose virginity they can take. While this type of crime was first sought by Asian men driven by the fear of AIDS and the belief that they could rejuvenate themselves by sleeping with a virgin, it has become increasingly prevalent among western men, who are willing to pay up to $500. As a consequence there has been an increasing number of cases in Asia of local men either kidnapping children or luring the poorer ones with the promise of money or jobs. They then sell them to the highest-bidding tourist before selling them on to a brothel.

The American television programme 'Dateline' broadcast an exposé of sex trafficking in Cambodia in 2005. As part of the undercover report they interviewed the owner of a brothel.

> Madam Lang tells us her virgins go for $600, and for that price she says we can take a girl back to the hotel and keep her there for up to three days. When she brings out the girl, the fifteen-year-old looks paralysed with fear.
>
> A child's tragic journey into the sex trade often begins in a family struggling for survival. This is a country where the average income is less than $300 a year. Some children are sold by their own parents. Others are lured by what they think are legitimate job offers, like waitressing, but then are forced into prostitution.

One of the women who is leading the fight to eradicate child-sex tourism in Cambodia is Somaly Mam, herself a victim of some of the worst abuse that has been documented. This is not her real name; she does not know her original name, or her age. When she was young—she estimates about ten years old—a man came to her claiming to be her grandfather and offering to bring her to her mother, who she did not know. After one day with this man she was forced to work for him, firstly as a slave. He would rape her while holding a knife to her head. Then, when she was about thirteen, he sold her to a brothel, where she was forced to have sex with western men for almost five years.

Throughout that time she frequently tried to escape but was caught. When captured she would be put in a cage with snakes or would be stunned with electric shocks. One night she watched a friend being murdered by one of the pimps.

When she was approximately nineteen she was set free, her captors saying she was no longer attractive to their paedophile clients. Though she claims that the years of abuse have left her dead inside, she was determined to help other girls who were faced with the same ordeal.

She first trained to be a midwife, working at a local hospital. She moved to France, where she met and married Pierre Legros before returning to Cambodia to work with the French organisation Médecins Sans Frontières ('doctors without borders'). With Pierre Legros she then set up Agir pour les Femmes en Situation Précaire (AFESIP)—'acting for women in distressing circumstances.' She opened her first shelter for victims in 1997; now the Somaly Mam Foundation works with almost 220 girls aged from four upwards. The foundation estimates that between 2 and 4 million girls and young women will be sold into sex slavery in the next twelve months.

Irish involvement in child-sex tourism is not confined to using the children, as was shown in 2003. A former member of the RUC, Richard Agnew, was described that year as being at the heart of the Philippine sex trade, running bars for tourists seeking out underage girls. He had moved to the Philippines in the early 1990s amid allegations that he had abandoned a number of investors in a time-share company he had set up, and there he bought as many as seventeen clubs and bars in the Angeles area of Manila. It was widely reported that the dancers in those bars looked no older that thirteen. Men would pay the proprietors to take the girl of their choice away to have sex.

In August 2003 the police raided one of his clubs, the Blue Nile, after relatives of two teenagers claimed the girls were being held prisoner and being made to have sex with tourists. The police found British, Australian and American men watching young girls dressed in bikinis on the stage. They took away eleven of the girls for medical examination and to see if they were under eighteen; they discovered that six of them were between eleven and thirteen years old.

Agnew, known to the girls as Big Daddy, claimed that he did not own the clubs, and his name did not appear on the clubs' official documents. He was imprisoned, but a few weeks later the police dropped the charges for lack of evidence. He insisted to British journalists that he was simply working as a consultant in some of the bars, and he rejected any suggestion that he was involved in prostitution.

————

The simple and unavoidable fact is that the abuse of children, the urge among some adults to have sex with children, is going to continue unabated unless something is done about it.

In January 2009 the National Society for the Prevention of Cruelty to Children claimed that 20,758 alleged sex crimes involving children under eighteen were reported to the police in England and Wales in the previous year—that is, fifty a day.

What happens to children in private homes is exceptionally hard to prevent, but there is, at least to some extent, a social desire to prevent it. Where the abuse is organised, however, when men from the other side of the world can easily find the children, there is obviously a lack of the political will to battle the problem. Possibly this is due to an insular approach to child-sex tourism: 'It's not in our back yard, so we will ignore it.'

The Irish Defence Forces had possibly their least 'finest hour' while on duty in Eritrea in 2002 and again in 2003. In 2002 a soldier serving with the UN peacekeeping mission there was sent home after it emerged that he had made a pornographic video with a local woman. The 23-year-old woman said the soldier gave her money and promised to take her back to Ireland. She made her claims from her prison cell after being arrested. She was eventually sentenced to two years' imprisonment. At the time it was the Eritrean government press that brought the story to light. 'To him our rich and wise culture is of no interest,' it said. 'What interests him is fooling around and seducing girls to do these filthy acts, recording them and selling them.' The soldier, a private in his forties from the west of Ireland, was sentenced to sixteen days' detention and then discharged from the army.

Worse scandal was to follow a year later when it emerged that Irish soldiers had been paying local women and girls for sex, and there were allegations that one of them was only fifteen years old. A number of local women claimed to have accepted money from the soldiers in return for sexual favours. The incidents happened in a UN camp in the capital city, Asmara, and were described in a report produced by the UN Mission in Ethiopia and Eritrea. None of the seven accused were interviewed for that report, so a military police team carried out an investigation. The accused were offered tests for sexually transmitted diseases, as nearly one in every four street women in Asmara is HIV-positive.

As the investigation went on, the Defence Forces made it clear that none of the women were forced to have sex, and, as regards the fifteen-year-old, it was accepted that the men did not know her age. After a long and detailed examination, six soldiers were charged with misconduct. More serious charges, that they had sex with minors, were not proved. Announcing the findings, a Defence Forces spokesperson said the men had never had full sexual intercourse with the women. Instead, the women offered lap-dances and other sexual services, including oral sex.

Four of the soldiers pleaded guilty at arraignments before their commanding officers, one other was found not guilty, and the sixth man contested the charges. The four who pleaded guilty were fined different amounts, including two days' pay, €100 and €110.

Whatever justification the soldiers had for their lapse in standards—being away from home for long periods without their families—such acts are obviously very serious. But there is a swathe of Irish men travelling deliberately to abuse children in Asian countries. This is not just an assumption: it is anecdotally established. Yet in a search of any of the newspaper archives any mentions of Ireland's abusers of foreign children are few and far between. Likewise, mention of the Government actively exposing or legislating against the activity barely registers.

I asked the Department of Justice what legislation exists on the abuse of children abroad, what steps the Government has taken through information campaigns to prevent Irish men engaging in child-sex tourism, and whether there is any plan to introduce legislation or guidelines on this issue. The response was:

> Under the Sexual Offences (Jurisdiction) Act (1996) it is an offence for an Irish person, or a person ordinarily resident in the State, to commit a sexual act against a child in another country which is an offence in that country and if committed in the State, would be an offence under the Schedule to that Act. In such circumstances, the person can be charged with the offence in this country. The offences listed in the Schedule (as amended) are carnal knowledge, rape, buggery and sexual assault offences.

The department said it was an offence under the act to publish information that is intended to or is likely to promote, advocate or incite the commission of a sexual offence against a child in another country. However, it made no reference to any concerted effort to tackle the problem. The rest of the response was predicated on the Government's long-overdue efforts to tackle human trafficking.

———

The penchant of Irish men for child prostitution was displayed in a chilling degree by the actions of what had been a respected former Garda sergeant. Kieran O'Halloran was caught trying to pay for sex with a child not once but twice. In both instances he tried to pay a prostitute to get the children for him.

On the first occasion he was jailed for three years, in February 2003, for paying a prostitute £100 to 'find him a seven to ten-year-old girl for sex' in 2001 and for the possession of child pornography at his home at Five Oaks, Drogheda.

In court the investigating gardaí testified that O'Halloran, who held a command position for twelve months in Croatia while working for the United Nations, picked up a 21-year-old prostitute in Blackhall Place, Dublin, before going to her flat, where he told her he was looking for a young girl. He told the woman he did not view such a request as sexual abuse, because he was willing to pay for the service. He paid the woman £100, though her fee was only £80 and they did not engage in any sexual activity.

The prostitute, pretending to go along with the request, took his mobile phone number and said she would meet him later in the south of the city, but instead she contacted the Gardaí. Detectives were able to track him down because of phone records, the registration number of his car, which the woman also took down, and CCTV footage of him withdrawing cash at an ATM in James's Street to pay for the child services.

When gardaí went to his home he said he had been expecting them but asked that the search be delayed so his family could leave. When detectives examined computers in the house they found a number of pictures of children in naked poses and engaged in sexual activity. Some of the web sites he had visited were deleted, but detectives were able to trace them.

O'Halloran, of Liffey Court, Clane, Co. Kildare, and Westminster, Blackrock, admitted possession of the material found on the computers but denied he had solicited the woman to find him a child. He was suspended from the force after his arrest and then resigned before entering his plea of guilty.

One positive aspect of this case was the praise given to the woman who had the courage to notify the Gardaí. The judge said she had 'put her credibility on trial because of her circumstances' but had done the right thing.

The court owes this lady a debt. I appreciate that it could not have been easy for her to do it. She saw him as a potential threat to young females and did what she thought was proper. The court commends her for that.

In sentencing O'Halloran, the judge imposed twenty years' post-release supervision and suspended the last year of the sentence, because, he said, O'Halloran had 'suffered greatly.' He must not have suffered enough, or played enough of an active role in the supervision, because within a few years he was once more trying to buy a child for sex, in even more despicable circumstances.

This time he offered two prostitutes up to €10,000 to obtain the children and asked one to organise 'three or four children in a hotel room' for him to have sex with. He also asked one to get him a picture of a new-born baby with her genitals on view. Again it was thanks to a right-thinking prostitute, who notified the Gardaí, that he was caught.

O'Halloran met the first prostitute at a brothel in Wolfe Tone Street, Dublin, in October 2005. He asked her to get him an eight or nine-year-old girl, telling her he wanted to 'fuck' the children, and offered her €1,000 for every one she could get him. He left, but kept in contact with the prostitute. She stored his phone number under 'pervert' before giving it to the Gardaí and making a detailed statement. Unfortunately, when an identity parade was arranged she could not pick him out, and the Gardaí were obliged to let him go. However, they continued to monitor his mobile phone.

In March 2006 O'Halloran visited another prostitute in Dublin and asked her to get him girls from eight years old but 'no older than eleven,' because he wanted an 'innocent face.' He told her he expected her to show them how to give him oral sex before leaving him alone with them. He even asked the woman if she had any friends with young children, because 'he liked to watch girls as they leave school.' He also said he had visited other countries, including Thailand, to abuse children, though his defence counsel denied that O'Halloran ever travelled abroad for child abuse and said the Gardaí could find no evidence of such travel.

It emerged in court that he had later sent this woman several text messages repeating his request and offering her €10,000 for a five or six-year-old child. He also requested a picture of a naked new-born baby.

O'Halloran visited her again in April and this time brought a child pornography DVD with him, which he showed to the prostitute and her partner. It featured an Asian girl, about twelve years old, performing oral sex on a man. O'Halloran told them: 'That's what I like: deep throat with girls like that.'

He visited her a third time that month and again requested a girl under thirteen to have sex with. Since the first incident in October the Gardaí had been monitoring his phone traffic and were able to track down the prostitute, who made a full statement.

This time in court O'Halloran said he never intended to harm any children and that it was part of a 'sexual fantasy'; but he pleaded guilty to inciting the women 'to organise or knowingly facilitate the use of a child for the purpose of sexual exploitation.'

Judge Katherine Delahunt sentenced O'Halloran to six years in prison. She suspended the last fifteen months on condition that he engage with the probation service for those fifteen months on his release. She said she had taken into account the fact that he was still under post-release supervision because of his previous conviction and was registered as a sex offender, she noted that there was no evidence that O'Halloran had ever abused a child, and she accepted that he had been abused himself when he was young, had low self-esteem and had a history of depression and alcoholism. She also said she had noted defence counsel's claim that the 'requests were unreal,' and that O'Halloran had been unemployed at the time and had no chance of paying the fees he had offered. Defence counsel had also pointed out that though O'Halloran had pleaded guilty to incitement it did not mean that he had any intention of actually sexually assaulting children, and he claimed that O'Halloran had said these things to 'get a reaction.'

Judge Delahunt said that not only had the probation service been active with O'Halloran but they had been 'consistently proactive in the manner in which they had dealt with him.' She accepted that O'Halloran had attended regularly at the Granada Institute for intensive treatment, but despite this it was considered that there was a high risk of re-offending.

This was picked up by Fergus Finlay, chief executive of Barnardo's. He said it was clear that O'Halloran had been skilful and manipulative in the way he had sought out the children, and he expressed the fear that when O'Halloran was freed he would remain a constant risk to children. 'The Gardaí are going to have a hard job,' he said. 'They are going to have to watch this man exceptionally closely for the rest of his life.'

O'Halloran's case was extreme, but there are others in which the perpetrators can simply convince themselves that the child in front of them is a willing participant and that therefore they are doing nothing wrong.

————

In 1998 Frank Hamilton, a Limerick journalist, appeared in court charged with sexually assaulting a fourteen-year-old girl in a hotel room in 1994 and 1995. The first reports in the media suggested that the girl had been viciously sexually assaulted, but it quickly emerged that she had in fact been there to have sex with him as a prostitute. Hamilton, editor of the former *Limerick Weekly Echo* and former press officer of Shannon Development, was arrested following a raid on a Limerick premises as part of an investigation. The Gardaí found sixty-nine child pornography and bestiality videos.

Hamilton, formerly of Shanabooley Avenue, Ballynanty, Limerick, made statements in which he admitted sexual activity with schoolgirls. He pleaded guilty to sexually assaulting one girl twice on unknown dates between 10 July and 30 November 1994 and between 1 January and 30 July 1995 at Jury's Inn, Christ Church Place, Dublin.

When his case came before Dublin Circuit Criminal Court gardaí testified that Hamilton told them he liked young girls with

big breasts. The gardaí admitted under cross-examination by
Hamilton's defence counsel that the girl was a willing participant,
and that her pimp was in the room at the same time, and also that
Hamilton had helped identify the pimp, so allowing him to be
prosecuted.

The defence made much of press reports that, it claimed,
attempted to reduce Hamilton in the public eye to the level of ver-
min by making out that the girl had been unwillingly subjected to
a sexual assault, and that she was only twelve at the time. Hamilton's
barrister said his client had been viciously attacked twice and his
home attacked, forcing him to move a number of times.

The gardaí said the girl was aged fourteen or fifteen at the time
of the incidents. She said she had been befriended by the pimp
when she was ten or eleven, and he had groomed her for child
prostitution. Hamilton made contact with the man and the
girl through advertisements in *Hot Press* and *In Dublin*, and
arrangements were made for an appointment. At the hotel room,
sandwiches, crisps and soft drinks would be provided for the girl.
Hamilton would pay the man £40 to £50 after each session.

Defence counsel pushed the point that the girl was 'sexually
mature' and 'had a mind of her own.' The gardaí admitted that the
girl had also operated in an apartment in Bachelor's Walk, Dublin,
where she went willingly for paid liaisons.

The judge said there was nothing in the probation or
psychotherapy reports that suggested that Hamilton had anything
but sexual fantasies about young girls.

> In my view, he will pose a continuing threat to girls of this age.
> The fact that the offences as shown by the evidence were
> premeditated, preplanned and prearranged and the hotel paid
> for, and that he should have known she was under age from
> the first offence, makes these two distinct offences, so that the
> sentences must be consecutive.

He imposed two consecutive sentences of three-and-a-half years
on each count, meaning that Hamilton faced seven years in

prison. However, less than six months later that sentence was cut to a total of three years by the Court of Criminal Appeal. The court said that the charges related to a time when the victim had reached fourteen years of age but was not quite fifteen, and that one had to be bear in mind that Hamilton was not the prime mover in the events that had taken place. It said the victim had been lured into a form of prostitution by another person. The court must approach the case on the evidence before it, namely that whatever was done was done with consent. There was no question of violence or threats or of assault in the ordinary sense of that term. The court pointed out that there was no question of any dominance on the part of Hamilton or any question of an abuse of trust, such as could arise where an accused person was a relative or a teacher.

Therefore the Court of Criminal Appeal decided that the Circuit Court judge had been wrong to impose consecutive sentences, and it would substitute concurrent sentences, in other words a total of three-and-a-half years.

———

The face of child prostitution in Ireland has changed markedly in the last ten years. Up to 2000 the children involved in the sex trade were mostly Irish, usually homeless, and more often than not addicted to drugs in some form or other. In 1997 the Eastern Health Board pinpointed a minimum of fifty-seven people under the age of eighteen who were or had been involved in prostitution. It said that girls and boys as young as thirteen were working on the streets and that it was apparently possible for paedophiles to specifically request a child prostitute from some brothels or massage parlours. At about the same time there were twenty people involved or suspected of being involved in prostitution in Cos. Limerick and Clare.

At the time of the Eastern Health Board report it was a well-publicised fact that a lack of accommodation for homeless children was forcing the children to sell their bodies on the streets, and the board did act to an extent by offering to provide an additional thirty emergency places for homeless children.

Two years later a Waterford outreach team told the South-Eastern Health Board that prostitutes as young as twelve were working in the city. The DORAS initiative said it was in regular contact with three male and seven female prostitutes in the city, including one twelve-year-old and another aged thirteen. This finding followed a report published two years earlier by Waterford Institute of Technology that claimed that thirty-five children were among up to ninety prostitutes working in the city.

Astonishingly, the author of that report, Dr Niall McElwee, who went on to become head of child care and learning at Athlone Institute of Technology, was himself convicted on two charges of attempted indecent assault involving two teenage American girls at a hotel in Amsterdam in 2004. He was allowed to continue in his post at Athlone IT, despite the health authorities, the Gardaí and Government officials being informed of the allegations against him. He had even been warned previously about using explicit pictures of sexually abused children during his lectures, causing some of his students to complain to the health board.

———

By 2000, the level of child prostitution, particularly on the streets of Dublin, seemed to have abated little if any. The RTE programme 'Prime Time' interviewed a number of young people as young as twelve who turned to prostitution.

Christine told the programme that at fourteen she had no way to get money to pay for heroin, to which she had become addicted since going onto the street. She said the only way to find the money was to turn to prostitution. A friend told her how much to charge and what to do only minutes before the first car pulled up. Her story was typical of those of dozens of children on the streets of Dublin and, to a lesser extent, around the country.

A graphic example of the failure to protect children in care in the late 1990s and early twenty-first century was the case of Tracey Fay, who was taken into care at the age of fourteen in 1998. When she was first brought in by her mother, those who dealt with her considered that she had no real problems with drugs or crime. However, the kind of care and guidance she received from then on aided her spiral into self-destruction. Over the next four years she was shifted around between twenty bed-and-breakfasts as well as numerous emergency care establishments, none of which she could return to during the day. She began coming to the attention of the Gardaí for numerous crimes, including prostitution, as well as drug-taking. There were long delays in assessment and treatment by the relevant health professionals, including psychological assessments.

One of the most damning things to emerge was a comment made by one social worker who worked with Tracey, who said she 'was poorly clothed for someone so heavily pregnant.' This health professional said the young woman expressed fears for the future care of her baby and asked if it would be best if the child was taken from her. 'Could someone please tell me how this extremely vulnerable girl is still wandering around with no care in her condition?'

Tracy Fay's body was found in a disused coal bunker used by drug addicts in the north inner city. A post-mortem examination found that she had died from an overdose of drugs, including ecstasy and heroin.

———

In recent years, the profile of those who are being exploited as child prostitutes has changed. Irish children in state residential care are now accommodated in centres that are much better regulated and have a better level of staffing and can offer the children much better support.

Instead, the victims now appear to be children trafficked into Ireland. As was reported in 2007, the health authorities admitted that these foreign children were being housed in accommodation centres that did not go anywhere near meeting the standards required.

In 2009 Denis Naughten TD was able to claim that four hundred children who had arrived unaccompanied had disappeared. He suspected that a number had been trafficked into Ireland and forced into prostitution. This opinion was borne out by research completed in the same year by the Immigrant Council of Ireland. (This report is examined in more detail in chapter 9.) Over a 21-month period in 2007–08 it recorded 102 women and girls who presented themselves at services that, using the internationally agreed definition, classed them as victims of trafficking. Of these, eleven were children at the time they were trafficked.

07 | WATCHING FROM AFAR

A s should be clear by now, many men are having sex in many ways with many prostitutes, all within a short distance of where you are reading this. That cannot be put down simply to speculation. It is a fact.

But how many of the prostitutes are doing it solely for their own profit and of their own free will? That is a question that is very much up for debate.

Given the size of the 'industry', it is surprising that more pimps have not appeared in the courts for their crimes. Certainly there are more than a handful of people running brothels in Ireland. A number have as few as one premises, operated by a few women. However, there is a small number of big operators who have chains of businesses around the country, both north and south of the border. Bearing in mind that this is Ireland, not Los Angeles or New York, one is not likely to see these men gaining international celebrity, such as the likes of Heidi Fleiss—though if one were to dig deeper it is more than likely that there are also a few very well-known figures among their regular clients. Given the number of men using the services, it would be a statistical anomaly if there weren't.

For the most part, the brothel-owners are male, intelligent, and highly skilled at avoiding any contact with the Gardaí. They are shrewd financial operators who are able to gauge the best areas in each of the cities and towns in which to set up an operation without attracting too much attention from neighbours or police.

While the majority of the big players in the prostitution industry have brothels in Dublin, mainly in apartments in the richer parts of the city, few actually live within close proximity of the operation. In most cases they are family men with a family home in one of the wealthier suburbs, where they may be members of the residents' association, their children play merrily with the other upper-class infants, and their wives enjoy a skinny mocha and a gossip with the other well-to-do partners. Their neighbours probably think they are doing well in IT or have a marketing business with premises in the city. They would be shocked to learn where these men are making the money that pays for their four-bed detached.

The most infamous of the country's pimps is 'the Policeman'. Peter McCormack, now in his early fifties, got his nickname from his short service in the RUC. In another life he worked in the hotel and catering industry, both north and south of the border, including a period in a bar in the 'bandit country' of south Armagh—a brave move for a former member of the Northern police in what was one of the IRA's heartlands.

McCormack did not appear to be particularly happy in any of his previous roles, as the financial rewards were nowhere near what he had set his heart on. In 1995 he made up his mind to move to Dublin; there he found his niche in the murky world of the sex industry. Among his first and most lucrative brothels was one in Camden Court, off Lower Camden Street, where up to five women worked at any one time. The women charged €60 for half an hour, and McCormack and his business partner, Martin Morgan, took a third of this.

The operation was so successful that McCormack and Morgan were able to set up at least fifteen other operations in quick succession, including businesses in prime city-centre districts, such as Leeson Street. The businesses were advertised in the now defunct *In Dublin*.

The men were picky about what women they would allow to offer sex on their premises, and it was the attraction of the good-looking women, previously not on offer, that made their operation highly popular with the punters of Dublin, who had never had such a choice in different parts of the city. The decision to offer a comprehensive 'out-calls' service meant that both men, at least in the early stages, were constantly driving women all over the city to service their clients.

Obviously, with such a wide range of businesses taking in hundreds of thousands of euros, McCormack's enterprise was going to come to the attention of the Gardaí, as well as the Criminal Assets Bureau. However, he and Morgan were slippery customers and difficult to pin down. Several times when these businesses were raided one of the men would be there; but through fast talking and a tight control on what the women said they always managed to evade prosecution. They had their operations well protected. They had the properties rented under false names, and could close up quickly if the attention of neighbours or police became too intense. On one occasion they took on a manager who, after McCormack had his lease cancelled by a vigilant landlord, immediately took over the lease and continued to operate on his behalf.

However, McCormack, then of Lawnswood Grove, Stillorgan, Co. Dublin, was not smart enough to evade capture indefinitely. In 2003 he appeared in court charged with organising prostitution between 10 September 1999 and 14 April 2000. The Gardaí had set up a surveillance of the Camden Street operation and watched the steady queue of men entering and leaving the premises.

Men departing were interviewed and admitted receiving sexual services for money, while several of the women who worked there were observed going to Bishopsmede Apartments in Lower Clanbrassil Street, which the Gardaí claimed was used as a clearing-house for the brothel. When gardaí finally raided the apartment a number of the women were there, with nine mobile phones and bundles of cash. The court was told that seven of the mobile phones had numbers that linked them to the Camden

Court premises. Callers were put through to an answering service for the brothel. Though McCormack was discovered in the apartment, he refused to admit his involvement, even when it was put to him that he was seen entering and leaving the premises regularly.

At McCormack's trial the court was given details of the Clanbrassil Street clearing-house, including details of how the women who worked for him in the brothels would go there to be despatched for appointments.

Despite McCormack's best efforts to conceal his part in the operation when he was arrested, it was unlikely, with the weight of evidence presented, that he would be able to convince the court of his innocence. After eventually pleading guilty, he was given a two-year suspended sentence and fined €3,000.

In sentencing him, it was clear that Judge Desmond Hogan was unaware of the extent of his criminality. He said that McCormack had pleaded guilty to a serious offence but had come to court and ultimately pleaded guilty, sparing the embarrassment of a number of men being forced to give evidence at a trial. He also believed evidence given that McCormack was no longer involved in the sex trade and was now running a bed-and-breakfast with his wife. 'He has no previous convictions and it does appear he has now ceased his activities and gone into legitimate business with his wife,' he said. 'I don't propose to impose a custodial sentence, but I do have to mark the seriousness of the crime.'

However, McCormack's withdrawal from the prostitution trade seems unlikely, given subsequent events. In 2006 an RTE 'Prime Time' investigation claimed that McCormack had taken half the earnings of an eastern European woman who had been forced into prostitution. He refused to respond to the programme's allegations from his home in Chester, England. Furthermore, newspapers in the North claimed he was still operating a number of brothels around the country, including one in Portrush on the Co. Antrim coast. This has also not been substantiated.

As for Morgan, he too eventually faced the wrath of the law. The Gardaí could not believe their luck when the distinctively stocky and bald figure of 'the Beast' walked into a Dublin brothel that they had been watching for three months. They had been patiently building up a case before raiding the apartment at Bachelor's Walk. They were about to bring the curtain down on the surveillance when the man who had for so long evaded prosecution came into view and walked into the brothel.

The 44-year-old former hotel doorman was infamous in prostitution circles as one half of one of the most successful pimping duos in Ireland. And he was not nicknamed 'the Beast' without good reason. Given his size, his sheer presence meant that few would dare mess with any business in which he was involved.

As Morgan began his three-year sentence, and with a fine of €24,000 hanging over him, he must have been kicking himself that he was so careless as to be caught red-handed. He did not need to be in the building when gardaí swooped in October 2005. The luxury apartment that housed his operation had a capable manager in the person of Deena Edridge, the woman who described him as her 'good friend', with whom she 'occasionally slept.' Morgan could have afforded to sit back at his London address and wait for the money to pour in. However, he had more than just business links with Ireland. As he admitted during his eighteen-day trial, he has eight children in five different families here.

When arrested, Morgan said he was a builder with no business interest in Ireland, and when asked why he preferred living in London replied, 'They have nice, friendlier police . . . Only joking!' But the weight of evidence against him was overwhelming.

When the gardaí entered the brothel Morgan was sitting in the living-room beside a small table on which there were six mobile phones—the communication method of choice for prostitutes trying to avoid unwanted attention—as well as a large bunch of keys. Despite protestations that he did not own the brothel, he would have found it hard to explain away an unsigned contract between himself and Edridge—who herself would be given a twelve-month sentence for managing the business—found by gardaí in a house in Ballsbridge.

Whatever the arrangement was between the two, there was no doubt it was highly successful; and even more details emerged about just how much was being pocketed.

One of the women in Morgan's employ, Vanessa, gave evidence that clients were charged €120 for thirty minutes or €220 per hour. She herself would have five clients per night, and every Sunday she would pay €130 to the owners. She said she earned €1,400 between late September and early October and gave half of that to 'Chloe Taylor', an alias of Edridge's. In one shift of only ten hours the brothel made a profit of €4,100.

The gardaí found rosters with women's names, expense claims and thousands of euros in cash when they raided the Bachelor's Walk apartment.

The size of the operation was evident from what they found when searching another apartment being used as a call-centre for the brothel. When gardaí entered an apartment in Malton House, Custom House Square, they could hear buzzing coming from a drawer in the kitchen. In it they found thirty mobile phones, being inundated with calls from potential punters. In fact the reception-ist of the brothel said she would be expected to answer as many as fifty phones during her employment. She said she got calls from men asking if women were available and where they could go to see them. She said that, depending on where the men were, she would give three access points for the Bachelor's Walk apartment. Once the men were at the place she specified she said they would ring her back to get further directions to the apartment. She had to describe the appearance of the women on duty at the brothel over the phone and the price of sessions. It looked like an open-and-shut case against Morgan.

However, there was one big snag for the prosecution. Deena Edridge, brought from her prison cell to his trial, claimed in court that she owned the 'whole escort operation.' She said she had carried on a sexual relationship with Morgan and had considered dropping her brothel to go into business with him, running escort web sites that he owned. In admitting that Morgan ran such sites, she was not getting him into any trouble, as these sites are operated outside the state and are therefore beyond prosecution, even though they advertise sex for sale in Ireland.

But the prosecution found a flaw in Edridge's claim. She could not tell the court what the precise income and outgoings of the operation were. Furthermore, she said that envelopes found at another address marked 'Chloe wages' were records of the money she was taking for herself.

The jury of eight women and four men saw through the tissue of deceit put together by Morgan and Edridge and, after eleven hours, unanimously found Morgan, of Herbert Row, Blanchardstown, and Blackstock Road, London, guilty on the two charges, and he was sentenced to the three-year term.

Ruhama said it was delighted that one of the most well-known figures in the trade had been brought to justice.

> We welcome the outcome of the court hearing and an outcome which emerged because of the commitment of gardaí to tackle the criminality that is inevitably linked to prostitution. This case also highlights a situation where women were essentially controlled within a criminal environment so as to generate massive profits, not for themselves but for our criminal underworld.
>
> It is important [that] the Government and its agencies continue to investigate and prosecute the criminals in all aspects of prostitution in Ireland.

Once the trial was over it was no time before the authorities began to try to seize some of the assets that Morgan had built up over the previous years.

———

The name Hutton, while it has not been heard in the courts for several years, is still synonymous with prostitution in Ireland, years after two family members made a dramatic appearance in the dock.

Reggie and Samantha Blandford Hutton came from a privileged background but were both driven to crime by failure at other occupations. Reggie failed to make it as a jockey or to successfully market a range of dodgy 'alternative medicine'. His sister failed at modelling and at female boxing and was spectacularly poor at selling herself as a Dublin socialite. She also had such a gripping cocaine habit that she was dubbed the 'snow queen'.

However, when Karen Leahy entered the Huttons' lives they suddenly found their forte. Leahy had been operating a successful brothel empire for some time before she met Reggie. They began a relationship in 1998, with Reggie taking on a chauffeuring and enforcement role in his new girl-friend's operation. Being heavily pregnant, however, Leahy needed help in running her growing enterprise, so she took on Reggie's sister, offering to pay her 10 per cent of the turnover—a handsome share in what would amount to more than ten brothels over time.

With all her airs and graces, the tall, blonde Samantha believed she could bring a more upper-class air to the business by developing a separate 'Executive Club', where the men would be expected to pay much higher prices but in return could expect to spend time in the company of a better class of woman than those operating in the cheap 'massage parlours'.

In a series of interviews with the *Evening Herald*, Hutton said she wanted to make sex in Dublin erotic rather than tawdry. The women would be able to have a drink and a meal and talk intelligently with the client before, as she put it, 'getting down to business.' The idea was that the men would feel as if they were on a date with these attractive, intelligent women, yet at the same time knowing that they would always be invited in for coffee. After a while the Executive Club was marketed, the women having been selected, and housed separately. Business cards were even printed for giving to prospective clients.

Though the women did indeed hire a 'better class' of prostitutes, despite all Samantha's wishes the trappings of Leahy and the Huttons' business remained the same as any other brothel enterprise. A number of mobile phones were used to direct clients to a variety of apartments and hotel rooms and to give directions for the women in providing out-calls.

In fact Samantha's 'Executive Club' nearly brought the curtains down on Karen Leahy's well-crafted empire, because she badgered the customers with inflated prices. Punters receiving the special treatment were expected to pay £300 for the pleasure rather than the usual £150 per hour. As it turned out, in many cases they were receiving the same service and from the same women. Some inexperienced punters fell for the duplicity, not knowing what such money would entitle them to normally. However, in several instances the men who had been told over the phone that they would be expected to pay €300 smelled a rat and would pay only €150 when they got the service. This was much to the displeasure of Samantha, who would still badger them with calls to their mobile phones at all hours in an attempt to recoup the money she felt her operation deserved.

In his book *Sex in the City*, Paul Reynolds refers to 24-year-old Frank, who turned up for the executive treatment. 'I didn't want to walk in off the street,' he said. 'I wanted something more personal.' However, when he was directed to one of the bog-standard brothels he looked around him and realised pretty quickly that he had been there previously. When he pointed this out to Samantha she managed to keep her cool and claimed there was a separate apartment in the complex for the Executive Club. However, it appears that she didn't tip off the prostitute to keep up the act. First he was kept waiting in a bedroom, then the woman refused to wear the special underwear he had brought. To add insult to injury, he was asked to pay £300—which should have got him one-and-a-half hours—for a service that lasted twenty minutes.

With such poor business acumen it's hardly surprising that Leahy and the Huttons became careless and allowed their operation to be infiltrated by the *Sunday Independent*. Not only did they give explicit details to a reporter posing as a would-be prostitute but Samantha allowed herself to be photographed being paid by a male reporter. The details were splashed all over the newspaper.

Among the titbits Samantha let fall was the fact that she wanted to set up a 'Cobra Club'. While the veneer of men wearing evening dress meeting women in high-class Dublin houses sounded attractive, it was actually a code for orgies that she intended to meticulously organise if she could drum up enough interest. The men would be expected to pay £1,500 each, for which they could have sex a number of times with a choice of women, in a bedroom, a sauna or a jacuzzi.

However, her dream never came true. Things began to go wrong for the trio when a caretaker noticed a large number of men entering and leaving one of the apartments. He could not help noticing that there were a number of exotic-looking women occupying the residence for long periods. He began to keep a closer eye on the place and established that there were up to five women carrying on business from there. Their movements left him in no doubt that this was a brothel. When he rang the Gardaí they were able to tell him they were already watching the apartment, which was operating as the 'Winter Garden' brothel, as part of Operation Gladiator. In the previous days they had been interviewing dozens of men entering and leaving the premises. Some admitted they had paid for sex, others said they had not gone through with the act.

In September 1999 gardaí raided the apartment and found Reggie, Samantha and the heavily pregnant Karen *in situ*. They also found a man lying naked on a bed with a woman in a black mini-skirt and black bra sitting on top of him.

A quick search of the premises revealed all the trappings of an active brothel, including ample supplies of condoms and sex toys. The gardaí arrested the trio, assuming that they were the ringleaders after they were searched and found to have in their possession a number of cheques worth thousands of pounds.

However, despite the fact that all three admitted that the premises were being used as a brothel, they were released without charge, and they were back in business within a few days. But they were back in Garda custody by February the following year, charged with managing brothels and organising prostitution.

Their court appearances became the stuff of legend. The three would arrive in a cortege of individuals all dressed in long dark robes and wearing masks. They would remove the masks only on arriving in the court.

Despite a fairly protracted legal battle, by October 2001 Reggie and Samantha, of St Patrick's Park, Clondalkin, and Karen, of Collins Avenue, Whitehall, Dublin, had been given eighteen-month suspended sentences and fined £6,500 each—a small price for them to pay, having earned several hundred thousand pounds a year.

Ironically, having exploited the sexual services of women in prostitution, Samantha Blandford Hutton would go on to exploit women in a new line of work. She set up a cleaning business, At Hand Cleaning Services Ltd, based at her own home in Clondalkin. The promise of £1,000 per month for an eight-hour working day attracted a Brazilian widow, Neusa da Silva Resende, to come to Ireland to work for Hutton. She ended up working up to fifteen hours a day, was not given even the minimum pay she could expect, and at times was left without food for days on end. In one week she worked 105 hours, for which she was paid £155. Two of her relatives who came to Ireland to work with her were left no better off. Neighbours found them sharing a cheap packet of biscuits for their lunch. For a total of seven months they were ferried to a variety of commercial and residential premises in a van with blacked-out windows.

If it was not for the generosity of a barrister and solicitor who took on the Brazilians' case free of charge, Hutton might have got away with what was in essence slave labour. When they brought the case before the courts it was clear that Mr Justice Peter Kelly had no time for Hutton's claim that she was at her wits' end over what she described as illegal immigrants. 'The working conditions were reminiscent of those which obtained in the times of Charles Dickens,' he said in his summation. He awarded against Hutton and ordered that almost £50,000 be paid to the Brazilian women.

———

It is not solely the capital city that houses the country's leading pimps, although, given the apparent Dublin-only remit of

Operation Quest, arrests elsewhere have been few and far between. Cork appears to be the place that attracts most Garda attention outside Dublin. The city has a booming 'escort' and prostitution industry. However, while there have been a few arrests, prosecutions have been thin on the ground.

This is not to overlook the fact that one man has been hit hard in the pocket for his transgressions, to the tune of €4 million. This man, in his fifties and dubbed 'Mr Big', has been involved in the sex trade in Cork, Waterford and Limerick for about twenty years. In that time he is believed to have amassed a substantial fortune.

Described as the kingpin of the Munster sex industry, Mr Big was one of six people arrested in April 2007 in a series of raids on brothels and homes in Cork. Three men and three women, ranging in age from early twenties to mid-fifties, were arrested in various parts of the city and suburbs and one premises north of the city as a follow-up to the Criminal Assets Bureau's 'Operation Boulder' in the city the previous November. That operation was investigating money-laundering through sex shops, 'massage parlours' and lap-dancing clubs. Seventeen private and commercial premises around the city were identified. At least three of the premises were owned by the same person, and at least two sex shops were uncovered as a front for upstairs 'massage parlours'.

During the raid miniature cameras were found hidden in the smoke alarms, which were used to record people visiting the premises. The Gardaí seized substantial amounts of cash, bundles of documents, videotapes and DVDs. The Criminal Assets Bureau spent several months trawling through boxes of the seized documents as part of an investigation into the proceeds of crime. Forensic accountants also looked at the documents to examine alleged money-laundering and tax compliance issues.

As a result of this trawl officials were able to serve a claim for €4 million on the man for tax liabilities and penalties. Then, in January 2008, the Criminal Assets Bureau arrested him for the second time during a dawn raid on his home in north Cork. The CAB said the arrest followed from Operation Boulder.

Once again during the raids gardaí seized a substantial amount of cash, DVDs and videotapes and a significant number of documents for the forensic accountants. However, again the man was released without charge.

———

One of the country's few female brothel-owners, Paula, worked in the sex trade as a receptionist and then owner in several counties for most of the last decade and so is better placed than most to give an interpretation of the sex trade in Ireland from the side of the procurer. In an interview with the author she described what she believed were the arguments in favour of prostitution.

> There are hundreds of women offering sex in Ireland. They would not be doing so if the demand was not there. The simple fact is that demand is not going to go away. Sex is a basic requirement for a lot of people. Men have a higher sex drive than women, and they look for an outlet to have that drive satisfied. By using the services of a reputable agency they are satisfying their demand for sex while the woman earns a living. Whether people agree with it or not, there are men out there who either cannot attract a woman for whatever reason or who have been in a marriage which they do not want to end, but they still desire sex.

Paula insisted that she and the women who worked for her were not out to hurt anyone. She claimed they were operating a business like any other—except that in the case of her business it was outside the law.

She gave an insight into the dangers women in her employ had faced and information about the security system she had established to try to negate as much of that danger as possible. Her years of working as a receptionist had given her a healthy distrust of the men who would ring up looking for sex. She would look for the slightest intonation in the voice at the other end of the phone that would suggest that the man could pose a risk to the women for whom she was taking appointments. 'I would turn away an awful lot of men,' she claimed. Those who did not get past her voice test would simply be told that the agency was closed and to call back another time. Her caution worked: during the time she was answering the phones none of the women working for her experienced a dangerous client.

However, when Paula began running her own agency she said she often found herself worrying that the receptionists in her employment might not be so cautious, particularly given that they were working for commission. She would ask them to look past the financial gain and be watchful, but still there were men coming through who would never have passed her own vetting system.

Given the danger, she decided to exploit the spread of mobile phone technology to her advantage. The receptionists were introduced to a system with which they could tag the phone number of clients they believed to be dangerous. If that person rang, the receptionist would either not answer or say the agency was closed.

Even when the men arrived at the agency their demeanour was assessed. 'If they throw the money down or appear in any way aggressive they will be told to leave,' she said.

She was equally strict with the women in her employ. It was drummed into them that they must remain professional, almost aloof, to ensure that what they were offering was construed as a business transaction and nothing more.

Paula believes that the best agencies are run by women.

> Men tend not to consider the dangers that the women can find themselves in, and in some cases it is the male pimps that are the danger themselves. The women who have come to work for me have done so because they have heard about my operation from other girls. I do not have to advertise my agency to attract escorts. Unfortunately ours is not a large operation, and sometimes the women are attracted by other agencies to go to the bigger client lists, even though they are

run by men. There, while they do earn more, because there are more clients, they are not treated with the same respect. Often they will come back.

Like many brothel operators in Ireland, she had heard of—and encountered personally—intimidation by rival owners. 'They would openly attack the agencies, beat up the security that was in place, and tear apart the apartments to take any money that was there,' she said. In particular she referred to two men in the midlands who had a reputation for using the threat of horrific violence to drive away competitors. However, she said that she, and others like her, could do little or nothing about it.

> If I identify someone who is intimidating me, or if I identify a punter who has done something to one of my women, the Gardaí will tell me they can only seek a prosecution if I am willing to be prosecuted myself. That means both the agencies and the women have to fight for themselves.

In spite of this, she did have one success with the Gardaí. A client came to her agency looking for under-age girls. She was horrified. After building up her courage, she was able to notify the Gardaí, and after undercover surveillance was secured they brought the man to court.

One of the things Paula was keen to stress was that, despite the public perception, brothel-owners did not all amass a huge fortune.

> In some cases they do, but I just earn enough to keep my family in a comfortable existence. While I do take them on holidays twice a year, I don't drive a new car, and I don't own my own home.

The reason she rented a house, however, was that she feared that any property she owned would be snapped up by the Criminal Assets Bureau if her operation was raided.

Three months after I first interviewed Paula she left the sex industry and started a legitimate business. It was something she said she had been wanting to do for a number of years, particularly as she was terrified that her children might find out where the money she was raising them with originated.

Despite her defence of the brothel industry and her place in it, she never seemed to me to really believe what she was saying. It was quite evident from her demeanour that she had encountered some terrible things while involved in prostitution. Certainly at least one of the women she had worked with had been brutally attacked by a client, and she was very distressed about that. It was also evident that she herself had borne the brunt of quite considerable violence from men in her life, though she never elaborated on what had happened to her.

———

Another woman who encountered violence but on a much grander scale was one of Ireland's best-known but ultimately most tragic brothel-owners, Marie Bridgeman or, as she was also called, Madam Mean. Unlike many of Ireland's pimps, she herself began working as a prostitute to support her two boys after the break-up of her marriage. She also came late to the 'profession', starting when she was in her forties. She worked for a number of pimps for several years before finally building up the wherewithal to go into business for herself.

After humble beginnings, with a couple of women working out of a small rented house, she gradually rose through the ranks of the brothel elite in the 1990s. She advertised her businesses in the telephone directory as health studios and in slightly more direct terms in *In Dublin.*

Out of every £60 she would take £20. According to Paul Reynolds's book *Sex in the City,* one of the businesses was so successful that Bridgeman provided a condom bucket, placed at the bottom of the stairs in the house, where the women would throw the used condoms. She developed the nickname Madam Mean after she and one of her sons, Paul Bridgeman, who was working with her, installed a coin-box phone in one of her operations. The reputation was compounded when she provided only a small heater to warm the whole building. She would also use video footage to make sure the number of men going in corresponded to the amount of takings the women were leaving for collection.

Bridgeman first came before the courts in March 1998, when she was convicted of running a brothel, called 'Tiffany's', in Wexford Street, Dublin. She was fined £500 by Dublin District Court. Then she and others became the subject of a large-scale Garda investigation, Operation Gladiator, directed at *In Dublin* for advertising brothels. As a result the Gardaí selected a number of specific brothels and brought charges against twelve of the principal owners. This led investigators to Bridgeman's main brothel, 'La Mirage', in Wexford Street, and a second one, 'Escort Studio', in Beechwood Avenue, Ranelagh.

On 13 February 2001 she was back in the dock in Dublin Circuit Criminal Court. She was fined £1,500 and given an eighteen-month suspended sentence for running the two brothels. Her son Paul should have been in court also to answer charges relating to the brothels, but he fled the country before the case came up. He had a further reason to run, having been caught with a large consignment of cocaine at his home.

She received a third conviction, a six-month suspended sentence, in October 2001 for failing to make tax returns. However, little did she or anyone else suspect that within a very short time after her sentencing she would be dead.

In January 2003 Marie Bridgeman, then aged fifty-six, was found dead following what was first described as an altercation outside her home in Ratoath, Co. Meath.

In court it emerged that on the night of her death she travelled by bus from Dublin to Ratoath. She phoned her son Kevin, and he met her off the bus. Shortly afterwards a number of neighbours heard a commotion in the grounds of a nearby house. They looked out and saw Kevin Bridgeman jumping up and down in what was described in court as a most agitated and furious manner. What he was jumping on was, in fact, his mother's body. While in custody he told gardaí that 'I battered her to death with my fists . . . I kept hitting her with my fists . . . I hit her and I gouged out her eyes.' He also said he stabbed her. As it turned out, the injuries he described were exaggerated. No knife was used, and her eyes were not gouged out. However, he had done more than enough to kill her.

Kevin Bridgeman of Old Mill Estate, Ratoath, Co. Meath, was found guilty but insane and was ordered to be detained at the Government's pleasure in the Central Mental Hospital, Dundrum.

———

These are all people who made a fortune from organising prostitution, exploiting women for gain. But one case reached the courts in 2004 that confused the stereotype. The man in this case was seen to have been the victim.

Given that he was seventy-one years old, Geoffrey Browne, a Co. Sligo pensioner, should really have known better; but, as he later told gardaí, he just wanted a friend. Neighbours of the elderly man became concerned when they heard strange noises coming from his house at the most unearthly hours. Suspecting that something was amiss, they alerted the Gardaí, who went to the house on 23 August 2003.

No doubt they had been informed that normally the house's only occupant was the elderly bachelor. One can imagine their surprise when they encountered a naked man who was considerably younger and what was described in court as a 'scantily clad lady'. Also discovered were three used and fifteen unused condoms, a sex aid, and six pornographic videos.

Whether it was the shock of the raid or the embarrassment of being caught, it was all too much for Geoffrey Browne, who had to be taken to hospital in what gardaí described as a 'distressed state'. The man discovered in a state of undress admitted paying the woman, a prostitute from Dublin, £100. But as the gardaí dug deeper they unearthed what could only be described as a bizarre arrangement.

Browne, of Scardenmore, Strandhill Road, Sligo, had been letting the woman, and several others, use his house for their business for several years. They would advertise their services in the local media and then travel there. Browne would act as their receptionist, taking bookings and giving directions. For all this he received nothing—not even the services of the women for himself. In court it emerged that when his brother died some years earlier Geoffrey was left on his own. He responded to an advertisement in a local newspaper and allowed his premises to be used. In court his defence counsel claimed that the women had exploited his loneliness, adding that he appeared to have fallen completely into their power.

The judge also appeared to see Browne as a victim. Handing down a six-month suspended sentence, he said: 'If he has been the victim of heartless harlots of one kind or another, let this be a message to them.'

———

One of the few brothel-owners to serve a significant term of imprisonment was Tom McDonnell, who chalked up a tax bill of nearly £2 million over eleven years of trading. In fact he had operated brothels for almost twenty years when he was finally caught and imprisoned.

A Clare man, McDonnell was more than due a long stretch in prison, if only because of his violence towards the women under his control. After 'road-testing' them himself and getting them to service his criminal buddies, he expected the women to pay him a whopping £60 out of every £150 they earned. He was almost paranoid in suspecting that they were stealing from him and would go so far as to count the towels used in the premises to work out how many men had been seen that day. If there was a discrepancy, one of the women would often feel his fury. His violent and criminal tendencies were exemplified by convictions for common assault in 1975 and three subsequent convictions for burglary and larceny.

McDonnell set up brothels all over Dublin, the first in Capel Street in 1984. Over the following eighteen years he would open and close many more, operating up to five at a time.

His brothels were raided for the first time in 1990, but it would not be until mid-1991 that he would make his first court appearance. On that occasion he was charged with running a brothel between February and April 1990. That particular brothel, the 'New Pleasure Palace', was charging punters £25, of which he was keeping £15. He walked from court a free man, only having to pay a fine of £4,500—a snip compared with what he was making— and to carry out a hundred hours of community service.

However, he was undeterred and was soon in business again in a number of places around the city. It is said that a fool and his money are soon parted, and McDonnell was a fool not to conceal the wealth he was earning from his enterprises. He would frequently fly from Dublin to his native Co. Clare in a helicopter he bought himself for £140,000. His notoriety was such that he was abducted by the INLA, which wanted a piece of his action. He escaped his captors, but only after being shot in the shoulder and leg. However, while he did not pay for his crimes at the hands of the gunmen, he paid for them in the courtroom in 2002.

McDonnell, then aged fifty, appeared in Dublin Circuit Court on both tax evasion and prostitution charges. He pleaded guilty to brothel-keeping between 4 September 1999 and 12 February 2000 and to knowingly or wilfully failing to make tax returns between 1987 and 1998 and three charges of knowingly or wilfully making incorrect returns for the years 1992–97 on a date unknown between 1 May and 30 May 1998.

Gardaí testified that the man before the court owned four premises in Dublin and one in Co. Clare and had other money squirrelled away in accounts in the Isle of Man and elsewhere. They also said he ran a series of 'health studios'. They were able to inform the judge that the accused had declared an income between £35,000 and £42,000 for the years covered by the charges but had in fact earned between £160,000 and £190,000 per year.

In the time between their investigation and the court hearing, McDonnell managed to cough up £197,000 of the £1.88 million he owed by selling off two houses. The Gardaí said it was intended to receive more when he sold a further two. Several months later only three houses in total had been sold and £700,000 seized.

Gardaí said McDonnell was arrested on 11 February 2000 following a five-month surveillance operation on a house in Grattan Street, Dublin, as part of Operation Gladiator. Interviews were conducted with various men leaving the house, and they admitted paying £60 in return for sexual favours for half an hour. They even recorded McDonnell leaving the brothel to get the towels washed. Finally, when they raided the house they found one customer in an embarrassing state of undress, as well as two women and McDonnell. They retrieved a number of business cards and change-of-address cards containing McDonnell's mobile number, and also £2,500 in cash. The women confirmed that of the £60 they would take in from a customer £20 went towards the house. The brothel would have up to thirty clients a day.

The judge was more than satisfied that McDonnell, of Grattan Street, Dublin, and originally from Cooraclare, Co. Clare, had been involved in prostitution for a considerable time. He jailed him for eighteen months.

> He was given a chance in 1991 but chose not to mend his ways. This health studio business is a euphemism for prostitution ... I don't know if the Revenue got him for all he earned, but they will only get one-third of the full liability. It's a very substantial shortfall.
>
> It's quite clear that he was making in excess of £500 a day and had substantial tax liabilities that he sought to evade.

A highly successful pimp-turned-businessman had his own message for the courts after he appeared in the dock in Dublin in 1998.

Brian O'Byrne, a former shop manager, had just been caught running two city-centre brothels. The evidence was compelling. Prompted by complaints from people living and working in the area, the Gardaí had established surveillance on the properties in North Lots and Parnell Street and had watched the goings-on of the punters and prostitutes for a considerable period. When they finally struck they were given more evidence, some of it graphic. Five people were found on the premises in 'compromising positions,' according to the investigating gardaí. Around the properties they found all the usual trappings of a brothel, including piles of condoms and a variety of sex aids. On closer investigation they were able to calculate that the four prostitutes on duty were each charging up to £60 to several clients each day for full or oral sex or masturbation. O'Byrne benefited by up to £20 from each punter, and in court it was estimated that he cleared £19,000 from the efforts of the women in his employ.

As part of his defence, O'Byrne's counsel pointed out that he had made an admission of what he had done, saving those caught *in flagrante* from having to sully their own names by giving evidence in the case.

O'Byrne was given the choice of paying £5,000, with a short time to come up with the money, or going straight to prison. He opted for the latter.

After he returned to the court, however, he had a lot to say. Firstly he stated his intention of gathering all his fellow brothel-owners into something of a union to lobby the Government for a relaxation of the laws that, he claimed, were discriminating against them. He maintained that at least six men and women had been discommoded by the courts for operating businesses that might otherwise be contributing to the state's coffers through taxes. The *Irish Independent* quoted him as saying:

> Guys like me want to pay tax and be above board. We're being discriminated against at the moment because since homosexuality was legalised none of the gay saunas have been closed down. What the authorities seem to be saying is that it's

okay to have places catering for homosexuals, and I've nothing against those guys, but it's not politically correct for consenting heterosexuals to do the same. The gays got their act together and lobbied to have the law changed, and maybe it's time we did the same. It's a bit like the pirate radio stations, which were being closed down for years and eventually they came along and legalised the whole thing.

But any efforts he made to rally his former pimps into action failed, because within three years he was in trouble with the law again. This time he would not have the option of a fine. The Garda investigation that led to his conviction must have begun very soon after he left court for his infractions in 1998, because the Gardaí recorded his new crime in 1999.

This time the surveillance operation concentrated on a premises in Synge Street, off the South Circular Road, Dublin. Once again the punters were watched entering the premises and leaving after about thirty minutes. Each red-faced man was stopped on his way out and was asked to sign a statement about what went on inside. On each occasion they said they became aware of the premises from advertisements in a Dublin magazine, the numbers in which would later be linked to the brothel.

O'Byrne was also seen entering and leaving the building. A search warrant was executed on 11 November 1999, and inside the gardaí found a man and two women and O'Byrne in an office on the upper floors. Both women admitted receiving money for sex, and the man confirmed that he had paid £60 for his time with them.

It emerged in court that O'Byrne had changed his pricing structure slightly. This time the women were expected to give him £100 a day when it was busy and £20 for each customer when it was not.

Once again O'Byrne came clean immediately, but his prompt plea was not enough to keep him out of prison. When Judge Patrick McCartan was told that O'Byrne had two previous convictions in 1998 for the same offences he said:

The disturbing factor in this case is that you have been convicted of such activity before and committed the offences while under bond from the District Court. It would be asking too much of the court not to impose a custodial sentence, and I must do so.

He sentenced O'Byrne, of Temple View Row, Donaghmede, to two years in prison.

08 | THE LAW OF THE LAND

According to the Central Statistics Office, 137 prostitution offences were recorded in Ireland in 2008. That includes the women arrested for working on the streets and in apartments and the men who were using their services. Given that every day there are probably up to a thousand interactions between prostitutes and punters, that is a pretty unimpressive arrest count.

If any member of the public with internet access and a car can go and find these women in their droves, both on the streets and in apartments and hotels, why can the Gardaí not simply do the same research, go to the source, arrest the punter, the brothel-owner and the women and close down the illegal enterprise that has facilitated their union? On the streets it should be easy to watch a known prostitute and, once a punter leaves the side of the road with her, move in.

However, the success rate for the Gardaí cannot simply be blamed on a lack of effort. They can only enforce the laws that are put into their hands by the Oireachtas, and there are a number of ways in which those laws fall far short of what is required to truly address the problem of prostitution in the 21st century.

Some might say this is due to public perception, or the lack thereof, of the situation. For many people a brief mention in a

Sunday tabloid is the only reminder that prostitution exists in Ireland. They believe it is confined to the darker streets of Dublin and is linked somehow to the criminals that lurk there. A simple search in the newspaper archives for 'prostitution law' will uncover hundreds if not thousands of articles. However, start to go through them and you would find it exceptionally hard to see any actual reference to the laws that govern prostitution. Practically every article is about trafficking, the exploitation of women, or the international dimension of the global sex trade.

Those are admirable concerns, but what does that tell us about the knowledge of what is happening in our communities? What information does that give the public about the laws against all the crimes that relate to prostitution?

The lack of reference in newspapers to the specific prostitution laws is not because of a lack of effort by the papers themselves. The frequently quoted maxim 'Sex sells' applies in newspapers as much as anywhere else, and a salacious story about prostitution will command column inches without a doubt. The exposé of a prostitution racket will sell many more copies of a newspaper than if economic forecasts are dominating the front page. However, there is little fodder for that demand, because there are very few court cases or exposés to be had. Why? Because there are very few laws that bring prostitution into the public eye.

That leads to a vicious circle of apathy. As there is no breach of laws to make public, there is no universal cry for prostitution to be stamped out, and that leads to a lack of pressure on the Government to address the laws that are so weak.

Firstly, a brief outline of what laws do exist in the area of prostitution.

The Criminal Law (Sexual Offences) Act (1993) is the main law governing prostitution. It is supplemented by a number of smaller pieces of legislation. It makes the following provisions.

SOLICITING

Under section 7 of the 1993 act it is an offence to solicit or impor-tune another person in a street or public place for the purposes of prostitution. That offence applies to everyone, whether male or female, prostitute or client, or a third party (such as a pimp), and includes kerb-crawling.

LOITERING
Under section 8 of the 1993 act a member of the Garda Síochána may direct a person in a street or public place to leave the vicinity if they have reasonable cause to suspect that the person is loitering in order to solicit or importune another person for the purposes of prostitution. It is an offence for a person without reasonable cause to fail to comply with such a direction.

LIVING ON THE EARNINGS OF PROSTITUTION
Under section 10 of the 1993 act, any person who knowingly lives in whole or in part on the earnings of the prostitution of another person and aids and abets that prostitution is guilty of an offence. The 'aiding and abetting' provision protects from prosecution any innocent dependants of a prostitute, such as a child or parents.

ORGANISING OF PROSTITUTION
Under section 9 of the 1993 act, any person who controls or directs the activities of a prostitute in respect of prostitution, organises prostitution or compels or coerces a person to be a prostitute commits an offence. This offence can be tried on indictment and carries a maximum prison sentence on conviction of five years.

PROCURING
Procuring a woman or girl to become a prostitute, to leave the country to become a prostitute or to leave her usual place of abode to become a prostitute in a brothel, in Ireland or abroad, is an offence under section 2 of the Criminal Law Amendment Act (1885).

BROTHEL-KEEPING
It is an offence under section 11 of the 1993 act to keep, manage or assist in the management of a brothel. It is also an offence to be

the tenant, lessee or occupier or person in charge of a premises and to knowingly permit the premises to be used as a brothel or, if the landlord or lessor of a premises, to let the premises knowing that it is to be used as a brothel.

DETENTION OF A FEMALE IN A BROTHEL

It is an offence under section 8 of the 1885 act to detain any woman or girl against her will in a brothel. A women or girl is deemed to have been detained in a brothel where, *inter alia*, property belonging to her is withheld.

ADVERTISING OF BROTHELS AND PROSTITUTION

Section 23 of the Criminal Justice (Public Order) Act (1994) prohibits the advertising of brothels and prostitution. It created the offence of publishing or distributing an advertisement that advertises a brothel or the services of a prostitute in the state or any premises or service in the state in terms, circumstances or manner that give rise to the reasonable inference that the premises is a brothel or that the service is one of prostitution.

In summary: It is illegal to solicit for prostitution, to loiter for the purposes of prostitution, to organise prostitution, or to live off the earnings of prostitution. It is not illegal to be a prostitute or to have sex for money.

Leaving aside the trafficking issue (dealt with in detail in chapter 9), there are two glaring failures in Ireland's legal framework regarding prostitution. Firstly, one of the biggest promotional tools of prostitution, the one that is facilitating thousands of liaisons between prostitutes and punters every day, is not in fact illegal. There are, as has been said previously, a hundred or more brothels operating in Ireland. All, bar none, have a presence on the internet. All bar a few have a web site that is hosted outside the state. For example, *sexysirenscork.com* had more than twenty women advertised on its web site in May 2009. It gave naked or semi-clad pictures of the women, a brief outline of their statistics, and a contact number. While it made the usual statement that the women charge for their time and companionship only and that 'anything else that may occur is a matter of coincidence and choice between consenting adults,' it was to all intents and purposes selling sex. The registrant of the site is E Designers Ltd of 29 Harley Street, London—the same people to whom the *escort-ireland.com* site is registered.

The Internet Service Providers' Association of Ireland says there is nothing it can do to stop a web site hosted outside the country advertising sex for sale here. Paul Durrant of the ISPA says:

> We have codes of practice which cover advertising and posting of illegal behaviour in this country. However, we have no jurisdiction over what is posted in other jurisdictions, irrespective of what we think about it. If there is a potential crime being committed as a result of the advertising it is a matter for the gardaí.

He says the real issue is that the sites are carefully managed with regard to the law in the countries where they operate. They will not contain anything that is considered illegal where they are hosted. Under the ISPA's code of practice,

> Members must use best endeavours to ensure that Services (excluding Third Party Content) and Promotional Material do not contain anything which is Illegal and is not of a kind likely to mislead by inaccuracy, ambiguity, exaggeration, omission or otherwise.

Where the ISPA's code of practice is breached, as would happen if prostitution was advertised, the association would act quickly.

> We would simply tell them to remove the material, and if it was not we would remove it.

The other glaring omission in the Irish legislation on prostitution is that the punter using the woman is rarely given more than a slap on the wrist. Most will see the inside of a courtroom only if they are summoned to give evidence against a brothel-owner. The low level of prosecutions for the purchasers of sex sits heavily with anti-prostitution campaigners, who point out that if the demand is eradicated the trade will surely die away.

The Swedish legal model on prostitution is the envy of many European countries, and is having demonstrable success, leading to calls for it to be copied widely in the rest of the world. Sweden introduced legislation in 1999 criminalising the purchase or attempted purchase of sex but decriminalising its sale. The aim was to reduce the level of prostitution and the trafficking of women by cutting demand. The legislation views prostitution as male violence against women and children, officially acknowledging it as a form of exploitation that is a barrier to equality between men and women. In January 2008 the *Guardian* (London) showed exactly how effective the system is.

The white envelope that arrived at the family home would have been innocuous enough, were it not for the emblem in the top left corner. For the married father-of-two to whom it was addressed the words Polismyndigheten i Stockholms län—Stockholm County police—were the first clue that his visit to a prostitute had not been as discreet as he might have imagined. Unknown to him, police surveillance officers investigating a suspected pimping operation were watching from an unmarked car as he arrived in his Volvo at the apartment building in the suburb of Bromma on a summer's day in 2006. They filmed him going in at 5.47pm, and leaving at 6.10pm. Eight months later they wrote to him telling him he was suspected of buying sex. He denied it, claiming he and 'Lia', the 25-year-old Estonian woman whose services he found on the internet, had done nothing but talk. But after being tried as part of a case against five men accused of procurement, he was found guilty and fined 15,000 kronor (£1,200).

Agneta Bucknell, former head of the Prostitution Centre, Social Services, said:

In 1998 when no one was speaking about trafficking properly and it was seen as quite a new problem, Nordic countries had a fairly even problem with regard to street prostitution, indoor prostitution and the trafficking problem. Today, we can say that our national rapporteur thinks there are between 400 and 600 people transported to Sweden each year for sexual services. In Norway and Denmark the police forces are counting 5,000 to 6,000 and in Finland somewhere around 12,000. I am not sure anyone can say it has decreased in Sweden but we are 100% sure there has been a tremendous increase in the number of victims of trafficking in the other countries.

The police are saying when they investigate different criminals in Europe, those criminals are saying 'Sweden is such a complicated country. There is too much focus on prostitution, we will have to take much more precautions not to be caught.' It costs them more to have people in Sweden than to put them into Norway. The whole grounds for the criminal network is to earn as much money as possible.

There has been about 1,000 people who have been taken by the police for investigation after using prostitutes and about 250 of them have been prosecuted.

They can get six months in prison but no one has been sent to prison so far. They all got fines sized depending on their income. The lowest fine was €20 and the highest was €6,000 for a very well paid man.

However, not all are so enamoured of what Swedish law has actually achieved—most particularly the prostitutes working in the country. They argue that the law has made life more dangerous and precarious for them. Rather than reducing prostitution, Swedish prostitutes say it has merely driven it underground. They say that customers are much less likely to reveal personal information, which makes it tougher to sort safe clients from the dangerous variety. Also, it has made clients far less likely to report situations where there is a suspicion of trafficking.

Isabella Lund, spokeswoman for the Sex Workers and Allies network in Sweden, stated:

> The law has increased the risks and violence against sex workers and the law forbidding procuring or pimping makes it impossible for sex workers to work safely and securely.
>
> Those who are worst afflicted are unfortunately the most vulnerable sex workers, the street prostitutes, addicts and sex workers from other countries. New and/or young sex workers are also more vulnerable from the law's negative consequences than their more experienced colleagues.

She said the legislation reinforced the 'whore stigma', the social shame, and the stereotypical and biased image that surrounds the sale of sexual services.

> Some customers are afraid to get caught for buying sex and that makes the clients more nervous and stressed. On the streets the negotiations must happen a lot faster than before since the police can be around the corner. If you market your services through the internet a customer can suggest the meeting should take place in a remote location where no one can see you or demand an arrangement where he/she cannot get discovered at all.
>
> During the negotiations with the client it is therefore hard to do a correct risk assessment. Is the client stressed, anxious and nervousness due to the fact that he/she is afraid to get caught by the police or is it a customer that wants to hurt you?

Anti-prostitution campaigners in Ireland are adamant that a similar system to Sweden's must be brought in. Fiona Neary of the Rape Crisis Network in Ireland said:

> If the Government is serious about tackling prostitution and its associated exploitation and trafficking, then criminalising those individuals who sell their bodies is hardly an effective

way to go about it. What does it achieve to prosecute people in prostitution? Our legislators continue to persecute these soft targets of the sex industry which has little if any impact on the industry as a whole. The Irish State seems powerless to make legislation on brothel-keeping stick. It is slow to bring into effect legislation on trafficking and has no legislation which makes it a crime to pay for the use of the bodies of women, girls and young men.

What are the alternatives? What would make it safer for the women? Would regulating the sex trade lead to more stringent health checks? Would it stop women having to stand on street corners?

As is to be expected, there is a clear divide between those in favour and those against. Those in favour argue that prostitution will exist in society whether it is legal or not. They view the sex trade as a financial exchange between two consenting adults, who are not hurting anyone else. Proponents say that legalising it is in the best interests of the prostitutes and the public. They claim— and this is subject to debate—that in countries where prostitution is regulated, the spread of sexually transmitted diseases is reduced through the encouragement of safer sex practices and regular STD testing.

There are some grounds for that argument. In the Netherlands, particularly in Amsterdam, the authorities offer free or heavily subsidised rates for sexual health screening, allowing the women to be regularly tested.

Advocates of legalisation also claim that making sex for sale legal reduces the incidence of rape and sexual assault, because the would-be attacker is given a legal outlet for his sexual desires.

The fact that the practice has been legal in several countries for a number of years does give an indication that those in favour may be correct. If it has not created a safer environment for prostitute and punter, would those countries not be the first to abandon the practice? As we will see below, some countries, such as Norway, have done so, but there are many others that continue to condone prostitution and even thrive on the income it creates for their economy.

Some opponents of legalised prostitution believe that the sale of sex is immoral and that the women, as well as their customers, should be prosecuted so as to eventually eradicate prostitution. They say a prostitute is likely to encounter abuse, exploitation, harassment, and in some cases death. In 2003 Janice Raymond of the Coalition Against Trafficking in Women International published ten reasons why she believed prostitution should not be legalised. Some of these reasons seem a little repetitive, but her points are well made.

1. **The legalisation or decriminalisation of prostitution is a gift to pimps, traffickers, and the sex industry.**
   Raymond pointed out that the legitimisation of the sex trade in the Netherlands, while making businessmen and 'legitimate sexual entrepreneurs' of the pimps, did not dignify the women working in the industry, even though it attempted to professionalise them.

   > People often don't realise that decriminalisation, for example, means decriminalisation of the whole sex industry not just the women. And they haven't thought through the consequences of legalising pimps as legitimate sex entrepreneurs or third party business-men, or the fact that men who buy women for sexual activity are now accepted as legitimate consumers of sex.

   > CATW [the Coalition Against Trafficking in Women] favours decriminalisation of the women in prostitution. No woman should be punished for her own exploitation. But States should never decrim-inalise pimps, buyers, procurers, brothels or other sex establishments.

2. **The legalisation or decriminalisation of prostitution and the sex industry promotes sex trafficking.**

3. **The legalisation or decriminalisation of prostitution does not control the sex industry, it expands it.**

    These two arguments can be considered together. Again using the Netherlands as her case in point, Raymond stated that one argument for legalising prostitution there was that the decriminalisation would help end the exploitation of immigrant women trafficked for the sex trade. She said that the government there had promoted itself as a champion of anti-trafficking policies and programmes,

    > yet cynically it has removed every legal impediment to pimping, procurement and brothels. In the year 2000, the Dutch Ministry of Justice argued for a legal quota of foreign 'sex workers,' because the Dutch prostitution market demands a variety of 'bodies'.

    She said the legitimisation of prostitution enabled women from the European Union and countries formerly part of the Soviet Union to obtain working permits as sex workers in the Dutch sex trade if they could prove that they were self-employed.

    > Non-Governmental Organisations in the Netherlands have stated that traffickers are taking advantage of this ruling to bring foreign women into the Dutch prostitution industry by masking the fact that women have been trafficked, and by coaching the women how to prove that they are self-employed 'migrant sex workers.'

    On the expansion of the industry since legalisation she said there had been a 25 per cent increase in prostitution in only the first decade since pimping was legalised and brothels were decriminalised.

    > There are now officially recognised associations of sex businesses and prostitution 'customers' in the Netherlands that consult and collaborate with the government to further their interests and promote prostitution. These include the 'Association of

Operators of Relaxation Businesses,' the 'Cooperating Consultation of Operators of Window Prostitution,' and the 'Man/Woman and Prostitution Foundation,' a group of men who regularly use women in prostitution, and whose specific aims include 'to make prostitution and the use of services of prostitutes more accepted and openly discussible,' and 'to protect the interests of clients.'

Legalisation of prostitution in the State of Victoria, Australia, has led to massive expansion of the sex industry. Whereas there were 40 legal brothels in Victoria in 1989, in 1999 there were 94, along with 84 escort services. Other forms of sexual exploitation, such as tabletop dancing, bondage and discipline centres, peep shows, phone sex, and pornography have all developed in much more profitable ways than before.

4. **The legalisation or decriminalisation of prostitution increases clandestine, hidden, illegal and street prostitution.** Raymond's arguments on this point seem a little tenuous. She claims that many women don't want to register and undergo health checks, as required by law in certain countries that have legalised prostitution, and so legalisation often drives them into street prostitution. However, this seems to be at odds with the evidence. Street prostitutes in Dublin told the author on several occasions that the legalisation of their status would enable them to feel safer and to be able to get the support they required.

More understandably, Raymond claims that many women choose street prostitution because they want to avoid being controlled and exploited by the new sex 'businessmen'.

In the Netherlands, women in prostitution point out that legalisation or decriminalisation of the sex industry cannot erase the stigma of prostitution but, instead, makes women more vulnerable to abuse because they must register and lose anonymity. Thus, the majority of women in prostitution still choose to operate illegally and underground.

5. The legalisation of prostitution and decriminalisation of the sex industry increases child prostitution.

On this point Raymond has statistics to back up her assertion. She points out that in the Netherlands child prostitution increased dramatically during the 1990s.

The Amsterdam-based ChildRight organisation estimates that the number went from 4,000 children in 1996 to 15,000 in 2001. The group estimates that at least 5,000 of the children in prostitution are from other countries, with a large segment being Nigerian girls.

6. The legalisation or decriminalisation of prostitution does not protect the women in prostitution.

Again this point is backed up by statistical analysis. Raymond referred to two studies on sex trafficking and prostitution by the Coalition against Trafficking in Women. These studies involved interviews with two hundred people whom she described as victims of commercial sexual exploitation.

In these studies, women in prostitution indicated that prostitution establishments did little to protect them, regardless of whether they were in legal or illegal establishments. The only time they protect anyone is to protect the customers.

In a CATW 5-country study that interviewed 146 victims of international trafficking and local prostitution, 80% of all women interviewed suffered physical violence from pimps and buyers and endured similar and multiple health effects from the violence and sexual exploitation. The violence that women were subjected to was an intrinsic part of the prostitution and sexual exploitation. Pimps used violence for many different reasons and purposes. Violence was used to initiate some women into prostitution and to break them down so that they would do the sexual acts. After initiation, at every step of the way, violence was used for sexual gratification of the pimps, as a form of punishment, to threaten and intimidate women, to exert the pimp's dominance, to exact compliance, to punish women for alleged 'violations,' to humiliate women, and to isolate and confine women.

She said that the women who did report that sex establishments gave some protection qualified this by pointing out that no 'protector' was ever in the room with them where anything could occur.

One woman who was in out-call prostitution stated: 'The driver functioned as a bodyguard. You're supposed to call when you get in, to ascertain that everything was OK. But they are not standing outside the door while you're in there, so anything could happen.'

7. **The legalisation or decriminalisation of prostitution increases the demand for prostitution. It boosts the motivation of men to buy women for sex in a much wider and more permissible range of socially acceptable settings.**

A visit to Amsterdam at any time of the day proves this point. The number of stag parties, lads' weekends away and single men on a 'voyage of discovery' means that the women behind the glass doors are not short of business.

Raymond points out that in countries that have decriminalised the sex trade many men who would not risk buying women for sex now see prostitution as acceptable.

When the legal barriers disappear, so too do the social and ethical barriers to treating women as sexual commodities. Legalisation of prostitution sends the message to new generations of men and boys that women are sexual commodities and that prostitution is harmless fun.

She said that as men have an excess of 'sexual services' offered to them, women must compete to provide services by engaging in anal sex, sex without condoms, bondage and domination and catering for other proclivities of some clients.

Once prostitution is legalised, all holds are barred. Women's reproductive capacities are sellable products, for example. A whole new group of clients find pregnancy a sexual turn-on and demand breast milk in their sexual encounters with pregnant women. Specialty brothels are provided for disabled men, and State-employed caretakers who are mostly women must take these men to the brothels if they wish to go.

8. The legalisation or decriminalisation of prostitution does not promote women's health.

Raymond's essential point here is that a legalised system that has a dedicated approach to screening the women for disease does not take into account the fact that the men who use them are the ones more likely to spread any sexually transmitted disease.

'Women only' health checks make no public health sense because monitoring prostituted women does not protect them from HIV/AIDS or STDs, since male 'clients' can and do originally transmit disease to the women. It is argued that legalised brothels or other 'controlled' prostitution establishments 'protect' women through enforceable condom policies. In one of CATW's studies, U.S. women in prostitution interviewed reported the following: 47% stated that men expected sex without a condom; 73% reported that men offered to pay more for sex without a condom; 45% of women said they were abused if they insisted that men use condoms. Some women said that certain establishments may have rules that men wear condoms but, in reality, men still try to have sex without them. One woman stated: 'It's "regulation" to wear a condom at the sauna, but negotiable between parties on the side. Most guys expected blow jobs without a condom.'

9. **The legalisation or decriminalisation of prostitution does not enhance women's choice.**

Raymond argues here that rarely do women make a conscious decision to become prostitutes. She said this choice is better termed a survival strategy.

> Rather than consent, a prostituted woman more accurately complies to the only options available to her. Her compliance is required by the very fact of having to adapt to conditions of inequality that are set by the customer who pays her to do what he wants her to do.

She said that of the women spoken to by the Coalition Against Trafficking in Women many described prostitution as the last option, or as an involuntary way of making ends meet.

> In one study, 67% of the law enforcement officials that CATW interviewed expressed the opinion that women did not enter prostitution voluntarily. 72% of the social service providers that CATW interviewed did not believe that women voluntarily choose to enter the sex industry.

There is no doubt that a small number of women say they choose to be in prostitution, especially in public contexts orchestrated by the sex industry. In the same way, some people choose to take dangerous drugs such as heroin. However, even when some people choose to take dangerous drugs, we still recognise that this kind of drug use is harmful to them, and most people do not seek to legalise heroin. In this situation, it is harm to the person, not the consent of the person that is the governing standard.

10. **Women in systems of prostitution do not want the sex industry legalised or decriminalised.**

This point is contentious. Raymond argues that in the five-country study on sex trafficking carried out by the Coalition Against Trafficking in Women, most of the 146 women interviewed expressed the strong opinion that prostitution should not be legalised or considered legitimate work, warning that legalisation would create more risks and harm for women from already violent customers and pimps. Again this goes against the evidence the author found when speaking to women involved in the sex trade in Ireland.

There are varied reports about the effect that legalising prostitution has on a society and economy. It is worth considering how legalisation or the weak regulation of existing laws has affected society.

AUSTRALIA

Australia is one of the few English-speaking countries that have a lenient approach to selling sex. Australians make between 12 and 16 million visits to an estimated 20,000 sex workers every year, to more than 5,000 legal brothels, 'escort agencies' and sexual massage services, and to 2,000 illegal brothels. It is estimated that one in every six Australian men has availed of the services of a prostitute.

Prostitution in Australia is governed by state (provincial) laws that in themselves vary greatly. Street prostitution is illegal in all states of Australia except New South Wales, where it is prohibited only near churches, schools, hospitals, and similar venues. There are tolerance zones in Sydney where sex workers can pick up clients and not get into trouble, and council-accredited 'safe house' brothels where prostitutes can take their clients.

One of the most abiding images of prostitution in Australia used to be the red-light district at King's Cross in Sydney, where, much like its counterpart in Amsterdam, the ambience was unmistakable. Those visiting the area knew what to expect: it was unashamedly sex for sale. Scantily clad women stood in brightly lit doorways twenty-four hours a day, seven days a week. From the outside the upper floors appeared bathed in light; in reality, the lights hid dingy little rooms with small single beds that witnessed little if any sleeping. Surrounding the brothels were numerous 'adult' theatres, sex shops, and strip clubs.

Today there are still some of the trappings of sex tourism, but they are rapidly being swallowed up by the opening of new shops and restaurants and masses of hoardings behind which large redevelopments are shooting up.

In the state of Victoria the decision by the government to legalise prostitution was based on the idea that not only would it make the industry less dangerous by putting the women into a safer, more controlled environment but it would also eradicate sex trafficking and child prostitution. It was also hoped that women in street prostitution would be taken off the main thoroughfares, where they were in full view of the public.

From 1984, when the state legalised brothels, to 2004, the number of licensed 'sexual services providers' increased from 40 to 184, according to Mary Sullivan, author of *What Happens When Prostitution Becomes Work: An Update on Legalisation of Prostitution in Australia*. According to Sullivan, Victoria's legalisation of prostitution has created a two-tier system: a regulated and an unregulated prostitution industry.

> There exist minimal opportunities for self-employment for prostituted women and no exit programs have been established for the huge majority who want to leave. Street prostitution, which is illegal, has not disappeared but risen commensurate with the overall demand for prostitution sex. Organised crime also remains inherent across the industry, blurring the boundaries between legal prostitution and unregulated sex businesses. Sex exploiters indiscriminately traffic women for commercial sexual exploitation, into both legal and illegal brothels, the former often a safe entrepot for the illicit trade. Sexual exploitation of children continues. The

increased tolerance of prostitution in Victoria, in effect, requires a steady flow of women and girls to meet the demands of the vastly expanding and lucrative market. And sex business interests are quick to devise new forms of sexual exploitation to ensure continuing profits and meet consumer demands.

Project Respect, an outreach project that works with prostitutes in Australia, estimates that there are typically up to a thousand women in Australia under contract at any one time—women still paying off a debt to those who brought them into the country. It says that the number of women trafficked for prostitution to Australia is difficult to estimate, for a number of reasons, not least because trafficking is obviously illegal and therefore often occurs undetected. It says that most women trafficked to Australia are from south-east Asia and China; however, there are also indications that women are at times trafficked from Europe and Latin America.

The majority of those trafficked to Australia in recent times appear to be Thai women. Among these are women who were abused by Wai Tang. Her case came to light in 2003 following a police raid on Club 417 in Brunswick Street, Fitzroy, Melbourne. According to the evidence at her trial, five Thai women were found to be working six days a week to serve nine hundred customers. The women were recruited in Thailand for $20,000 each. Their debt was set at 45,000 Australian dollars and was then reduced by $50 per customer; if they worked a seventh day they could keep the $50 per customer. While the women were not prisoners—they were able to come and go from the brothel—according to testimony in the court they had little money, had limited English, worked long hours, and feared that they would be found by the immigration authorities. Their visas had been obtained illegally, and their passports were held by Tang. Two of the women paid off their debt in six months, and restrictions on them were lifted: their passports were returned, they were paid, and they could choose their hours of work.

In June 2006 Tang became the first person in Australia to be convicted by a jury of possessing and using a slave since the federal anti-slavery laws were introduced in 1999. However, the following year she successfully appealed her conviction in the Victoria Court of Appeal, which quashed the convictions and ordered a new trial.

In turn the Commonwealth Director of Public Prosecutions appealed to the High Court against the quashing, and in August 2008 the High Court upheld the slavery conviction and over-turned the order for a new trial. The court held that the Federal Parliament had the power to make laws as part of its obligations under the international slavery convention, and it found that enough evidence was provided during the trial of Wai Tang to meet the definition of slavery. Tang was ordered to serve six years' imprisonment before being eligible for parole.

This was not the first time that Asian women had been lured into sexual slavery in Victoria. In 1999 a Melbourne man, Gary Glazner, was charged with breaches of the Prostitution Control Act for crimes relating to trafficking. The investigating police believed that Glazner had bought up to a hundred Thai women, enslaved and then prostituted them.

Evidence that legalising the sex trade in Australia has failed to raise awareness of the health risks in using prostitutes was brought into full clarity in September 2008. It emerged that rates of HIV infection in Australia had increased by almost 50 per cent in the previous eight years. The latest figures show that Australia had 10,000 cases of AIDS, while more than 27,000 people were infected with HIV. The upsurge was blamed on Australia's mining boom, as a result of which well-paid miners and wealthy businessmen were taking holidays overseas and contracting the virus while having sex with prostitutes. The Australian Federation of AIDS Organisations said it appeared to be chiefly men who were holidaying in south-east Asia and Papua New Guinea and having unprotected sex with women who they were unaware were HIV-positive. Health officials in Cairns, Queensland, said that a cluster of six middle-aged businessmen who had tested positive for HIV following trips to Papua New Guinea could be the beginning of a serious outbreak in the city.

NEW ZEALAND

Just across the Tasman Sea the New Zealand authorities have gone
one step further than Australia. Until 2003 the laws on prostitution
were similar to those in Ireland, with advertising the sale of sex,
running a brothel and living on the earnings of prostitution all
illegal, while prostitution as such was not. Under those laws,
anyone who solicited for the purposes of prostitution faced a significant fine, five years in prison for keeping a brothel or living on
the earnings of prostitution, and up to seven years in prison for
procuring anyone for the purposes of prostitution.

However, in 2003 the country seemed to go completely the other
way—though only by the narrowest of votes. Of 120 members of
Parliament, 60 voted for change and 59 against, while one—
Ashraf Choudhary of the Labour Party, the country's only Muslim
MP—abstained.

The Prostitution Reform Act (2003) decriminalised almost
every aspect of prostitution in New Zealand and at the same time
introduced provisions to protect the health and safety of sex
workers and their clients. It had only three stipulations. Firstly, it
prohibited the use in prostitution of people under the age of
eighteen. Secondly, and just as crucially, it stipulated that no
permit could be granted to anyone who is not a resident of New
Zealand. Thirdly, any prostitution business was expected to hold a
certificate issued by the Auckland District Court.

Supporters of the reforms argued that the act would eliminate
rogue operators and take sex out of the side streets into the safer,
more regulated brothel environment. The New Zealand Prostitutes'
Collective said that under the new law safe working practices were
now the norm, women were now aware of their rights, and there
were far fewer exploitative brothel-owners. Women who faced
crimes committed by punters were free to approach the police,
knowing that they themselves would not face charges.

The law also resulted in an increase in prices, with brothel-
owners arguing that increased competition, as well as stricter
standards for the conditions under which women could expect to
work, would detract from their profit. In the immediate aftermath

of the introduction of the new law many women left the brothels
and set up on their own.

In 2008 the Prostitution Law Review Committee reported on
how successful the Prostitution Reform Act had been. It found
that the sex industry had not increased in size, despite fears of the
country turning into a place of low morals.

> Many of the social evils predicted by some who opposed the
> decriminalisation of the sex industry have not been
> experienced. On the whole, the PRA [Prostitution Reform Act]
> has been effective in achieving its purpose, and the Committee
> is confident that the vast majority of people involved in the sex
> industry are better off under the PRA than they were
> previously.

However, the committee was not entirely happy.

> Progress in some areas has been slower than may have been
> hoped. Many sex workers are still vulnerable to exploitative
> employment conditions, and there are still reports of sex
> workers being forced to take clients against their will.
> Nevertheless, it is encouraging to note that most sex workers
> contacted during the research for this report were aware of
> their right to say 'no', and that some brothel operators'
> behaviour in this respect has improved since the enactment of
> the PRA.

The committee said that the prohibition on non-residents working in the sex industry, coupled with New Zealand's geographical
isolation and its robust legal system, provided a protection against
it being singled out as a destination for human trafficking.
This opinion was supported by statistics that showed that no
women had been trafficked into New Zealand up to 2007 for the
purposes of prostitution.

This was not to say, however, that crime in the sex trade had
vanished with the new act. Within weeks of its being enacted a

man was caught offering sex with a sixteen-year-old at a 'massage parlour'. Several more under-age girls were detected in various areas.

The National Council of Women of New Zealand had supported the new law, because it believed it would 'validate and protect human rights.' However, it found that all the law did was condone prostitution. Its opinion was confirmed when it found that even though new protection was meant to be given to children under eighteen, there were still numerous cases of girls as young as thirteen and fourteen on the streets or in supposedly certified 'massage parlours'.

As with any law, there were teething problems. Auckland City Council immediately came under pressure to introduce a by-law banning clusters of brothels in suburban commercial areas as well as any sex business within 250 metres of homes. The council was also forced to examine ways of ensuring that the city did not develop a glitzy red-light district akin to that of Amsterdam. It listed many other restrictions on the setting up of brothels, including that they not set up business in a residential area or close to a place of worship, a school, or a community facility. However, the High Court quashed the by-law, saying it was too restrictive. The court said that it prevented prostitutes from plying what was now their lawful trade and that the council could introduce such by-laws only on legal and not on moral grounds.

There were other teething problems, with fears that chains of 'McBrothels' would spring up without proper regulation. The Society for the Promotion of Community Standards said that a loophole in the law would allow chains to be set up without the authorities knowing where they were, with only a postal address for the certificate.

One community group in South Auckland decided it had had enough and declared war on street prostitution in its area. The Papatoetoe Community Patrol wanted to get rid of about twenty prostitutes who worked at the notorious Hunter's Corner. The group began to track down the clients through their vehicle registrations and sent letters to them warning of the dangers associated with their pastime and also warning that some people there were only intent on robbing the clients.

It was not only the prostitution they were unhappy with but also the rubbish they left, including condoms and human waste, and the fact that the street workers often propositioned teenagers when they were walking through the area. The community also sought a reform in the law to make street prostitution illegal.

However, the Australian Prostitutes' Collective attacked the community for treating the prostitutes 'like they were criminals' and for dehumanising the women by suggesting that they were despicable.

NETHERLANDS

Prostitution has been legal in the Netherlands since 1830. Until 1980 there was a law forbidding a third party from making profit from prostitution. In practice, this law has rarely been applied, and prostitutes were not in fact protected. In 1988 prostitution was recognised legally as an occupation. A new law introduced in October 2000 makes prostitution legal, subjecting it only to municipal regulations about the location, organisation and practice of a business.

There are on an average 25,000 sex workers in the Netherlands. They work the streets, behind windows, in nightclubs, in small-scale brothels, the so-called private houses, in 'massage parlours' and in 'escort agencies'.

There are 140 brothels in Amsterdam's red-light district and 500 prostitute display windows. They bring in an income of approximately €100 million a year. The blatancy of prostitution in Amsterdam is evidenced by the web site *www.amsterdam.info*, which actually describes the etiquette of picking up a prostitute in the city's red-light district.

> You will have to talk with her at the door—tell her what kind of sexual pleasure you have in mind, and agree upon the price by forehand—usually around € 50. You step inside and the curtain on the window is tightly closed and the door locked.

The fee is to be paid in advance. You will have your 20 minutes of pleasure you paid for. The condom is a must, whatever you both agreed upon, for your own safety.

The Dutch authorities say they are trying to regulate prostitution, aiming at protecting minors, eliminating forced prostitution, and combating human trafficking. Any sex business must obtain a licence, certifying that it has fulfilled the legal requirements needed to operate.

The city health services inform the prostitutes about a free or low-cost clinic for sexually transmitted diseases, and provide free or low-cost medical care. The prostitutes are fully open to the rigours of the tax system.

Prostitutes in Amsterdam have a support organisation, called Red Thread. It was founded in 1985 by former sex workers with the aim of fighting for the rights of all prostitutes working in the Netherlands, Dutch and foreign, male and female. It maintains that it is in a good position to understand what is happening in the industry, because its expertise comes straight from contact with sex workers. Like Ruhama in Ireland, Red Thread regularly visits the prostitutes. However, while Ruhama is gently trying to persuade them to escape the exploitation while still offering support, the prostitutes that Red Thread meets in the red-light districts, the brothels and the street-walking areas are informed about working conditions, tax, rights, and privacy regulations.

The sex industry in Amsterdam may be a legal business, but social exclusion, discrimination and exploitative working conditions still exist. This was made clear in an article by a Dutch economist and lawyer, Helen Mees, writing for Project Syndicate. She claims that the legalisation of prostitution in 2000 merely codified a Dutch tradition of tolerance towards the buying and selling of sex in the Netherlands.

But is legalisation the right approach? Even in the Netherlands, women and girls who sell their bodies are routinely threatened, beaten, raped, and terrorised by pimps and customers. These women are Amsterdam's leading tourist attraction (followed by the coffee shops that sell marijuana). But an estimated 50% to 90% of them are actually sex slaves, raped on a daily basis with police idly standing by. It is incomprehensible that their clients are not prosecuted for rape, but Dutch politicians argue that it cannot be established whether or not a prostitute works voluntarily.

The situation is so bad, she wrote, that police from the city's vice squad had begun to ask in large numbers to be transferred to other departments, because they were so appalled by what they were seeing. 'Only this year,' Mees wrote, 'the city administration has started to close down some brothels because of their ties to criminal organisations.'

In 2008 two German-Turkish brothers, Saban and Hasan Baran, were charged with running a large-scale prostitution operation, assaulting prostitutes, and forcing some of them to undergo breast-enlargement operations. According to reports, some of the women were tattooed on the neck with the brothers' names, and those who became pregnant were forced to have an abortion.

The gang was active in Germany and Belgium as well as in the Netherlands. More than a hundred women were caught up in their network. According to the legal counsel for one of the victims, most of them came from families marred by incest, alcohol abuse or parental suicide and from countries in eastern Europe or south-east Asia that have fallen victim to human trafficking, lured by offers of decent jobs or sold by their parents.

The gang took the women's passports and threatened and intimidated them and their relatives at home. One prostitute was beaten with a metal baseball bat and then forced to sit in a bath full of ice-cold water to prevent bruising. The women were kept under constant observation by an ever-changing group of pimps, guards, and chauffeurs.

The two brothers were among six traffickers given prison sentences ranging from eight months to seven-and-a-half years. In addition, three men were ordered to pay compensation of up to

€50,000 to several victims. All six accused were found guilty of trafficking in women and of abuse. The court, however, cleared several suspects of certain aspects of the trafficking charges, in part because of the public prosecutor's formulation of the charge, which could not be proved. According to the European Network Against Trafficking in Human Beings, the sentences given were also lower than the ones demanded by the public prosecution office.

The low sentences were also the result of the fact that few women dared to testify against their traffickers, for fear of reprisals, emphasising the need for better witness protection, including the possibility of testifying anonymously.

It is clear that the legal status of prostitution in the Netherlands does not sit well with everyone. Every town and village has the liberty to develop its own prostitution policy. As a result, the regulations vary widely between municipalities. Some villages will try to prevent sex workers from operating near their homes.

Eindhoven's designated sex work zone is due to close by 2011. The city began awarding prostitutes 'credits' in return for good behaviour under a new scheme to encourage them to abandon their occupation. The prostitutes would receive 'street miles' that they could use to acquire free clothes or furniture, provided they take up an offer by the city council to take steps leading to a career change and a safer life. 'We needed to come up with incentives that these women might latch on to,' said Veronique Beurskens of Eindhoven City Council, who led a drive to rid the city of street prostitution. The city also began funding assertiveness classes to help sex workers sever ties with their pimps, as well as workshops, advice, and courses on how to find new jobs.

> For every step they take to get out of their trade, they'll get vouchers that they can cash in to go shopping. They will be assigned a coach, whose first job will be to help them muster enough courage to stand up for themselves and break free from the trade.

Another scheme in the pipeline is the creation of a fashion label conceived by the prostitutes themselves.

> This has worked well in Amsterdam, where the women have launched their own label and can make money from it. We have plenty of designers at the college who could show them how to get started and teach them about clothes-making.

However, Red Thread, the Dutch prostitutes' union, objected to the scheme. Metje Blaak of Red Thread stated:

> This is fine if they actually want to move on to something else but some might not want to. At the end of the day, this is a step towards making street prostitution illegal, and what will happen to the women then?

She said that prostitutes do not easily make the switch to a normal job.

> They often miss the adrenaline rush. They need work where they feel they are really achieving something.

Eindhoven is among many Dutch cities that are clamping down on the country's famously liberal sex trade. In 2008 Amsterdam began shutting down part of its red-light district, a sprawling network of streets where prostitutes display themselves in shop windows lit by neon lights. The city is buying up scores of the buildings that now house the sex trade, with a view to closing down the windows.

NORTHERN IRELAND
Until July 2008 kerb-crawling in Belfast was not an offence, and it was driving local people in parts of the city centre to distraction. There was a running joke that the women operated 'around the Albert Clock,' but the reality was that new business areas of the city, particularly in the south, were overrun with women parading

the streets as soon as those businesses shut their doors. A network of streets stretching across a square mile rapidly became Belfast's red-light district. Women were selling any sexual services men could imagine for as little as £25, often without protection.

The numbers of women operating grew rapidly. At one point in the early part of the twenty-first century thirty women could be on the darkly lit street corners at any one time. The reason there were so many was that the men who wanted to use their services could kerb-crawl to their hearts' content, knowing that only if caught in the sexual act would it lead to prosecution. Therefore they would pick the women up, bring them out of the area to a number of different rendezvous sites, and proceed undetected.

The men seemed almost immune from prosecution, and the situation grew out of control. Members of a local gym were being propositioned every time they left after an evening's work-out. Female employees of the business were propositioned or shadowed by men in slow-moving cars every time they left work.

The matter came to a head when some of the businesses whose doorways were darkened by the women were closed down and replaced by trendy restaurants and apartments. People were unwilling to pay high prices for apartments or town houses when there was every likelihood that the used condoms and other wares would be found in their doorway each morning. They were unwilling to move into the area knowing that every night wives, girl-friends or mothers would have to run the gauntlet of kerb-crawlers.

A public meeting was called in City Hall, and the residents bombarded the police and local politicians with their concerns and demands. They were preaching to the converted, with one senior detective pointing out that some of the laws on kerb-crawling in Northern Ireland were 150 years old.

What has emerged and what has been highlighted in tonight's meeting is that there seems to be a gap in legislation. Currently, we deal with legislation which is 150 years old. Our colleagues in police services elsewhere in the United Kingdom, in mainland England and Wales, have a more updated legislation specifically designed against kerb crawlers.

Finally, in July 2008, legislation was introduced that put the kerb-crawler on the wrong side of the law. It became an offence to

solicit another person for the purpose of prostitution—
(*a*) from a motor vehicle while it is in a street or other public place; or
(*b*) in a street or other public place while in the immediate vicinity of a motor vehicle that he has just got out of or off, persistently or in such manner or in such circumstances as to be likely to cause annoyance to the person (or any of the persons) solicited, or nuisance to other persons in the neighbourhood.

NORWAY

For many years prostitution was legal in Norway. The only element that was outlawed was procuring or pimping. This tolerance made it a haven for foreign women flocking to the country to sell themselves. Unlike many countries where the practice was illegal, it was estimated that more than 40 per cent of the country's estimated four thousand prostitutes sold themselves on the street, while the rest of the activity took place indoors, in hotels or 'massage parlours'.

In fact the liberal laws on street prostitution in Norway worked against local women. For many years they had stuck to their specific areas of the cities and let customers approach them. In 2004, however, the Norwegian prostitutes began having to tour around the country, because their main patch, Oslo, had been overrun by foreign women, in particular eastern Europeans and Africans. The new influx of women did not stick to the unwritten rule of not hassling every man who passed. Some began walking up to men in shops and propositioning them. In one case the managers of a convenience store pressed charges, and one prostitute was convicted of disturbing the peace after she yelled at the shop's lone employee and made threats after being told to leave.

In 2007 the news agency AFP reported that 80 per cent of Oslo's prostitutes came from abroad, especially from Romania, Bulgaria, and Nigeria, by means of trafficking. It said the rest were Norwegians who tended to be drug-abusers.

Street prostitution, as we have seen, is the main source of criminal activity, both in danger for the women and in the prevalence of women from poor countries in trafficking. Despite the legality of the trade, women were still in mortal danger.

One Norwegian prostitute, Rebecca Rist, went missing in Bergen at the same time that the five prostitutes were murdered in Ipswich at the end of 2006. However, while Steve Wright's killing spree made national headlines, little was written about Rist's kidnapping and murder. She was last seen alive on 2 December, when she and her attacker were seen buying cigarettes. Eighteen days later her body was found near the man's house.

According to the US State Department's *Trafficking in Persons Report, 2008,* Norway is a destination country for women and children trafficked from Nigeria, Russia, Albania, Ukraine, Latvia, Lithuania, Estonia, Brazil and east Asian countries for the purpose of commercial sexual exploitation. It found that victims were sometimes trafficked through transit countries, such as Sweden, Denmark, Italy, and the Balkan countries, en route to Norway. Children in Norwegian refugee centres are vulnerable to human trafficking.

The country has done its best to combat the trafficking. Between 2006 and 2007 it carried out more than fifty investigations into trafficking, and eleven people were convicted over the two years. The government identified 190 victims of trafficking in 2007 alone, and it allocated $18 million to international anti-trafficking projects.

It was the high level of trafficking, as well as the hugely detrimental effect on tourism caused by the pushy new prostitutes, that led in 2007 to the country finally taking steps to stamp out the high levels of sex for sale. The government looked at the Swedish model of criminalising the men who were buying sex and introduced laws that could put those men in prison for up to six months as well as imposing heavy fines. As in Sweden, the women selling the sex would remain within the law.

In formulating the law the Minister for Justice, Knut Storberget, said it was designed to send a clear message to men that buying sex was unacceptable, because they were contributing to the international crime of people-trafficking. However—again much like Sweden—the women argued that it was actually taking the safety away from the street prostitutes. They said that while previously they could choose who they would get into a car with, with the new law they would have to rely on illegal pimps to find them clients.

In addition to the six-month prison sentences and heavy fines for the users of prostitutes, the law that the Norwegians formulated and that became effective in January 2009 also proposed jail sentences of a year for aggravated cases involving adult prostitution and up to three years where child prostitutes were involved. The law also affected Norwegians who buy sex abroad.

The decision to begin actively combating prostitution gained support. There was a realisation that there were thousands of foreign women who would no longer be able to ply their trade. The city of Bergen decided to take the novel approach of offering language courses and information about the women's legal rights.

The authorities took into account the fact that when the law came into force there would be a number of women who would continue to operate, so they introduced self-defence classes for them, because they realised that the women would have to operate in a less visible, and therefore less safe, environment.

The results of the new laws could be seen very quickly. The media reported that in one area of Oslo that might have had a woman at every street corner there were only two or three in the whole area. Men, fearful of being arrested and given the six-month prison sentence, simply stayed away. Women who expected to make up to €600 in a few hours were having to stay out all night to make €200. The men who would previously have driven the women to somewhere close by to have sex began taking them miles from the centre for fear of being caught.

By mid-February twenty-three men had already been arrested under the new law. All but three accepted on-the-spot fines of nearly €900; three others took their chance, refused to pay the fine and opted to be brought to court.

The fact that there were so many prosecutions in January 2009 and such a drop in business for those women still going on the streets was a testimony to the success of the law.

The news agency AFP spoke to one prostitute, Nadia, who at twenty-two had already been a prostitute for eight years. She said: 'The clients are extremely nervous. Most of them don't dare come here.' She said that one of her clients was caught after the law came into force.

> It was embarrassing, because we were busy when the police came. I told the guy he should say I was feeling unwell and that he was driving me home. I stuck to the story but he spilled the beans immediately.

Her colleague Michelle said:

> The men are afraid to drive by, so they walk up to us, tell us 'My car is parked around the corner, meet me there.' Before we would go down to the harbour and be back in fifteen minutes. Now they drive us out of town, where there is no one, and we're back one hour later.

SWITZERLAND

In 2008 it was reported that the Swiss Child Protection Association had called for the age of consent for prostitutes to be raised from sixteen to eighteen, because teenage girls were increasingly turning to sex work to be able to afford expensive consumer goods. It warned that because the legal age for prostitution in Germany was twenty-one and in France and Italy eighteen, Switzerland risked becoming a 'paradise for tourists seeking teenage sex'. Prostitution is legal in Switzerland, though pimping is banned.

The Swiss AIDS Federation estimates that 14,000 women work as prostitutes in Switzerland and that about 550,000 male clients use their services at least once a year. The practice is so accepted that there are full pages of advertisements for 'massages' in Swiss tabloid newspapers.

Though the age of consent is sixteen, if the age gap between parties is three years or less, for example between a thirteen-year-old and a fifteen-year-old, no charges can be brought. Karolina Frischkopf of the Swiss AIDS Federation told Swissinfo:

> The UN Convention on the Rights of the Child as well as the Optional Protocol to the Convention on the Rights of the Child on the sale of children, child prostitution and child pornography—both ratified by Switzerland—foresee the protection of children against sexual exploitation until the age of 18
>
> The problem is that the law does not mention the situation where [sixteen or seventeen-year-olds] voluntarily prostitute themselves. All other situations are covered by current law. It's a question of closing a legal gap.

The association demanded that the legal age for prostitutes be increased to eighteen and that paying for sex with a sixteen or seventeen-year-old should become a punishable offence.

In what has become known as 'label sex', more and more teenage girls in Switzerland are turning to part-time prostitution as a source of pocket money for designer dresses or expensive accessories. Girls advertise on line or visit upmarket clubs. One Zürich nightclub even organised a theme event, including sixteen-year-old guests. The web sites advertising these Swiss women, which can be viewed in Ireland, verge on child pornography. The on-line demand for young prostitutes is high, and advertisements emphasise the fact that sixteen and seventeen-year-olds are available.

Legalisation has not made it any safer for the women working in Switzerland. In August 2008 a Thai prostitute who had been

working for a Zürich 'escort agency' went missing. On 26 August
she was driven by one of the agency's chauffeurs to a client. She
failed to appear when the chauffeur went to pick her up the next
morning, and he raised the alarm. Her body was eventually found
in a forest near the home of the alleged killer in Thurgau in north-
east Switzerland. Her alleged murderer, a 41-year-old Swiss man,
was a known client of the prostitute and had spent more than
eight years in prison during the 1990s on various charges of rape
and violent assault.

It must be pointed out, however, that while the risks for prostitutes in Switzerland are the same as in most other countries, the
rate of sexually transmitted infection seems to be fairly low.
A study of HIV among prostitutes in Zürich found that out of a
little over 120 sex workers only 15 had contracted the disease, and
13 of those were intravenous drug users. That sounds like a high
proportion, but it must be pointed out that almost all the women
not using drugs were free of HIV.

Not so optimistic, however, is the level of trafficking to which
Switzerland is susceptible. According to the US State Department's
Trafficking in Persons Report, Switzerland is primarily a destination
and, to a lesser extent, a transit country for women trafficked from
Hungary, Poland, Bulgaria, Slovakia, the Czech Republic,
Slovenia, Ukraine, Moldova, Brazil, the Dominican Republic,
Thailand, Cambodia, Nigeria and Cameroon for the purpose of
commercial sexual exploitation. Figures showed that more than
two hundred trafficked women had to receive support within
two years.

ENGLAND AND WALES

In November 2008 the British Government made it an offence in
England and Wales to have sex with a woman trafficked or forced
into prostitution as well as introducing tougher new laws aimed at
penalising the punter.

The act of purchasing sex was not a criminal offence, and this,
the Government believed, had made it a soft target for people
profiting from the exploitation of others. However, in London the

Metropolitan Police estimated that 70 per cent of the 88,000 women involved in prostitution in England and Wales were under the control of traffickers. An estimated 100,000 men pay for sex in Britain every year.

Introducing the new legislation, the Home Secretary, Jacqui Smith, said that the laws would leave men with no excuses if caught using women who were not having sex for money voluntarily. Controversially, the new law left no room for men claiming they did not know the women were being exploited: paying for sex with a woman 'controlled for another's gain' was made a 'strict-liability offence', meaning that prosecutors would not have to prove that the man knew a prostitute was being exploited in order to charge him, and ignorance of the woman's circumstances would not be a defence. Those convicted would get a criminal record and a fine of up to £1,000. In more serious cases, where it could be proved that the man did know the woman was working as a prostitute against her will, he could be charged with rape, which carries a potential life sentence.

Furthermore, the new law toughened up kerb-crawling offences. Until the new legislation the men had to be found to be 'persistent' offenders, identified as making regular visits to pick up women. However, first-time offenders are now also subject to the full rigours of the law. Brothels were also a target, and the police were given greater powers to shut down brothels associated with sexual exploitation.

The new legislation was drawn up following a six-month review of the vice laws in other countries, including Sweden and the Netherlands. In announcing the changes, the Home Secretary said:

> I want to do everything we can to protect the thousands of vulnerable women coerced, exploited or trafficked into prostitution in our country and to bring those who take advantage of them to justice. That is why I am determined to shift the focus onto the sex buyer, the person responsible for creating the demand for prostitution markets which in turn

creates demand for the vile trade of women being trafficked for sexual exploitation.

There will be no more excuses for those who pay for sex. This new criminal offence of paying for sex with someone who is trafficked or pimped will apply even if the buyer claims he did not know the woman was being controlled for gain.

I also want to tackle kerb crawling. In my book, once around the block is once too many, and so I'm making kerb-crawling punishable as a first offence. I also want to see more naming and shaming of persistent kerb crawlers.

She said the government had considered banning payment for sex altogether but had ruled this out, as there was no public support for such a move. However, Cari Mitchell of the English Collective of Prostitutes warned that laws supposedly aimed only at women suffering exploitation would have a damaging effect on those who sell sex by their own choice.

Bitter experience tells us that any law against consenting sex forces prostitution further underground and makes women more vulnerable to violence. Under the proposed offence, any client of a woman working for another could be convicted. But what is his crime? The woman is working voluntarily and is likely to be making a better income than most women in commonly available low-waged jobs.

09 STOPPING THE TRAFFIC

OLENA, UKRAINE

I am 23 years old. I come from a very poor area of Ukraine. I was not happy there. I lived with my father, mother and brother and my child. I was not married and my father and my brother did not like that. They beat me and called me names for not being married but having a child. I did not have a proper job and spent a lot of time looking after my child and my sister's. After a while I could not bear to be there any more, so I went to Moldova with a friend of my sister who said he could help me get work there in a restaurant, and help me start a new life. But when I got to Moldova he sold me to some Albanians who took me to their house. They locked me in, raped me and made me watch pornography. They beat me regularly. I was forced to work at that house as a prostitute for two months, and then I escaped. They found me and brought me back to the house, but they decided I was trouble and they sold me again, to more Albanian men. These men got me a false passport and took me by plane to the UK, to a massage parlour in Sheffield. There were other women there, but none of them was British. When I was in Sheffield I was forced to see many clients per day—as many as 15. I worked every day, even during my periods; they made me put a sponge inside me to stop the blood. I got a very bad infection doing this and was very ill.

I was expected to make up to £400 per day for the men. I was not allowed to keep any of it and the other women would tell the men if they did not think I was working hard enough. They did not let me contact my family, but they had connections in Ukraine and they visited my mother and threatened her. They told her that if I returned home they would kill me.

I was able to escape when I was sold again. The maid helped me to run away before the new gang arrived to fetch me. Altogether I had been kept as a prostitute for nearly two years. Since I escaped I have had to have a big operation inside, as a result of my infection while working during my periods. I am not really sure what the operation was for, as I did not understand what the doctors said in the hospital. I have very bad headaches now, and I am scared to go out. But mainly I am angry. I am very angry that this happened to me and I can't control myself. And I do not trust anybody any more. [From a case study, by courtesy of the Poppy Project.]

In June and July 2006 the soccer World Cup attracted more than three million visitors to Germany to enjoy what was generally regarded as the sporting spectacle of the year. It was envisaged that as the drink flowed there would be a demand for some 'action' off field; and even though Germany legalised the prostitution business in 2002 and has 400,000 sex workers, it was feared that the country's significant red-light districts would not be able to cater for the demand. Not unexpectedly, the fear emerged that, among the thousands who would arrive in the country to take up the shortfall, there would be very many who would be trafficked.

The International Coalition Against Trafficking in Women launched what it later described as 'an extraordinarily successful international campaign,' called 'Buying Sex Is Not a Sport,' to protest against what it saw as Germany's promotion and public display of prostitution during the games.

Malka Marcovich, European director of the coalition, co-ordinated the campaign, as a result of which an on-line petition, available in five languages, was signed by more than 150,000 individuals and organisations from 125 countries and delivered to German embassies around the world at the start of the games.

The petition called on the thirty-two countries participating in the World Cup to oppose Germany's promotion of prostitution and to publicly dissociate their teams from the prostitution business. It urged the Committee and President of FIFA to oppose the link between football and the sex trade and called on the German government and its head, Angela Merkel, to stop this traffic in women for prostitution and to discourage the demand that fosters prostitution.

The German sex industry erected a massive prostitution complex for the 'booming business' expected during the games. The 3,000-square-metre 'mega-brothel', called Artemis, which could accommodate 650 male clients, was built next to the main World Cup venue in Berlin. It was described as an organised sauna club, similar to those in several other German brothels, where the customers and prostitutes paid an entry fee of approximately €70, after which they could use all the facilities for as long as they wanted. Food and non-alcoholic beverages were included, though no alcohol was served. On a typical night there would be thirty to forty women, all nude, available to the men, who were somewhat more modestly clothed in robes. Payment for sexual services was made directly to the women.

For those looking for something a bit less chic, the sex industry also erected wooden 'sex huts' or 'performance boxes' in fenced-in areas the size of a football field, with condoms, showers and parking for the buyers and a special emphasis on protecting their anonymity.

In the end it was estimated that forty thousand extra women were brought into the country to 'sexually service' the excitable football fans. However, the campaign by the Coalition Against

Trafficking in Women and the pressure brought to bear on the German authorities meant that, while the coalition's aim of eradicating the exploitation of women was not wholly successful, the authorities did at least appear to crack down heavily on the industry to ensure that there was no flouting of the country's lenient prostitution laws.

The police carried out large numbers of searches for forced prostitutes or women without legal papers, which might indicate that they had been trafficked. In the end, Artemis had fewer than three hundred customers per day; its profits were even less during the big matches.

The *New York Times* had a reporter in the brothel on the night before Germany played Argentina in the quarter-finals of the World Cup. He reported that, while tens of thousands of soccer fans would be piling into Berlin, 'the mood in the club was as subdued as the lighting.' Luna, a 33-year-old Serbian woman, told him: 'The last time Germany played, not that many men came here. Maybe they went out to a pub and drank instead.' The paper reported that while clubs like Artemis had been busier than usual after the games, the tournament had generated nowhere near the surge in demand for prostitution—or the influx of temporary prostitutes from eastern Europe and Asia—that many experts had predicted.

'Our business is okay, but it's not great,' said Egbert Krumeich, public relations manager for Artemis. 'We get 250 to 260 customers on a game day. We'd be happier getting 600 a day.'

'The police carried out a lot of searches to look for forced prostitutes or women without legal papers,' said Stephanie Klee, a prostitute who leads a group that lobbies for the rights of sex workers. 'When clients see police at the brothels they think that sex work is linked to crime.'

Government officials said they found no evidence or information about any cases of forced prostitution during the World Cup. However, just because no evidence of trafficking was found does not mean it did not happen.

In Germany in 2003 it was established that 5 per cent of trafficking victims were aged between fourteen and seventeen. An analysis of the German situation revealed that 45 per cent of victims had been deceived about the purpose of their migration, while 32 per cent had agreed to work in prostitution. Of the suspected traffickers, 39 per cent were German and 31 per cent from central or eastern Europe. Dispelling the myth that all traffickers are men, it was found that 21 per cent of trafficking suspects in the German research were women, often former prostitutes.

This situation is mirrored throughout western Europe and is made all the clearer by statistics compiled by Europol, in conjunction with the Council of Europe, in 2005–06. It found, among other things:

• In the European Union, most women and girls are trafficked from the Russian Federation, Ukraine, Bulgaria, Romania, Lithuania, Moldova, and some countries of south-eastern Europe, and half or more of the victims are below the age of eighteen.

• Greece is the primary destination of children trafficked from Albania, while the regions of the Czech Republic bordering Germany and Austria are the target of child-traffickers from other eastern European countries. The victims serve as prostitutes for clients from Austria, Germany, and other western countries.

• In the Baltic Sea region, Estonia, Lithuania and Russia are reportedly the countries of origin of most child-trafficking, with the destination countries being Germany, Sweden, and the United Arab Emirates. Most victims in this situation appear to be girls aged between thirteen and seventeen.

• In Italy in 2005 it was estimated that the number of victims of trafficking was more than five thousand a year, with estimates of the annual profit from their sale and sexual exploitation ranging from €380 to €950 million. Italy appears to be a common transit route for traffickers.

So how much can the traffickers expect to make in general for their human goods? It has been established that trafficked Lithuanian women are being traded for between €2,200 and €6,000 each. They may be re-sold up to seven times along the way. Europol quoted one barman who had made a profit from one trafficked girl of between €10,000 and €15,000 per month.

As we have seen, while the victims of sex trafficking can be any adult or child, in most cases they are women and girls and in a smaller number of cases young boys.

There are innumerable reasons why they end up being trafficked and why, in some cases, they allow themselves to be put into that position, and innumerable characteristics that tend to identify them as victims of trafficking.

Ruhama and a number of agencies have identified some of the common characteristics of the victims of trafficking, mainly as regards women, as they are by far the most often exploited. They say that such a woman will be constrained in her freedom—will not be free to socialise and build social networks. When the punter arrives, the woman will be locked in, or there will be evidence of permanent surveillance. She will not be free to dispose of her earnings or will have no access to them; often she will receive none or only a small proportion of the money, with the owner of the brothel or the pimp paying part or all of the woman's income to a third party. In those cases it is more than likely that the woman will be in debt to the brothel or pimp because of travel arrangements and will be forced to keep working to pay the debt. She will therefore be expected to earn a clearly defined minimum amount of money per day or per week.

As to how the woman was trafficked into prostitution, Ruhama says that a number of methods are used by the traffickers. She may have been given a false promise about an opportunity; she may not even have been informed about her impending involvement in the sex trade. Otherwise she may have known she was going to be involved in such work but was misled about the circumstances or the conditions. Other things that can be picked up by punters include signs that the woman cannot make decisions about services offered or cannot refuse any clients, or that she has to work long hours with no breaks. There is often evidence that her place of work functions as her living quarters.

The backgrounds of these trafficked women are much like those of the bulk of women in prostitution: no family links or an abusive family background, a history of sexual abuse, psychological or mental health issues, a predisposition towards submissive behaviour, poverty, not speaking the local language, poor education, or discrimination and lack of opportunity in their country of origin.

In a large number of instances the woman will have no passport or identity card, will be frightened, and may even show signs of bruising or battering. In some instances, particularly with women from African countries, she may even believe she is under the control of a 'hex' or curse: she may have sworn an oath to obey the trafficker and may fear the consequence to herself or a family member if the oath is broken.

The low value placed on the women themselves is evidenced by a report in the *Independent* (London) in January 2008. It told the story of 29-year-old Lena Suriane, brought to London from her home town of Kaunas in Lithuania in the winter of 2004. Soon after she arrived she realised she had been sold to an Albanian pimp. She had two young children and had been living in poverty, and she jumped at the chance when a woman approached her and told there was well-paid work in London. Suriane told the *Independent*:

> She hinted that the work was in prostitution. I had tried so hard to find other jobs and my plan was to do it for a while then come back to Lithuania and set up a business or something like that.

As soon as she arrived in England her passport was given to two Albanian men, one of whom said to her, 'Do you know that you've just been sold for £4,500?'

The day after her arrival she was set to work on a daily twelve-hour shift, from 11 a.m. until 11 p.m. 'On average I had sex with fifteen men a day,' she says; on one particularly busy day that number rose to thirty-seven. Charges started at £20 for ten minutes, rising to £140 for an hour. The takings were huge, but Suriane received only £10 a day.

———

With all this evidence pointing to a lucrative trade in women and children throughout western Europe, are Irish people naïve in thinking that a country with such a porous border is not a haven for trafficking?

Brian Lenihan, then Minister for Justice, told the Dáil in 2007 that human trafficking had 'the potential' to become a significant problem in Ireland. Speaking during a debate on the Criminal Law (Human Trafficking) Bill, he said the Government was committed to tackling the crime and that he appreciated that there was a need to draw together various departments in combating it. However, his view had been made clear two weeks earlier, while welcoming the participation of the Garda Síochána in Operation Pentameter II, an investigation into worldwide human trafficking for sexual exploitation being run by the police in Britain and Northern Ireland. At that point the minister said there was no evidence of a significant problem of human trafficking in Ireland.

His view was reinforced by that of the US State Department, which in June 2007 drew the wrath of anti-prostitution campaigners and human rights activists in Ireland by claiming in a report on international human trafficking patterns in 2006 that Ireland had only a 'potential problem', though the presence of foreign women in prostitution and the growing immigrant labour population raised concerns.

> Ireland is a potential destination country for women and girls trafficked internationally from Eastern Europe, Africa, Latin America or Asia for the purposes of commercial sexual exploitation and forced labour. Unaccompanied minors from various source countries, particularly in Africa represent a vulnerable group in Ireland that is susceptible to trafficking and exploitation.

It went on to say, however, that the Irish Government 'continued to demonstrate strong efforts to protect and assist victims of trafficking in 2006' and that it had provided more than €580,000 to a non-governmental organisation (NGO) to finance care and living expenses for victims while they awaited court appearances. It also said that while the Gardaí were investigating a small number of possible trafficking cases, the Government had reported no trafficking prosecutions or convictions in 2006.

A joint NGO group that included Ruhama, Amnesty International and the Ad Hoc Working Group on Trafficking of the Conference of Religious of Ireland (CORI) quickly issued a response to the claims made in the American report. It accused the United States of minimising the challenge facing Ireland with regard to human trafficking and questioned how the State Department had received and compiled the information.

> In our considered view, this year's report departs from standards of objectivity and lack a checking of data, thereby drawing inaccurate conclusions. The document refers to Ireland as a 'potential problem' and says there are 'only a small number of cases'. We wish to dispute this comment which is simply not factual. It may be in reference to the number of prosecutions but it does not refer to the cases presented to NGOs or cases investigated. There is definitive evidence to show that well over 100 people have been trafficked into Ireland for sexual exploitation and forced labour.

It was not aware of any Irish NGO receiving €580,000 from the Government for living expenses for victims waiting to go to court. The response also said that the State Department had not taken into account the legislative vacuum in Ireland in relation to trafficking, nor referred to the fact that the Criminal Justice (Trafficking in Persons and Sexual Offences) Bill (2006) had been sent to the Irish Human Rights Commission for an assessment of its compatibility with Ireland's obligations to human rights standards.

The group's diligence paid off. In their next report the American analysts changed their language completely, admitting that Ireland is an easy target for traffickers, as it has failed to comply with the minimum standards for eliminating the crime. In its

2006 report the State Department named Ireland in the first tier of countries for its efforts in fighting the illegal transport of vulnerable people; in its 2008 report it dropped Ireland into the second tier. Now the report says that women from eastern Europe, Nigeria and other parts of Africa, South America and Asia had been trafficked into Ireland for forced prostitution, and that people had also been trafficked for forced labour. The report further stated that Ireland did not fully comply with the minimum standards for eliminating trafficking, and that its prosecution efforts were hampered by a lack of comprehensive legislation during the rating period and that this was why there were no prosecutions for the offence in 2007.

Ruhama welcomed the portrayal of Ireland's efforts in combating human trafficking in this report as well as the US government's call for Ireland to fully comply with minimum standards by enacting comprehensive anti-trafficking legislation.

So are women being trafficked into Ireland to provide sex or not?

A report in the Sunday media in April 2009 appeared to cast doubt on the belief that there was any significant problem. It claimed that the Gardaí had carried out an investigation into prostitution and 'had found no evidence of organised trafficking.' This was despite a report by the Immigrant Council of Ireland that found considerable evidence to the contrary only days earlier.

Fine Gael's spokesperson on immigration, Denis Naughten, said that as late as that month the Minister of State with Special Responsibility for Integration Policy, Conor Lenihan, had told the Joint Committee on Justice, Equality, Defence and Women's Rights that 149 investigations into human trafficking were initiated by the Gardaí. In his report to the committee Lenihan said:

> Of the 149 investigations commenced, 41 have been fully investigated and no evidence to support the allegation of trafficking has been disclosed. However, in some cases evidence of other offences, i.e. assault, sexual offences, employment permit offences, etc., has been established and

proceedings are being considered, commenced or are pending in these matters.

It is anticipated, at this time, that an Garda Síochána will be in a position to submit investigation files into a number of these cases to the Law Officers in due course, including recommendations that prosecutions be commenced/initiated for breaches of the Criminal law (Human Trafficking) Act 2008.

Naughten commented: 'Obviously [the] Gardaí believe there is an issue in relation to trafficking if 149 investigations have been commenced.'

In 2009, research commissioned by the Immigrant Council of Ireland identified 102 women and girls who had been trafficked into or through Ireland for the purposes of sexual exploitation over a period of less than two years. In their report, *Globalisation, Sex Trafficking and Prostitution: The Experiences of Migrant Women in Ireland*, the researchers collated information about the women who had been found by ten support services between January 2007 and September 2008. The largest number was identified by Ruhama. The Women's Health Project under the Health Service Executive, the Immigrant Council of Ireland and the organisation STOP Sex Trafficking of Cork also identified significant numbers. Of the 102 women, 26 were aware of a further 64 women who were trafficked into Ireland, bringing the number trafficked during that period to a possible 166.

This number of 166 trafficked women is an underestimation; trafficking is covert and illegal, and many women who are trafficked remain invisible. It is mainly women who escape, are rescued or who have paid off their indentured 'labour' that come to the attention of services.

Most worryingly, the research found that 11 per cent of the women were children (i.e. younger than eighteen) at the time they were trafficked to Ireland, and 7 per cent were children at the time of the research. The largest category—48 per cent—was of women between eighteen and twenty-four. The great majority of the women were from African or eastern European countries: 71 per cent from Africa, specifically west Africa, and 23 per cent from eastern Europe. More than half the women were resident in the greater Dublin area.

Information was also available on the type of prostitution involved for 84 women. The great majority (90 per cent) were in indoor prostitution, 6 per cent were involved in both indoor and outdoor, and 4 per cent were involved in outdoor prostitution only.

Women reported being transported by plane, train, bus, car or ferry, and many were transported by several means of transport. Some came from Britain via Belfast and were then transported to other parts of Ireland. A significant 9 per cent were trafficked through Italy, and some were prostituted in Italy before being brought to Ireland.

The report found that when women who were trafficked reached Ireland they were sometimes passed over to Irish brothel-owners, who prostituted them: others were held and prostituted by the original traffickers. In either event, the women's papers were usually taken from them. They were then not only in the country illegally but were also without documents of any kind. 'In this situation, the woman lives in clandestine conditions. Her existence is one of isolation and confinement, which makes it difficult for her to escape and seek assistance.'

In addition to poverty, this study found that family dislocation, war and violence and childhood abuse were predisposing factors leading to women being trafficked. Patterns of recruitment reflect patterns documented internationally, with the least common form of recruitment being kidnapping. Deceptive recruitment— where the women were promised an education and work in domestic and other service sectors—was common, while some women were recruited through the pledge of marriage or a long-term relationship.

Sister Stanislaus Kennedy, founder of the Immigrant Council of Ireland, said:

The physical and emotional harm these women experience, their real concerns about the health impacts of prostitution and the stories they tell of their unhappiness and abhorrence of their situation, the violence and the threat of violence, should dispel any notion that these women are involved in harmless commercial transactions.

The following is the story of Lisa, which was narrated to the authors of the report by a member of the Women's Health Project who worked hard to help the young woman.

Lisa, a 22 year old from Latin America, was a student at university and worked as a dancer in a bar to pay her fees. A friend who returned from Ireland informed her that she could earn a lot of money here as a dancer and could go to an English-language school during the day. She offered to arrange a student visa, a flight ticket and to give her a contact of an agency in Dublin who would employ her as a dancer. Lisa agreed as she was struggling to pay her fees and her father, mother and siblings needed money to survive.

When she arrived in Ireland, her dreams of earning high wages as a dancer faded. She realised that the contact was an escort agency. The agency was very pleased to see her. They kept telling her that she fitted the right profile in terms of beauty, bodily proportions and pleasing disposition.

She was brought to an apartment where there were three other very young women from other Latin American countries. She was told that her job involved having sex with men. She would get €180 per session and the agency would get €220. The agency operated at the upper end of the market, 'servicing' discerning professional customers. She was expected to ensure that the customers were satisfied. Lisa was shocked. She felt that she had little option but to concede as she now owed a large debt, knew no one in Dublin and needed money to cover her living expenses. Also, her mother and father at home had high expectations that she would send money home. However, no money was paid to her for six weeks.

Champagne and cocaine are offered to the women and she has started to take them to ease the pain of having sex with the stream of men who make their way to the apartment. The agency has also provided lingerie and cosmetics. Lisa says she is expected to provide a range of abnormal sexual acts, which she finds disgusting. She was told she could not attend English classes as she is on call 24 hours a day. She is required to travel around Ireland and service men in hotels and apartments owned by the agency. At the time of the interview, the agency had arranged for her to travel abroad with a client for the weekend.

When engaging in prostitution in Dublin from the agency apartment, security is on call, supposedly to protect the women. More often than not, they are there to ensure that customers are satisfied. One of the women was severely beaten by security when a customer complained. She suspects that the agency is owned by Irish and Russians and is linked to a Nigerian group that provides the security.

Lisa is in debt to the agency. Her family back home is very religious and does not know that she is engaged in prostitution. However, she is frequently in contact with them by phone and they fear that she is in trouble.

Isobel's account is much shorter but illustrates more graphically how these women are essentially sex slaves.

It felt like a prison, no time for lunch and I was on call 24/7. I saw between five and seven men a day, with occasionally a day off. There was no choice about which men you saw and some men wanted sex without condoms. If you refused to have anal sex you had to pay a penalty or the 'security' men would beat you up.

The International Organisation for Migration puts the number of people trafficked globally at between 700,000 and 2 million. An alternative statistic offered by the us State Department estimates that between 600,000 and 800,000 people per year are trafficked along a series of global routes. Of these it is estimated that 80 per cent are women and children, 70 per cent of whom are trafficked for the purpose of sexual exploitation.

Here in Ireland, apart from the report of the Immigrant Council of Ireland, no-one is able to put an exact figure on the number of women and children who have been trafficked into this country to be used in the sex trade. Even the Immigrant Council's report is only a snapshot of a two-year period. Similarly, research by Dr Eilis Ward of the National University of Ireland, Galway, and Dr Gillian Wylie of the Irish School of Ecumenics at Trinity College, Dublin, could provide statistics only for a certain period, though the research was very thorough and very enlightening. Their report, *The Nature and Extent of Trafficking of Women into Ireland for the Purposes of Sexual Exploitation, 2000–2006*, states that seventy-six women were known to have been brought into the country during the seven years studied. However, they surmised that the true figure is likely to be substantially higher, given the criminal nature of the business. In fact their two-year research uncovered a further seventy-five cases of probable sex trafficking into Ireland, but they could not include them in the final count because they could not be proved.

Like the research by the Immigrant Council of Ireland, their statistics revealed that the majority of women were trafficked from eastern Europe, as well as from Africa, Asia and South America, and that the majority ended up in private brothels. Country-by-country figures showed that nineteen women had been brought here from Nigeria; the next-highest was Russia, with eight. However, when the authors clustered the statistics regionally they found that the dominance of Africa shifted. A total of 34 women came from countries formerly part of the Soviet Union, and 29 were trafficked from Africa. The researches said:

> Our research revealed the use of force, coercion, deception and physical and sexual violence as part of the transit journey. In most cases, when contact was made with agencies and

organisations, the women were in states of distress, they frequently had little or no English and were extremely vulnerable.

They found that where information was available to them, a pattern emerged of many forms of force or violence being used during the journey, including sexual assault, physical assault, threats—including the use of firearms—and coercion. Women reported being kept under close watch and feeling great fear.

Contact was initially made with the majority of women by their traffickers in their home town or village and usually by a fellow national. In most cases contact was made on the promise of work or opportunities for betterment in Ireland. One woman travelled to Ireland after her 'boyfriend' promised her a better life. One woman was homeless and another was extremely vulnerable, arising from a sexual assault and resulting pregnancy which led to abandonment by her family. In all cases, where information was available, there was deception. In one case of particular significance the woman was first contacted in the hostel for asylum-seekers where she had been placed by the state following her asylum claim. She was promised lucrative work and a better life by her traffickers.

Once the contact had been made, the woman's life was inevitably thrown into turmoil.

In most cases the traffickers were men and travelled with the women to Ireland. In one case, a fellow national couple, a man and woman, travelled with the woman and it was not until they reached Ireland that they began to behave with hostility and use threats. They removed the woman's passport and it emerged that the intention was to prostitute her in a private house.

Of the 76 women included in this report, 36 disappeared from contact with the investigating organisations, and at the time of publication their whereabouts and status were unknown. Fourteen women were repatriated, and twenty-two were granted leave to remain or were in the asylum process in Ireland. Three were deported, and one woman was repatriated to a third country.

One woman was kept in an apartment in the Financial Services Centre in Dublin and forced to have sex with men. Another woman was regularly beaten by her captors, moved around in Ireland, and kept by means of physical force. The researchers came upon one woman who reported that she had been moved by her traffickers between Ireland and Britain. She told them that a gun was shown to her during her transit. While she met other women during this period, she was kept isolated from them. She was given clothes and make-up by her captors.

> In another case for which considerable details were available, a woman was brought to Ireland by a fellow national and once here was sold to an Irish person to work in a lap-dancing club and, it is believed, in prostitution. In one case a woman reported that she did manage to escape the debt which she 'owed' to her traffickers through her work in the sex industry and decided to remain working in that sector. In all cases where detail was provided the women were kept in off-street, private brothels in apartments or houses.

At a Garda Immigration Conference in 2006 it was revealed that in the space of twelve months almost 1,100 illegal immigrants had been stopped trying to enter the Republic from Northern Ireland alone. A total of 5,436 people had been refused entry at ports, an increase of 500 on the previous year.

Phil Taylor, Regional Director for Scotland and Northern Ireland of the British government's Immigration and Nationality Directorate, charged with stopping the flow from the North, said that as far his department was concerned the trafficking of girls and children was the area that caused his department most sleepless nights. He said there was clear evidence of sex workers being moved between Britain and Ireland.

Proof that women can be and are being trafficked between the two jurisdictions was shown in March 2009 when the Police Service of Northern Ireland confirmed that it had detected eleven victims of human trafficking in homes around the North in a period of twelve months. The police had rescued women from Africa, eastern Europe and Asia from local brothels run by international crime gangs. The Assistant Chief Constable of the PSNI, Drew Harris, was unequivocal. Describing what the police had found, even in rural areas, he said:

> They are being held in captivity. They live in fear of awful violence as well; we know an awful lot of violence is inflicted on them by those holding them and there's the threat of violence either to them or even to their families back home.

He insisted that the women could not be referred to simply as prostitutes, as they were imprisoned in brothels. 'Massive profits are made from this, so we can expect that this will be a continuing problem for us.'

———

The ability to move women across the border without any real obstruction led a group of Lithuanian men based in the North to try to sell one of their own countrywomen to a brothel-owner in Dublin. Such was the inhumanity of the abuse to which they exposed the woman that the courts in Belfast sentenced them to up to fourteen years in prison.

TR was a young Lithuanian woman living and working in the North. She first met a Lithuanian man, identified as Julius, when she was walking to work. He and another Lithuanian man, known as Andrius, offered her a lift. The judge in the trial said they had first spoken to her in English, and it must have been reassuring for her to discover that they were both Lithuanian.

She was in a foreign country, lonely, adjusting to her new circumstances. She accepted the lift to work and she and Julius exchanged contact details and met that evening. During the course of that evening Julius put into operation an inhumane and depraved plan to induct TR into prostitution. The aim was to cut her off from her family, her friends, her home and the person that she was—to utterly change her life.

During that first evening Julius told her how he had got another woman into prostitution, and that he and she had shared the profits. He then tried to have sex with her. When she became distressed he deleted his details from her mobile phone, pretending to cut contacts with her.

However, the other man who had been in the car, Andrius, contacted her to tell her he was having a party with other Lithuanians, that Julius would not be there, and that she was welcome to come. The woman agreed and was collected by that man and another. When she arrived, Julius was there. The evening spiralled quickly downhill for TR when she was forced to perform oral sex on one man and was then raped by him. She became distressed and locked herself in a bathroom, and her attacker relented. She was taken from the house, and as she was being brought home Julius told her that the rape would bring great shame to her family in Lithuania, and that no-one would be able to prove what had happened.

She thought her ordeal was over. However, she was about to be subjected to infinitely worse.

Over the following weeks both men bombarded her with phone calls, firstly saying they had a job for her in Dublin and then threatening that if they could not meet her 'other men would.' One afternoon Julius rang her and told her that if she did not meet him that day these 'other men' would go to her house and take her. She agreed to meet him in a pub near her home for five minutes, as long as he arrived alone. She thought that if she met him face to face in a public place she would be safe and she would be able to persuade him to leave her alone. She was also frightened by the threat of the other men.

The court was told that Julius went to the meeting with two other men, Audrius Sliogeris and Saulius Petraitis. These men got out of the car some distance from the pub and bought a case of beer and cigarettes before waiting for Julius to return from the meeting.

At the pub, Julius's threats changed. He told TR she was to come with him or else he would make a call now to other people. He began counting off the seconds before he made the call. The threat was that either she would have sex with him on one occasion and he would let her go or he would make a phone call and she would have to have sex with many others.

As a result of this pressure, she left the pub with him and got into his car. He stopped the car and picked up the other two men. They applied the central locking so she could not escape as they drove to a deserted track in a remote mountainous area. The woman was brutally raped by all three men and sodomised by at least one of them. Julius gave instructions to the men on what he wanted each of them to do to her: he wanted her to be forced to perform sex in as many ways as possible. The men also took her mobile phone, and tried to drug her. Julius also wanted her passport, for reasons that would become apparent.

She was then driven to a house occupied by two of the defendants and Julius. There she was raped repeatedly by at least six different men, sometimes by two men at once. Altogether she was kept against her will for twenty-eight hours and was raped countless times. During that time Julius told her he was going to sell her into prostitution for €15,000. He received a text message from a brothel in Dublin asking what she looked like. When he read it aloud, Sliogeris said that no-one would pay €15,000 for her and that she was worth less. Nevertheless a man came to the house to, as the judge put it, 'look her over.'

Because she was so afraid, TR suggested to Julius that she might be able to get a friend to give her £5,000 to secure her release. Julius took her up on the offer and got her to phone the friend and read out a prepared story. She was then released in order to meet him. When she did meet him she was obviously distressed, and this man persuaded her to report the matter to the police.

'As it turned out,' said the judge, 'she was neither sold nor ransomed, but there was an attempt to do both.' Summing up, he said the plan involved the use of a number of techniques.

The prospects of financial gain were held out to her. There were threats of violence and within a short space of time kidnapping and false imprisonment to facilitate the multiple rape of TR. The purpose of the multiple rapes, as far as Julius was concerned, being to force TR to experience intercourse during one day with numerous different men and thereby simulate and attempt to familiarise TR with the working life of a prostitute. Again as far as Julius was concerned to so degrade her in her own self esteem that she herself would perceive that prostitution was the only option open to her. To make her feel that there was nothing left of her and that she was completely helpless. To leave the fear with her that her family, her friends and people in general from her own home environment in Lithuania would find out what had occurred to her. That she would have to face the prospect that the way in which she was perceived in her own home environment would be irredeemably changed. The financial objective of the plan from the point of view of Julius being that once she was inducted into prostitution he would sell her to another unnamed individual from the Republic of Ireland for €15,000. In short she would be 'trafficked' by Julius.

While Julius was not brought before the court, Audrius Sliogeris and Saulius Petraitis received prison sentences of between eight and fourteen years and will be deported once their sentences are complete.

According to the victim impact statement, TR's suffering will go on much longer. She is still haunted by memories of the most minute details of her ordeal, such as the smell of the room in which she was kept. Having returned to Lithuania, she is deeply afraid that she will be attacked once more when the men are released from prison. The social worker concluded: 'TR came to

Northern Ireland as an energetic, quiet, sexually naïve young lady but has left a severely traumatised, fearful, sad and hurt person.'

———

This was not the first time that Lithuanian men have been identified as violently exploiting one of their own countrywomen. In another case of apparently blatant trafficking in late 2003 the perpetrators got away with it, but at least the woman was freed—thanks to the efforts of Anton McCabe, a SIPTU branch president with a special interest in immigrant issues. Details of places are deliberately obscured to protect the young woman.

> One Sunday morning I got up and I had a voice mail on my phone from a young lad. I could tell he had a few drinks on him. He said in the message that he wanted to report something to me. He told me he had got my number from a friend. He said on the night before he had been having a few drinks in a nightclub up the country when this big imposing guy, who he said had approached him, offered him what he described as a 'lady of the night'. He directed him to a house outside the town, and he went there. What he said in the phone message was 'I am 19 and was offered a ride.' It was €80 for full sex. He went into the room in the house and there was a young girl sitting on the bed and she was crying. All he could picture sitting on the bed was one of his twin sisters. So he spent about fifteen minutes just sitting there, talking to her, because she told him if he just left straight away she would have been beaten. So he gave her the €80 and he left. He said it terrified him.
>
> The problem was, I had no way of contacting this young fellow, because his number was blocked on the phone. He rang me back on the Wednesday and told me where she was. Through a friend of a man who was active in the particular community we were able to pinpoint the house and find

the girl. I went to the house that morning with another Lithuanian girl at about 10:30 a.m. and got her out. She was a very pretty girl. The other girl was able to explain who I was.

She was able to tell me that she was nineteen years old. I brought her up to a friend of mine in Dublin. She told me that she had expected to be there until she was twenty-five, which I found bizarre. I asked her what she meant and she said that in Lithuania girls were in these houses until they were twenty-five, and then they were put out onto the street and a younger girl would be brought in to replace them.

She said this guy that had brought her over first met her when she was fourteen to fifteen years old and she thought they were boyfriend and girlfriend. He then left to come over here to work before returning to Lithuania three years later, and they began a physical relationship. He told her he could bring her to Ireland and she could get a better life. She came over on a Sunday, and by Tuesday she had been brought to Dublin to meet a man who turned out to be a pimp, the big Lithuanian who lived in the town where she would eventually end up. She said the way they discussed her it was like discussing selling a cow.

On the way to the town she said she took her passport out of her bag and said she wanted to go home, on which he grabbed her passport and slapped her across the face, telling her she would do what he told her to do.

Initially she was expected to 'service' men from the Lithuanian community, and over time he decided he could expand his 'business'. She said she kept count of the number of men, and by the time I got her out of there she had seen twenty-eight.

She said if I brought her to the Gardaí he would destroy her in her own village back in Lithuania, and that she would be an outcast. I had her in Dublin and with my work I had several contacts all over the country, and she had told me she had been a trainee beautician, so I got her a job in the south of the country. She has a better life now.

I will never forget the young lad who rang me. I never met him, but he said his sisters were the same age roughly as this girl.

Until 2008 the legislation for tackling human trafficking in Ireland was at best weak and at worst negligent. The Child Trafficking and Pornography Act (1998) made it an offence to organise or knowingly facilitate the entry into, transit through, accommodation in or exit from the state of a child for the purpose of sexual exploitation. Sexual exploitation, as defined in the act, included inducing or coercing a child to engage in prostitution or the production of child pornography, using the child for prostitution or for the production of child pornography, and inducing or coercing a child to participate in sexual activity. The penalties were suitably severe, with a maximum penalty of imprisonment for life. Up to 2008, however, there was little or no specific legislation creating an offence of trafficking in adults for the specific purpose of sexual or labour exploitation.

Nothing substantial was done, therefore, to support one young Romanian woman who came to Ireland in the hope of making a better life for herself and ended up being forced to have sex with Irish men for money. Maria was seventeen when she was trafficked from Romania. She was one of two girls that 'Prime Time' found in 2006; the other girl was only fifteen.

I wanted more money, I wanted a better life. A friend of mine asked me if I wanted to go to Ireland with her after I have a problem with family and I have no money. She told me we go work in restaurant in Ireland.

She left her home and was driven across Europe with her recruiter. She had no reason not to trust her. They arrived in Cork Airport, where a sister of her friend and the pimp were waiting. She was driven to an apartment block in Arbour Hill, Dublin.

He told us to relax, to eat, to feel comfortable. After two days he went with us to buy clothes, and then he told us we were

> going to work in an apartment with men. I could not say
> nothing. I was only with him and I was afraid. He beat me.

She was then brought to Herbert Park Apartments in Ballsbridge,
where she saw the first man.

> It was horrible. I was crying all the time. When a client came I
> was crying and he still wanted me to go to him. They said
> nothing.

On the first day she saw four or five men. Over the following
weeks she would work six days a week, seeing eight to ten men
each day. The Irish pimp who ran the brothel, and who is well
known to the Gardaí, took half the money, the trafficker the rest.

Eventually she was picked up in a Garda raid. She was brought
to court and was given a choice of two months in prison and
deportation or leaving the country within seven days. She made it
back to Romania to a shelter miles from her home. She does not
want her family ever to find out.

———

The Government approved the general scheme of the Criminal
Justice (Trafficking in Persons and Sexual Offences) Bill a full two
years before it finally introduced it. This lack of immediacy hints
at a distinct lack of urgency. Finally, on 7 June 2008, the Criminal
Law (Human Trafficking) Act (2008) came into force. It created a
number of separate offences, including trafficking in children for
the purpose of their labour or sexual exploitation or the removal
of their organs and trafficking in adults for their sexual or labour
exploitation or the removal of their organs. It also made it illegal
to solicit or importune a trafficked person for the purposes of
prostitution. A person convicted on indictment could face a
prison term of up to five years.

The act also established the High-Level Group on Combating
Trafficking in Human Beings. According to the Government, this

group was charged with proposing to the Minister for Justice 'the most appropriate and effective response to dealing with trafficking in human beings.' Jointly chaired by the Director-General of the Irish National Immigration Service and the Assistant Secretary-General of the Department of Justice, Equality and Law Reform dealing with crime, the group will include representatives of the Garda Síochána 'and other Departments and Offices who have a contribution to make to the national response,' the Minister for Justice said.

> The Committee will decide the most appropriate way to engage constructively with NGOs and other interested parties to ensure the most effective response to this crime. The NGO community will have an important role to play, particularly in relation to service provision for victims. We now have a comprehensive, up to date set of criminal offences which will ensure that human traffickers will find Ireland a very unwelcoming country [in which] to pursue their evil trade.

Fine words; but, as is so often the case, the legislation has not had nearly the effect in practice that one would have hoped for. Firstly, while it makes it an offence to avail of the services of a trafficked woman, the defence for the punter is ready-made: 'How was I supposed to know she was trafficked?' Secondly, groups working with trafficking victims have claimed that little or nothing was done to improve the situation of the women and children who had been trafficked. The Council of Europe's Convention on Action Against Trafficking in Human Beings gives a number of guidelines on the rights of the victims of human trafficking. It aims not only to prevent trafficking and to prosecute the trafficker but also to protect the human rights of victims. It applies to all victims of trafficking, men, women and children alike; to all forms of exploitation (including sexual exploitation, forced labour, servitude, and the removal of organs); and it covers all forms of trafficking, national and transnational, whether or not related to organised crime.

The treaty came into force in February 2008 in the ten countries that ratified it: Albania, Austria, Bulgaria, Croatia, Cyprus, Denmark, Georgia, Moldova, Romania and Slovakia. On 1 May 2008 it entered into force in Bosnia and Herzegovina, France and Norway. Ireland was one of twenty-four member-states that only signed but did not ratify the convention.

The main features of the new convention are:

- Awareness-raising for persons vulnerable to trafficking and actions aimed at discouraging 'consumers' to prevent trafficking in human beings.
- Victims of trafficking must be recognised as such in order to avoid the police and public authorities treating them as illegal immigrants or as criminals.
- Victims of trafficking will be granted physical and psychological assistance and support for their reintegration in society. Medical treatment, counselling and information as well as appropriate accommodation are among the measures provided. Victims are also entitled to receive compensation.
- Victims are entitled to a minimum of thirty days in which to recover and escape from the influence of the traffickers and to take a decision regarding their possible co-operation with the authorities. A renewable residence permit may be granted if their personal situation so requires or if they need to stay in order to co-operate in a criminal investigation.
- The private life and the safety of victims of trafficking will be protected throughout the course of judicial proceedings.

The convention also provides the possibility of not imposing penalties on victims for their involvement in unlawful activities if they were compelled to do so by their situation.

Yet, according to Ruhama, in Ireland everything is premised on the person's willingness to co-operate with the prosecution of their trafficker, even when the women are afraid for their lives. The support and protection of the victims remains as a section in the Immigration, Residency and Protection Bill. Under this proposed legislation the granting of residence permits does not include this clause and continues to leave the granting of protection conditional on helping the criminal investigation.

On 4 December 2008 the flaws of that were exposed. At that point the Gardaí launched a series of raids on nine brothels in Cavan, Drogheda, Athlone, Mullingar, Sligo, Kilkenny, Enniscorthy, Newbridge and Waterford. Among the ten people arrested was one 48-year-old man, members of his family and his new South African girl-friend. He cannot be named because, at the time of writing, a case against him, his South African girl-friend and his daughter is in progress and they are contesting the charges against them.

Six homes and professional premises, including solicitors' and accountants' offices in Carlow, were also raided, and there was an arrest in the North in connection with the investigation. The alleged pimp and trafficker and his 31-year-old girl-friend were arrested in the Pembrokeshire area of Wales.

The seven people detained in Ireland were arrested on suspicion of organising and managing prostitution. No charges were made before their release, though files were prepared for the Director of Public Prosecutions.

The operation to track the brothel operators had begun several months earlier and involved the police in Northern Ireland and in Britain. It had been triggered by the findings of Operation Pentameter II, and the PSNI was a driving force in the arrests. It had been studying information on the sex trade south of the border for several months as part of a general assessment of the movement of non-nationals into the sex trade in Ireland.

There had been a number of arrests and prosecutions for human trafficking in the North in the preceding weeks, and it appeared in several cases that the women were destined for the sex industry in the South. This operation was the first significant attempt to crack down on the illegal sex industry outside Dublin—despite the fact that interest groups have been lobbying the authorities for years to extend Operation Quest beyond the capital. In fact one source within the PSNI said that its counter-parts south of the border seemed ill prepared and inexperienced in handling trafficking cases.

Ruhama took in two of the seven women rescued. It could have taken more, and wanted to take more, but did not know where they were. The organisation was worried that the criminal gang behind the alleged trafficking might try to get to them.

Within days of the raid the Minister for Justice, Dermot Ahern, said he would not sign deportation orders in respect of women who are subject to possible human trafficking. He said:

> We're passing immigration legislation where we will be putting in place a reflection and recovery period for people who are the subject of trafficking. They will obviously be required to cooperate with the gardaí in the investigation of the crime of human trafficking, because we want to prosecute the human traffickers. In the meantime, we have an administrative system in place in the interim period between now and passing of the legislation.

However, Gerardine Rowley of Ruhama said that having the administrative system was fine in theory but that only one person had in fact been granted the sixty-day reflection period that precedes a possible six-month temporary residence permit—and that happened to be within hours of her going on radio to complain that none had been issued.

She also said that the minister's claim about there being no deportations was inaccurate, as women they had encountered were in fear of deportation because of negative responses in refugee applications. She added that Ruhama was trying to support the women as best it could, but its resources were finite.

> In Ruhama we provide safe accommodation and try to get them access to medical care—all the different services. But many women have deportation hanging over them as a threat. Because we don't have a system that provides residency to the

women, the only route open to victims, the only avenue they can take, is the asylum route. It is not the most appropriate, but it is all there is. Even though they are co-operating with [the] authorities, telling their stories when seeking asylum, they get back letters saying they cannot have refugee status.

She said the women are coming out of dreadful situations, believing they are going to be protected, but find themselves being left with no state support and facing deportation to the country where their ordeal began.

We have an obligation as a country to provide protection and assistance to victims of sex trafficking. We have the obligation because many of the women have been used by Irish criminals in our state and many Irish men have purchased these women for sexual services, which is abuse and violence.

The one thing the victims need when they are traumatised is to feel safe and secure . . . if you could only imagine what these women are feeling when they are threatened with being sent back to the country where the traffickers took them from in the first place. They have death threats on them and they are terrified.

Denis Naughten TD picked up on the numbers of trafficking victims the PSNI had detected, and the failure of the Government in tackling the problem.

Ruhama offered services to 44 victims in 2007 alone. In a stark comparison, in the last year the Northern Ireland authorities identified 11 victims of trafficking and as a result are establishing new care facilities which will include secure accommodation, health care and counselling. We must urgently follow suit.

At present, there are no clear policies or guidelines as to what happens to women who were identified as having been victims of sex-trafficking. A purely criminal law response will not deal with the issue of human trafficking and we must address the issue of victim protection and assistance. We have no detailed data on the extent of the illegal sex trade in Ireland, no details on the number of victims of trafficking rescued annually, and most importantly, we have had no convictions for trafficking as a result of inadequate legislation. This problem arises because victims cannot be guaranteed adequate assistance and protection. Like many problems in relation to Immigration, the Government are awash in a sea of ignorance, with no knowledge of the extent of the problems they face. This government's record on trafficking is dismal. They must recognise that trafficking is a heinous activity and we must put support and protection services in place immediately to address the issue.

Just weeks after Deputy Naughten spoke on the issue a further six suspected victims of human trafficking were rescued from brothels in the North as police moved to smash a prostitution ring run by the Chinese mafia. A Chinese woman and a former police officer were arrested after morning raids by armed police on terrace houses in south Belfast and in Derry. The police officer had been stopped at a ferry port with two Chinese women in May.

While the court hearing was continuing at the time of writing, in court it was alleged that the women were forced into prostitution after answering advertisements for nannies.

Crown counsel in the case told the court the women had got on a bus to Newry and were taken to a house where one was told she would do massages and the other would be the brothel's madam. It was claimed that they were expected to work from 10 a.m. until midnight and told that because they were in the North illegally they would not be able to go to the police.

In 2009 Paul Goggins MP, the British government's Minister of State for Northern Ireland, launched a new care service for victims of human trafficking who have been rescued. With support from the PSNI, it is provided by the Women's Aid Federation (NI) and the Migrant Helpline. It offers access to secure accommodation, health care and counselling for victims of human trafficking. In the South, while Ruhama is funded partly by the Government, the backing it is given could not be further from that shown in the North.

Paul Goggins said that victims of trafficking should not be reluctant to contact the authorities because they are concerned about being deported.

> That issue is being 'taken off the table' to enable help to be given to the women. Northern Ireland is no longer immune from the vile crime of human trafficking. Human trafficking is modern-day slavery. All the law enforcement agencies in the Organised Crime Task Force are working as one to catch the criminal gangs who are profiting out of human misery and suffering. We are also committed to supporting the victims of human trafficking, and the measures that I am introducing will deliver a victim-led and comprehensive package of care and support services. The welfare of victims rescued from this vile trade will be given the highest priority. The new and extensive system of expert support that we are putting in place will help victims recover and rebuild their lives.

So what can Ireland do? According to the Immigrant Council of Ireland, there are a number of international practices that we could learn from.

- An inter-agency approach and political will on the part of the Government and public officials is needed to advance counter-trafficking objectives, to develop effective systems of identification of the victims of trafficking, and to provide support and assistance to victims. Co-ordination among the principal agencies at the government level and the police and immigration authorities, as well as with NGOs, particularly with regard to the identification and referral of victims, is essential if there are to be effective approaches.
- Trafficking for sexual exploitation is inextricably linked to the growth of the prostitution industry and must be seen in

the context of the internationalisation and feminisation of migration. This raises challenges regarding how to prevent, detect, identify and provide support services to victims, who are often invisible to the public authorities and who experience significant risks and harm.

- Effective data systems, including common indicators and mechanisms for monitoring counter-trafficking work, are necessary; this also includes common data collection on national support and assistance programmes to enable comparisons to be made and cases to be tracked.
- Training and capacity-building are essential in identifying victims, developing common standards, and identifying and learning from models of best practice. Immigration policies should aim to implement effective systems for identifying victims and provide for best practice in safety and support measures, based on human rights principles.
- Immigration policies can be developed to provide security and protection to victims of trafficking through the granting of residence permits on humanitarian grounds.
- Trafficking needs to be seen in the wider context of violence against women and placed within an equality and human rights framework. Trafficking therefore needs to be integrated in a national strategy for tackling all forms of violence against women within a human rights framework.
- Consideration needs to be given to best practice in the methods used for reducing the demand for commercial sexual exploitation. This should include legislation to criminalise the purchase of sex, while also ensuring that there are resources and training to ensure that law enforcement is effective.
- Rather than criminalising women victims it is important to provide effective forms of support that provide the women with realistic choices and support for leaving prostitution, for example through opportunities for training and work, and policies for reintegration in their countries of origin.

- There is also a need for awareness-raising campaigns in the media to publicise the harm experienced by women in the sex industry.

In June 2009 the Government did indicate that it wanted to address some of these shortcomings. It launched an 'action plan' to combat human trafficking and said its proposals would 'create a hostile environment' for traffickers.

However, rather than being decisive, the document merely set out measures already introduced and identified areas where further action was needed. For example, on protecting the victims of trafficking it reiterated its commitment to a 'recovery and reflection' period of sixty days and temporary residence permits where suspected victims co-operated with an investigation or prosecution. Sound familiar?

Dermot Ahern, the Minister for Justice, said the National Action Plan 'follows on from a public consultation process which took place in late 2007. . . Nearly thirty submissions were received from a variety of sources, but primarily from the NGO community working in this area,' he said. 'The submissions were carefully considered when drawing up the plan. A number of the NGOs also actively participate in an NGO/Governmental/International organisation working group structure within the Department of Justice, Equality and Law Reform and the views they expressed there have been taken into account in the preparation of the Plan.'

However, while Ruhama welcomed the fact that the Government was at least publicly acknowledging the problem, it was far from happy at the *ad hoc* way in which NGOs such as itself were consulted.

'Ruhama is disappointed that the Department of Justice published this Action Plan without presenting a draft copy to members of the Anti Human Trafficking working groups for consultation,' it said. 'We are also concerned that victims will still have to wait long periods of time before the recovery and reflection period is granted.'

Fine Gael's immigration spokesman, Denis Naughten, in an

interview with the *Irish Times* was critical of the plan's proposals to put suspected victims of trafficking into asylum centres, saying that these did not provide secure accommodation and in fact that some victims were actually groomed in the centres.

The failure to deal effectively with sex traffickers, whether through a lack of cases or, more likely, the failure of the authorities to detect them, means that we must look to Britain for an example of a successful, ruthless trafficker being made to face the full rigours of the law.

Few sex criminals have been as successful as Luan Plakici, who at twenty-six was able to afford houses the size of palaces in his native Albania and the world's most expensive cars, all paid for by the exploitation of women and girls as young as sixteen. When he was finally caught it was found that he had made more than £1 million from what were described as 'poor, naïve and gullible girls' whom he brought to England.

What the British police uncovered was horrific. Up to fifty or sixty women are thought to have been trafficked to work in brothels in London, Reading, Bedford and Luton, though Plakici would be found guilty only of three charges of kidnapping, one of procuring a teenager to have unlawful sex, incitement to rape, and three charges of living off prostitution between July and October 2002. Plakici admitted seven charges of people-trafficking.

He was caught only because one of the women he kidnapped and forced into prostitution told the police she had been raped. They suspected there was more to her case than she was telling them, and over time they built a rapport with her. Eventually the full story of how she came to be in England emerged.

When the police dug deeper they found that this woman was only the tip of the iceberg, as would be shown in the detail of the court case that followed. Plakici had run his business in a 'merciless' fashion, beating and kidnapping women and threatening to harm their families if they did not comply. They were forced to entertain up to twenty men a day as payment for the £8,000 'travel bill' they owed him after travelling from Moldova or Romania.

The prosecution based its case on that of five young women. Two Romanian sisters, aged seventeen and twenty-four, told the jury that their journey across Europe had taken them through the Czech Republic, Italy and France. They had been approached in Romania by a man who offered them the chance of work in England as waiters or bar attendants. He got them Romanian passports and told them to go to Prague, where they met Plakici, who arranged forged Italian identity cards for them.

He then handed them over to two Italian men, who drove them to Britain via France. Plakici met them at Dover and paid off the two Italians. Within hours they were trapped in a small room at his home with two other women, and they were told they were to work as prostitutes. When they complained they said they were beaten into submission.

One of Plakici's other victims was sixteen when she and approximately thirty other women were loaded into a crowded boat in Moldova and taken to Italy. In court this girl said she was very frightened, because the boat was so overcrowded she thought it might capsize and that she would drown.

Once Plakici got her to England he made her work in a brothel, where she would be given condoms and lubricating cream each morning. Plakici made sure she was working hard enough by counting the condoms at night. She told the court that she had to make at least £500 a day.

Plakici not only kept the women working for him: he also sold them on. In one case another pimp became angry because the woman Plakici had sold to him for £7,000 was allegedly lazy. Plakici was forced to buy her back, but she was still trouble for him, and managed to escape. He even married one woman in order to get her into the country. His new wife would earn him £144,000 within two years.

Plakici's history showed him to be a cunning and resourceful individual. He arrived in England in the late 1990s as an asylum-seeker but was able to secure himself a British passport, which gave him free access to the Continent. His skill at finding the loopholes in immigration legislation that allowed him to bring in the women was probably honed as he worked as a translator for a number of law firms specialising in immigration. His success at trafficking allowed him to build luxury houses for himself around Europe, including one in Albania that was described as a small palace. When arrested he was found to have £204,000 in the bank and drove a Ferrari Spider and a BMW convertible.

However, his ill-gotten gains were worth nothing when the court handed down a ten-year prison sentence, which was later more than doubled to twenty-three years when the leniency of the sentence was appealed by the Attorney-General.

———

If any more proof is needed that far more needs to be done to protect the victims of trafficking, here are three more cases of women who came to the attention of the Poppy Project in Britain, which has kindly permitted me to reproduce them.

ADA, SIERRA LEONE

When I was 23 I was trafficked by my boyfriend into prostitution. My parents had thrown me out of the house for converting to Christianity, and going against their religion, so I was living with a friend and supporting myself. My father had beaten me and was abusive verbally too. I was finding life very hard living with my friend, so when my boyfriend suggested that we move to the UK and get married, I was very excited. I thought it was a good chance to start a new life. He paid for everything and we travelled together straight to London. I carried my own papers and travel documents. I was happy. I thought I was leaving the past behind me and starting again. Three men picked us up from the airport. I thought they were my boyfriend's friends. They took us to a house and while we were there, my boyfriend left. I did not see him go but after he had gone one of the men raped me. They took me to a brothel and made me work there for six months. There were five other women there. I had to have sex with two or three men a day and I was kept locked in at all times. I was exhausted as I had to see customers at whatever time they came to the brothel, so I was often woken up in the middle of the night. The men had guns and I was threatened a lot with physical violence, so I was afraid to say no. I was also too afraid to ask the customers for help because the men told me they would find out and kill me. Usually the customers wanted safe sex, but sometimes they wouldn't let me use a condom. They paid more when they wanted this. I saw a lot of bad things while I was at the brothel. I saw the other women being beaten and raped. I was raped too. I escaped at New Year, when the men held a New Year's Eve party and I managed to run out of the back door. I find it very hard to trust people now and I do not like myself. I can't believe my boyfriend did this to me.

LIEN, CHINA

I was trafficked to the UK two years ago from China. I had tried to escape from my aunt, who had kept me as a prostitute in her house after my parents died when I was 13. Instead of looking after me she did not feed me properly and she kept me tied to a chair and beat me. I lived like that for six years. I was very depressed. I thought about killing myself and I wanted to run away. Then one of the men who visited me at my aunt's house offered to help me escape. He said he felt sorry for me and wanted to take me somewhere safe. He told my aunt he wanted to take me out for the day, and gave her some money. But instead he took me to the airport and brought me to England. He arranged my travel and told me that he had arranged immigration papers for me. He paid for everything too. He was nice to me but that changed when we arrived here. He left me at a brothel while he went for a drink with a friend. He did not come back. He had sold me and gone back to China. I did not know where I was. I was made to work as a prostitute again, with at least five other women. Only one other woman was Chinese; the rest were all white, but I don't know where they were from. They threatened me and kept me locked up. I was kept there for several months and then I managed to escape in the middle of the night. I walked for three days before anybody helped me, and then a stranger called the police for me. The police locked me up overnight before they came with an interpreter and realised I had been trafficked. I am very tired now, all the time, and I have very bad nightmares. I am still depressed. I think I always will be.

MEDIJA, ALBANIA

My name is Medija and I am 19. Before I was trafficked, I lived in a small town in Albania with my family. I left school when I was 14 so I could work in the market with my father. He was very worried all the time about money, and sometimes he would hit me. While I was working I met a man called Guri. He said he had seen me around and liked me. He became my boyfriend. My parents did not approve and said I must choose between him and them. I decided to go and live with Guri, as I was tired of living in a small house. After a few months he said he wanted to take me to live in Italy. I didn't want to go but my family had disowned me so I had no choice. I agreed to go. Guri paid for my travel and we travelled by speedboat to Italy, where he gave me false Italian travel documents. He said I would need them because the UK authorities were prejudiced against Albanians. From Italy we travelled across Europe by coach to the UK, where we were met by a friend of Guri's. He drove us to Bristol, to a house. That's when they told me that I would be working as a prostitute. I screamed and cried and refused. They beat me badly and raped me, and told me I had no choice. It was true. I had sex with between five and ten men every day, seven days a week, working in saunas during the day and massage parlours some nights. I was exhausted and often in pain, from all the men and from the beatings. I had no contact with my family and I was locked in the house all the time, only let out to go to work. I lived like this for six months until the police raided the sauna. They took me to the POPPY Project, who gave me shelter and are helping me recover from my experiences. I still have many problems. I can't sleep and have nightmares, and sometimes I have panic attacks. I am afraid of people and do not like to leave the house. I don't trust anybody. I sometimes drink too much, to help me forget what happened. But it doesn't work. I will never forget what those men did to me.

10 | CONCLUSION

SISTERS CAN'T ALWAYS DO IT FOR THEMSELVES

In this book it has been my intention to show that women rarely choose to work as prostitutes, that their lives are massively damaged by it, and that the state is sticking its head in the sand instead of legislating to tackle one of the most harrowing aspects of our society.

If the Government is not using tough laws to eradicate the problem, is it at least working to stop women believing they have no alternative but to enter prostitution? Is it looking at the root cause of the desperation that drives women to sell their bodies, at huge risk to themselves? The answer is quite plainly No.

As has been established in the preceding pages, there are a number of factors that force women to sell their bodies and to keep selling their bodies. For example with addiction, as we saw in the chapter on street prostitution, Emma said she would have to keep working the streets of Dublin for at least the three years it would take for her to get into the methadone programme. That may be an exaggeration, but the waiting time is at least a year, and there are now an estimated 16,000 heroin users in the country, with fewer than thirty drug detox beds in the whole country. And this will not get any better, given that the Government reduced the funding for a number of addiction services at the beginning of the economic crisis in 2009.

Certainly the Government may be saving money; but, as seems to be the norm for the Government, the savings will no doubt fail to be passed on to society but will be wasted on trips for politicians to faraway destinations on St Patrick's Day or to pay for yet another layer of administration in an already over-managed but under-staffed health service. It misses the point that every addict who is not helped continues to claim social welfare benefits and remains an unwilling burden on the state. To get them clean and actively contributing to society through working and paying taxes would make them less of a burden. The women working in street prostitution, 95 per cent of whom are drug users, are servicing punters to feed their habit. They are also costing the state in Garda hours and the time of the legal system. They could be contributing meaningfully to the country if given the treatment they require. They want to be off drugs and away from the men whom they fear but whom they depend on to finance their habit.

The state is also failing the women in the shortcomings of its welfare system. The findings of Ruhama's Next Step initiative illustrated that failure. It found that the women the researchers encountered had no alternative means of supporting either themselves or any children they have: their choice was limited by the constraints society had put upon them. Ireland's care structure may be run to the best of its professionals' ability, but when they are operating on a shoestring their services are always going to be limited. Yes, the country has been in the economic doldrums since the end of 2008, but the failures that now exist remained throughout, or emerged during, Ireland's boom 'Celtic Tiger' period. That has left thousands of children in care services that cannot adequately cater for their specialist needs, and over time those children develop habits that may lead them too onto the streets. Even the more straightforward issues, such as adequate child care—issues that are easily fixed—keep the women on the streets.

The authors of the Next Step Initiative have said:

> In terms of seeking out alternatives to prostitution, some of the women did not know where to turn, did not know how to

exercise their choice. Choice can only really be considered in terms of the real and perceived alternatives available. There is no doubt that women involved in prostitution enter it as a result of a limited pool of choices and alternatives given their background, education and life experiences.

Policy changes are required to better support the transition to education and training, removing structural barriers and poverty traps currently within the system. Policy changes are also required to enable women to access meaningful, secure employment providing them with childcare supports and secure and affordable accommodation.

What the Next Step Initiative recommended was a network of formal support for the women, based on specialist knowledge of the challenges those women faced. 'Funding for groups working with women involved in prostitution needs to be provided under the violence against women budget line,' it argued.

At present the only organisation dealing solely with support for women in prostitution is Ruhama. It is a heavy burden to carry and should not be borne by one group alone. Essentially, by giving a grant to that organisation each year the state believes it can abdicate its responsibility for caring for the women. With that meagre funding Ruhama is therefore expected to provide the women with:

> **Outreach**—Going out every night and communicating with the women, making sure they are all right, offering them a cup of coffee and a chat. This service is not to be underestimated. The women operate in areas of the city and at times of the night that present danger to the outreach workers themselves.
> **Advocacy**—Acting on the women's behalf when they need help with any number of aspects of their lives in which they are having difficulty, whether it be housing, social welfare, or drug addiction. Ruhama's workers also accompany women to court, medical appointments, or meetings with statutory agencies.
> **Befriending**—This is not some airy-fairy support. It is

estimated that it could take a woman ten years—if at all—to truly come to terms with having worked as a prostitute. Throughout that time she is vulnerable and at risk of returning to the sex trade if she finds it difficult to control her life. Therefore Ruhama must constantly be on call to offer support and advice in a non-judgemental manner.

Counselling—This speaks for itself. It involves issues in every aspect of the women's life that they may need to discuss and work through.

Development—Ruhama plans each woman's education programme according to her needs and abilities, from reading and writing to arts and computers, as well as group learning. Women have successfully completed training courses in, for example, Junior Cert subjects and FETAC courses, and some have been helped to take up third-level studies.

Unfortunately, Ruhama's support can only do so much. The state needs to take on a greater role.

In England, for example, a group of prostitutes got together about twenty years ago to offer better support to those on the streets. 'Prostitute Outreach Worker' (POW) was launched when local prostitutes volunteered to train as researchers to assess the health and intervention needs of prostitutes in a disadvantaged area of Nottingham. The World Health Organisation and Nottingham Health Authority financed the research.

The survey data the group generated was used to design an outreach and referral service that is now considered a robust independent charity. Rather than being shunned by society, the organisation is well supported: to celebrate its tenth anniversary its members were invited to hold a civic reception at the Council House in Nottingham to acknowledge its achievements. A few years later it was instrumental in the setting up of satellite genitourinary medical sessions throughout the area, where clients could receive sexual health advice, screening, and testing. That was all possible because the British government became involved and actively supported the efforts of the organisation.

Back in Ireland, Mary is one of the women who has become involved in street prostitution but has managed to find her way out of her predicament and has built a new life for herself. Here she talks about what she went through and how only one organisation helped her as she tried to get herself out of the sex trade. She was angry at the state for its failure to adequately support people like herself.

I got into this through drugs. It was actually my partner: he tried to push me into it. I didn't know much about it, but he said we could make money out of it.

I started off when I was in my late twenties. I was doing it for about eight months, and I got clean then.

I had sold drugs before that. I was actually in treatment and got clean, and then I relapsed. But when I came out I got a conscience. I had no bottle left for selling the drugs. My partner used to supply me, so I didn't have to find the drugs myself. He wouldn't go out robbing, because he had charges, and he said he was going to finish with me if I didn't help him to get money. So we began going out on the streets, and he would get me to bring a punter down an alley and then he would come down and rob him. That was how it started off, but it only lasted a few weeks, and then I had to do it for real.

You could be there for an hour and get €300, or you could be there for seven hours and only get €50, or the whole night and get nothing. Sometimes at the start I would go over about 1 a.m. so that no-one would see me. Then later on to get more money I might go over at midday. I robbed some of the clients as well. I used to dip into their wallet without them knowing.

A lot of the men would demand it without protection, but you would get extra money. A lot of girls would say they don't do that, but I did it. I was after being on drugs, getting them from different people. There's girls saying they always use protection, but if you get that extra bit of money—I mean I used to say I would never do that, but I did. I would never have admitted to myself before that I would have done it.

Most of the money I made went into the drugs.

Some of the punters were very rough, and I got a few slaps one night, but that didn't bother me. But how I ended up finishing was one night I got a clobbering from one guy. I went in the car and he actually took my money and gave me a few clatters and raped me. All the same, that night I got into another car anyway. The guy that did it to me was well dressed, had the good car, but he did it to me anyway.

Every time I got in the car I never knew if I would be getting out again. But it was a job. I had to take more drugs to keep doing it. I ended up taking cocaine.

The men were just a way of getting money. I think they were scumbags. I see some of them nowadays, out with their wives and children around the town. If only they knew. There was one fella who was actually okay, he was genuine. He didn't treat me like a piece of meat.

They were young and old. I mean there was one guy and he must have been nearly eighty. There were a lot of fellas there all the time, and there were loads of others driving past and looking and doing something to themselves. I was not doing it that long, but I'm sure if I had done it longer I would have been raped.

I was picked up by the Gardaí twice. I was brought to court, but the case was struck out, 'cause he gave me a choice. The man walked away, with nothing done to him except a warning. There was actually one garda in the Bridewell who was lovely. He actually used to follow you to make sure you were all right. He would drive by as well to make sure things were all right.

No-one knew what I was doing until the summons came to the house and my dad opened it. They were more angry with my partner for getting me into it, because I had being doing drugs for ten years and I had never done anything like that.

I felt trapped all the time I was doing it. There was nothing else I could do. If I could have got money another way I would have. I mean, I heard of other women getting bottles put up them and all that.

I was given support by Ruhama. They did everything. They got me into treatment, and I found out I was pregnant. Thankfully it was by my partner, not a punter; but that was a tough time, and Ruhama helped me through it. When I was ready they helped me get back into school by sorting out child care and giving me counselling. I actually then got work in child care.

I got no support from anyone else. There is nothing from the Government or anything like that. They should be helping to stop women get into prostitution by doing better drug treatment. And also if the fellas were getting more penalties. I mean, a load of the girls get sent to prison; they don't. They should be supporting the girls, not always going against them. They are not doing anything to anyone, they are not robbing banks, not harming anyone only themselves.

When I realised I had made the break, I felt lucky but also ashamed of my life. Even now I feel ashamed when I think that I done that.

I couldn't think about going back and doing it now that I am clear of drugs, but I do sometimes think about the money side of it when I'm getting things for my home or if I want spending money for my holidays. I think I could get the money from two hours on the street. But I would never do it. I am totally against legalising it. It makes me sick.

I have moved on with my life. I have my family. I am very angry towards the man who got me into this. Sometimes I ask myself, was that really me. I always have reminders. One of my family members keeps telling people when we fall out.

The dangers of not helping the women are evidenced by a report from Scotland, where the National Health Service cut funding for the Scottish Prostitutes Education Project, from £150,000 to £50,000. But the fact that this project was being funded for so much in the first place should be praised. The funding was cut because it was believed that prostitutes were no longer at high risk of HIV and other infections. The education group put up a good argument. It pointed out that it was organisations such as its own that were giving the women the knowledge with which to protect themselves. The manager of the project, Ruth Morgan, told the media that they had concerns about the services that would be available to sex workers now they had to stop their outreach work. It was likely that there would be less face-to-face contact with those seeking help and advice, and that the range of supplies available for prostitutes—such as condoms—would also have to be reduced. A representative of the National Health Service in Lothian, Mike Massaro-Mallinson, disputed that last point, saying: 'NHS Lothian is spending over £50,000 this year on direct HIV prevention work with female sex workers and is also investing an additional £20,000 in an increased condom budget ensuring [that] all female sex workers have access to free condoms.'

Obviously the effect of the cutback will not be known for some time, as infections like HIV take so long to detect. One can only hope that the groundwork the Scottish project has done in the past will have been enough.

———

I talked to a lot of prostitutes in researching this book, and it has been a sobering experience. The sight of Emma almost cowering in the shadow of a tree on what was a bitterly cold night was bad enough; but what made it worse was when she told me that her family would literally kill her if they found out, and what made it ten times worse was that she was terrified every time she got into a car. She was a fresh-faced young woman; she barely looked over the age of consent. Yet that fragility and obvious youth would have attracted every one of the men who used her that night. They did not care a jot about her past, or the fact that their money was paying to keep her on the drugs that were wrecking her present and her future. When they went home to their warm houses and probably cuddled up to their wives, she remained on the banks of the canal, and actively contemplated throwing herself into the freezing water rather than live with the thoughts of what she had just done.

And Emma is not the worst off in the sex industry. While she is fighting the demon of drugs that forces her to keep having sex with strangers, her breakthrough may finally come through counselling, or a prevailing will to live. However, there are hundreds of women behind closed doors in cities in Ireland and around the world who have been completely robbed of any choice. They are earning thousands of euros a week—and handing it over to scumbag traffickers and pimps.

Their day-to-day existence revolves around servicing men, to whom they must present the façade that they are there of their own free will. If they don't, they will be beaten mercilessly.

There is no doubt that the women in the indoor sex industry are not all trafficked, that a large proportion are not there because another individual is forcing them to be there. But if the men who are using them are aware of the torture that trafficking victims face, why do they allow themselves to avail of the service without a guarantee that the woman whom they are with is not a slave? How do they proceed with what could essentially be rape?

I hope I have made it clear that the people who run the web sites, who organise the women, deserve nothing but abhorrence. They are perpetuating a trade that is destroying families, marriages, and lives. In our newspapers we see page upon page about fat-cat bankers and their predilection for playing fast and loose with our money. But the pimps and web-site owners are making just as much money from the exploitation of other people's entire being. They hide themselves from the law by establishing themselves outside the state and rake in millions of euros each year.

However, they are not the only ones who are to be abhorred. It is Irish society that is perpetuating this abuse. It is the Irish Government that fails to act decisively to catch the pimps, to properly legislate so that the Gardaí can go ahead and deal with the issue. The fact that as late as 2007 senior ministers were not even acknowledging that there is trafficking into Ireland says it all. There is no political will, because it is so easy to turn a blind eye.

And that is because we as a society do not make a big enough fuss about what is happening all around us. Like so many other supposedly rich societies in western Europe and beyond, we are happy to live divorced from our social conscience. We give millions in charity for starving babies in Africa or disaster victims in southeast Asia because images of that suffering are shown to us daily— and because it makes us feel good about ourselves. The essence of such suffering is not hidden away behind closed doors. The knowledge that prostitution, trafficking and their terrible fall-out are in our back yards is too uncomfortable for us to contemplate, so we look the other way.

The other reality is that a significant proportion of Irish men want prostitution to remain. They are happily paying for sex, knowing that 21st-century Ireland does not care about the implications. Bluntly, Irish prostitution is a €180 million industry. At an average of €120 per half-hour session (roughly €80 on the street, €130 off), that is 1½ million sessions with prostitutes a year.

Given the amount of work that it does in trying to help women in prostitution, it is appropriate to give Ruhama the last word.

> Prostitution, in itself, is a form of violence against women that is intrinsically traumatising. There are many levels of harm implicated—as well as the physical harm and damage, there is the emotional and psychological harm of being sexually objectified. One study found that while there is more physical violence in street, as distinct from brothel, prostitution, there is no difference in the psychological trauma. The psychological damage is intrinsic to the act of prostitution.
>
> When a human being is reduced to a body, objectified to sexually service another, whether or not there is consent, violation of the human being has taken place.
>
> As well as the harm to each individual, there is the social, cultural and global impact—the damage to the social position and perception of women, both nationally and globally, the proliferation of sex tourism and trafficking and the normalisation of all forms of violence against women. The

sexual exploitation of prostitution is harmful to all women. The sexual degradation of any woman is the sexual degradation of all humanity.

Prostitution is not an isolated individual act. It is part of an organised system which feeds on abuse, distress, failure, vulnerability and inequality.

For those men who still think it is worth while visiting a prostitute, one punter on an 'escort' web site showed just what the money you are paying out could be spent on.

€250 an hour eh? Blimey and you come and go so quickly. So before handing over your hard earned beans, consider this . . .

€250 gets you . . .

A week's holiday in a European destination

First class inc accommodation to pretty much any sporting event inc the 6 Nations rugby decider

A couple of nights in most any of Irelands top hotels

24 hours in a Porsche Boxster

An iPhone

Blue ray player

Round of golf and change at a top Golf course

2 quad bike sessions or 2 flying lessons or 4x4 session or 1 x helicopter lesson

2 hovercraft sessions!

The list goes on and on

or . . .

About 1 hour of a divorce lawyer!

Anyone who bought or borrowed this book because they thought it might be a titillating read, or because they thought they could get tips on how and where to find a prostitute: no offence, but I hope you've been badly disappointed.